For Molly

"For over 20 years I have been impressed with both Denman Moody's wine tasting skills and his incredible ability to write about the vast world of different wines—all in a way anyone, from beginner to expert, can clearly understand and appreciate..."

— Kevin Zraly, author of *Windows on the World Complete Wine Course,*
over 3 million copies sold

"Denman Moody, one of America's most knowledgeable wine authorities, has put together an excellent and useful book for all consumers. He combines history with valuable wine recommendations at numerous price points. Perfect for wine lovers who would like to take it to the next level."

— George M. Taber, author of *Judgment of Paris, California vs. France and the Historic 1976 Paris Tasting that Revolutionized Wine* and *To Cork or Not to Cork, Tradition, Romance, Science, and the Battle for the Wine Bottle*

In Vino Veritas!

all the best,

Denman

The ADVANCED OENOPHILE

DENMAN MOODY

ISBN: 1468053647
ISBN-13: 9781468053647

For Marijo, Christy, Lindsay, Caroline, Catherine and Michael

TABLE OF CONTENTS

ACKNOWLEDGMENTS

This book has been evolving in my mind for more than 33 years spent tasting a wide range of wines—from some pretty bad ones to the very best—writing about wines, and serving as a consultant for restaurants, private clubs and avid collectors. Without the help and encouragement of my executive publishers and editor, the publication of this book would not have been possible at this time.

I'm indebted to four wine experts at Spec's Wines, Liquors and Finer Foods (undoubtedly one of the finest wine stores in the world) in downtown Houston for their help: Nate Rose for general help; Ross Tefteller for valuable additions to my chapters on Argentina, Chile and Australia; Collin Williams for valuable additions to my chapter on Spain; and Bear Dalton (certainly one of the leading wine authorities in the world) for leading me to Patricia Chapman, who wrote the exceptional chapter on the wines of Oregon and Washington.

I'm also indebted to Ralph Leibman, whose help was invaluable to my article on South African Wines. Ralph and his wife, Etienne, immigrated to Houston years ago from South Africa, where he was an extremely successful wine retailer. He and Etienne own Leibman's Fine Wine and Food in west Houston. I also acknowledge the assistance and friendship of David Orr.

The number-one expert in the world on Port and Madeira is Bartholomew Broadbent. Possibly because of my long-standing friendship with his father, Michael Broadbent (former chairman of the wine department at Christie's in London), and definitely because of a passion for educating wine lovers, Bartholomew has written the chapters on these two very important fortified wines. There is some information here that generally can't be found anywhere else, and you can take it to the bank!

Master of Wine Debra Meiburg's article on the wine scene in Asia is a real eye-opener, and is news to even the most advanced oenophiles. The bios of Bartholomew; Debra; Wes Marshall, who penned the intriguing article on the wines of Colorado, Michigan, Texas and Virginia; Richard Olsen-Harbich, who wrote a revealing article about sulfites; and Patricia Chapman appear under their bylines.

INTRODUCTION

Join me on a trip around the world of wine! From the renowned wine districts of Bordeaux, France, to the exotic foothills of Mendoza, Argentina, we will visit the great wine-growing regions of the world and explore the wines they produce. But the journey doesn't end there. Following each chapter, I have included bits of wine wisdom I've amassed throughout my 30-plus years as a wine critic and writer, traveling and tasting around the globe. My sojourns have led me to experience, or meet others who have experienced, some of the most exceptional and historical wine-tastings/dinners ever held. My goal is to provide you with thought-provoking, useful information on wine selection and consumption. Nothing difficult or esoteric, just what you need to know—actually, what the advanced oenophile must know!

So whether you are seeking out new destinations to uncover marvelous wines, an educational overview to take you to the next level of wine knowledge, or simply want to heighten your ability to discern wines that optimally suit your taste, consider this book an invaluable reference. Now let our journey begin.

UNDERSTANDING THE WINES
OF FRANCE—BORDEAUX

A well-rounded understanding of wine begins with Bordeaux. Histori-cally, the greatest modern red wines have been produced in Bordeaux. This region in the southwestern part of France is geographically compa-rable to California in the United States.

There are some 30 wine districts in Bordeaux, but let's hone in on the five that have brought Bordeaux her fame: the Médoc, Saint-Emilion, Pomerol, Graves (pronounced grahv) and Sauternes. The greatest reds of the Médoc are the most well-known wines of the region, and within the Médoc, from north to south, are four important villages: Saint-Estèphe, Pauillac (pronounced paw yack), Saint-Julien and Margaux.

Once you've mastered the names of this one region (Bordeaux), five districts (The Médoc, Saint-Emilion, Pomerol, Graves and Sauternes), and four villages (Saint-Estèphe, Pauillac, Saint-Julien and Margaux), you're already miles ahead of Bordeaux amateurs, and you have the foun-dation for understanding what comes next.

Now that's not all that difficult, is it? But if it hasn't stuck yet, don't worry. Go on. It will.

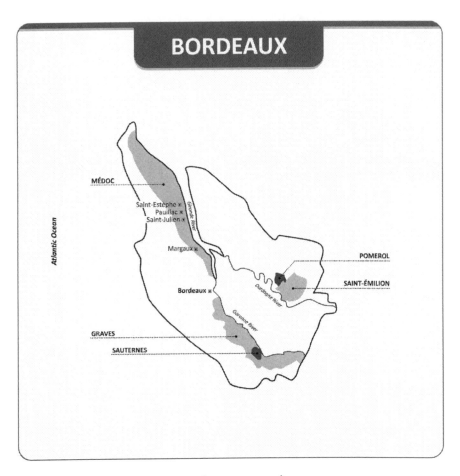

APPELLATION CONTROLÉE— LA CRÈME OF THE CROP

The words Appellation Controlée adorn the labels of the top French wines. With very few exceptions, this denotes the highest quality wines from France to be found for purchase and consumption in the United States. A label with Appellation Controlée appearing thereon legally guarantees that the wine conforms to the basic French standards for that wine. If a word appears between Appellation Controllée, such as Appellation Bordeaux Controlée, then the wine conforms to the more stringent standards of Bordeaux.

The better wines from Bordeaux usually reveal the wine district, such as Appellation Médoc Controllée, and the very best disclose the village name (which also signifies the highest quality), such as Appellation Saint-Estèphe Controlée, Appellation Pauillac Controlée, etc. A great vintage (year) combined with a red Bordeaux wine from one of the previously mentioned village appellations equates to a first-class bottle of wine. For example, even without knowing the chateau (winery), if you spot a red Bordeaux wine with Appellation Pauillac Controllée on the label from the famous 2005 vintage, it is probably a very good to outstanding wine.

THE MÉDOC

Although there are five principal districts in Bordeaux, I'll focus on the Médoc in this chapter.

The most lauded red wines of the world hail from Bordeaux. And as we shall see later, a growing number of the greatest rivaling red wines come from the United States, Australia, Spain and Italy. The premier red wines of Bordeaux, with some notable exceptions, are from the Médoc.

It is unfortunate that the complexity of the next subject discourages many wine lovers from truly gaining an understanding of the great red wines. But this piece of trivia is what I call a wine knowledge separator. It will easily separate you from the people who *think* they know about wine.

In order to discuss these greatest of red wines at any level of understanding, one must be familiar with the 1855 Classification of Red Bordeaux Wines—almost all being from the Médoc, which is where most all the great Bordeaux wines were made at the time. Here's where we separate the men from the boys, or we could even say the women from the girls. The latter phrase may be more accurate, because at their best, many of the wines of the Médoc, especially when mature, are beautiful and elegant.

In 1855, based upon prices each of the great Médoc wines had brought in previous years, the Classification was established. Most of these wines are located near and entitled to the village appellation of one of the four village friends we have previously met: Saint-Estèphe, Pauillac, Saint-Julien and Margaux. These wines—the best of the best—were officially named and divided into five categories. Instead of A+++, A++, A+, A and A-, they were called First Growths through Fifth Growths. The First Growths (or Premiers Crus in French) literally means the First Estates of the classification. They are:

Chateau Lafite-Rothschild—Pauillac
Chateau Latour—Pauillac
Chateau Margaux—Margaux

Chateau Mouton-Rothschild—Pauillac
Chateau Haut-Brion—Pessac

The entire 1855 Classification, as originally established, can be found in Appendix A.

Chateau Haut-Brion is not a Médoc wine—it's a Graves just to the south. But it was already so famous (it was mentioned in Samuel Pepys' diary in 1663 and later by Thomas Jefferson) that it was included. As early as the mid-1700s, those in the know had already established Lafite, Margaux, Latour and Haut-Brion as the four greatest wines of Bordeaux.

The 1855 Classification has remained mostly unchanged, owing to factors such as soil, weather conditions, tradition and strong lobbying efforts; however, there have been two execeptions, the most important being in 1973 when Chateau Mouton-Rothschild was elevated from a Second Growth to a First Growth.

Although some of these wines are no longer worthy of their positions, the wines, in the main, have retained their reputations and correspondingly high prices all these years. A few, such as Fifth Growth Lynch-Bages, Third Growth Palmer and Second Growths Pichon-Lalande, Léoville-Las-Cases and Cos d'Estournel, have consistently outperformed their fellow "Cru" wines, and are called Super Seconds by some.

If Chateau Lafite-Rothschild, Chateau Latour and Chateau Margaux sound familiar, now you know why—these are three of the famous First Growths of the 1855 Red Bordeaux Classification.

GRAPES

A majority of the grapes grown in the Médoc at the great chateaux are Cabernet Sauvignon. Some, like Mouton-Rothschild, use over 80 percent of this grape. Others, like La Tour-Carnet, use less than 50 percent. The grape peel imparts color to the wine along with tannin. Sometimes called the "backbone" of a wine, tannin is one of the elements necessary for a wine to improve in the bottle. Acidity is the other primary necessity for aging. As one of those "I'm not sure I need to know this yet" factoids, tannins, anthocyans and flavonoids—all present in wines to some extent, are phenols. One way to soften a wine that would otherwise be too tannic is to allow the grapes to fully ripen. During this period the phenols bond, resulting in extra texture and what some call tender tannins.

The tannins and other materials present in Cabernet Sauvignon can cause a harshness when the wine is young. To soften the Cabernet and add other desired qualities, vintners add Merlot (pronounced mehr low) in varying quantities to suit their fancy (which may be swayed by the consumers' preferences). For additional color, fruit, bouquet and other qualities, the winemaker may add Cabernet Franc, Petite Verdot and Malbec.

In Saint-Emilion and Pomerol, the Cabernet Sauvignon does not fare as well. The Merlot is king here with Chateau Pétrus, the greatest Pomerol, using almost 100 percent Merlot. Cabernet Franc and Cabernet Sauvignon are the primary blending grapes, with Petite Verdot and Malbec used at times in the blend.

FERMENTATION

The grapes are picked and allowed to ferment in the Médoc generally around the end of September. Fermentation is a natural process in which the sugar present in the grape juice turns into ethyl alcohol and carbon dioxide (CO_2). Yeast is the catalyst that engenders fermentation. For red Bordeaux wines, the sugar is almost all expunged during the fermentation process. The resulting dry wine, in a good year, will contain around 13 percent alcohol.

In some years, the grapes do not contain enough sugar for the fermentation process to yield a substantial amount of alcohol, resulting in a thin, weak and unstable wine. In such years, the winemakers are allowed to add sugar to the fermenting juice, called the must, to aid in the production of an acceptable percentage of alcohol. This process is called Chaptalization, named after Chaptal B. Moody from Grapevine, Texas. Okay, that's not really true. But now you might remember that Chaptalization is the process of adding sugar to the must to help produce an acceptable amount of alcohol in a poor year. It's actually named after a famous Frenchman, Chaptal, who was a pioneer in wine/sugar studies in the early 1800s.

WOOD AND BOTTLE

Following fermentation and some other necessary duties, the wine is transferred into wood. The very best Médoc wines are aged in small oak barrels. After several years, the wine will have developed further character and complexity.

When the expert tasters decide the time is right, the wine is bottled. In a very good to outstanding year, Médoc wines should further develop in the bottle for 10 to 25 years. In some rare vintages like 1945, given proper cellaring, the wine can ascend in quality after 30 years or more.

BORDEAUX PART II

Saint-Emilion and Pomerol are two of the five famous wine districts of Bordeaux. Unlike the Médoc, where Cabernet Sauvignon is King, Merlot is the reigning monarch here, producing a soft, round but full-bodied wine that matures more quickly than Cabernet Sauvignon. The primary blending varietal is Cabernet Franc, with various percentages of Cabernet Sauvignon and Malbec thrown into the mix. Petit Verdot is used sparingly.

SAINT-EMILION

Saint-Emilion is much larger than Pomerol and produces more than five times the wine. Until 1955, there was no official classification in Saint-Emilion. Today, this classification comprises Premiers Grands Crus Classés—roughly translated as First Great Classified Estates—and Grands Crus Classés.

Premiers Grands Crus Classés is divided into A. and B. The A. category has only two names: Chateau Ausone and Chateau Cheval-Blanc (the prized bottle cellared by Miles in the movie *Sideways*). These are considered the equivalent of the First Growth wines of the Médoc. The B. category is similar to the second growths of the Médoc. Those wines are (omitting the word "Chateau"): Angelus, Beau-Sejour Bécot, Beauséjour (Duffau-Lagarrosse), Bélair-Monange, Canon, Figeac, Clos Fourtet, La Gaffelière, Magdelaine, Pavie-Macquin, Troplong-Mondot and Trottevieille. Numerous other wines call themselves Grand Cru, but the absence of "Classé" renders the title meaningless.

Between 1956 and 1974, Ausone was, in my opinion, one of the most overpriced wines on the market. Beginning in the mid-1970s, Ausone gained ground but had some ups and downs. Since the late 1990s, and with the addition of the heralded Michelle Rolland as consulting winemaker, it is again the equal to Cheval-Blanc.

Cheval-Blanc has long been top notch. In fact, the 1947 Cheval-Blanc is thought by some connoisseurs to be the greatest of all wines. In the late 1970s and throughout the 1980s, I tasted this wine about six times, and I respectfully disagree. While unique, it is just too much like a vintage Port without the sugar—difficult to pair with a food it doesn't overpower. Figeac, which has the peculiarity of a large percentage of Cabernet Sauvignon, is only a stone's throw from Cheval-Blanc, and along with the other "B." wines provides luscious drinking.

These wines, even from a great vintage, could be purchased for $15 to $25 a bottle in the early 1970s. Now, at release, the Premiers Grands Crus Classés, Grands Crus Classés, and the First and Second Growth Médocs are exorbitantly expensive and mainly considered collector wines. But they have been and still are the most renowned red wines in the world.

POMEROL

Pomerol was little known until after World War II. The most famous Pomerol, which is on the same quality level of a First Growth Médoc—and even more expensive—is Chateau Pétrus. Like Saint-Emilion, Pomerol is primarily Merlot; however, unlike Saint-Emilion, it is sometimes all Merlot. Pétrus, for example, is sometimes almost 100 percent Merlot with just a percent or two of Cabernet Franc.

Although there has never been a classification of Pomerol wines, some of the very best, besides Pétrus, are Le Pin, Lafleur, Trotanoy, La Providence, Gazin, Clinet, Hosanna, l'Eglise-Clinet, La Conseillante, L'Evangile and Vieux Chateau Certan. These are very expensive wines.

GRAVES

The city of Bordeaux is located in the northeastern part of Graves (grahv). The red wines of Graves were officially classified in 1959, and although Haut-Brion (ō bree awn) was included in the 1855 Classification, it appears here again. Each wine is classified equally as a Cru Classé; however, each is listed here in the writer's order of preference (again, the word chateau omitted):

Haut-Brion
La Mission-Haut-Brion
Pape-Clément
Haut-Bailly
Smith-Haut-Lafitte
Domaine de Chevalier
Fieuzal
Carbonnieux

The others are: Latour-Haut-Brion, La Tour-Martillac, Bouscaut and Olivier.

For red Graves wines, the primary blending grapes are Cabernet Sauvignon with Merlot and Cabernet Franc, with Petit Verdot and Malbec playing a minor role.

The white Graves wines are made principally from Sémillon and Sauvignon Blanc. The best ones are typically dry, but not as full of depth and charm as the more famous white wines made from Chardonnay in Burgundy. The white Graves wines were also officially classified in 1959. Apparently the owners of Haut-Brion and Fieuzal asked that their white wine not be included, and therefore were not. Haut-Brion blanc is nevertheless one of the greatest white wines in the world, so I'll list it first here anyway, along with the rest of the classification:

Haut-Brion
Bouscat
Carbonnieux
Domaine de Chevalier
Couhins
Couhins-Lurton
Laville Haut-Brion
Malartic-Lagravière
Olivier
Latour-Martillac

SAUTERNES AND BARSAC

In the far south of Bordeaux lies the district of Sauternes (silent s) and its inner district of Barsac (bar sack). The predominant grape is Sémillon with Sauvignon Blanc not far behind. This region produces the famous Bordeaux dessert wines.

Pictures of the grapes that make up these wines could make one gag, so a written description will have to suffice. The grapes in this area are, in most years, attacked near the end of September by botrytis cinerea, a mold known as (in one of the best uses of prestige jargon), the "noble rot." It's a wonder that anyone had the temerity to make wine out of a bunch of rotten grapes, shriveled to the size and appearance of an oozing, decaying raisin. But after the grape skin has split and some of the juice, primarily water, has oozed out, the juice that is left is extremely rich in natural sugar content. Because of this, after fermentation, the residual sugar is high, as is the alcohol (unlike in Germany, where the alcohol in dessert wines is low).

Sauternes is traditionally served in France with foie gras at the beginning of a meal. This is one of the most complementary pairings possible. Sauternes and Barsac wines are usually served as or with dessert. When I wrote my first article on the subject in 1978, use of dessert wines was minimal in the U.S. and still is. One reason is that many young wine-sippers start with cheap, sweet whites or reds, progress to better dry whites and then to better dry reds. They've never tried a phenomenal dessert wine. Another reason is that even at dinner parties the dessert course is either omitted or typically served with coffee.

In 1855, there was also a classification for Sauternes and Barsac. Chateau d'Yquem was the only Grand Premier Cru. Eleven Premiers Crus appeared: La Tour-Blanche, Clos Haut-Peyraguey, Lafaurie-Peyraguey, Rayne-Vigneay, Suduiraut, Coutet, Climens, Guiraud, Rieussec, Rabaud-Promis and Sigalas-Rabaud. And there are an additional 12 Deuxièmes Crus (Second Great Estates).

Chateau d'Yquem is at the top—all by itself. The grape pickers are native to the area and return each year to harvest the grapes from October through November. These are the most skilled pickers in Bordeaux, picking over each vine every week or so to select grapes individually at the perfect stage of Botrytis attack.

The current plantings are 80 percent Sémillon and 20 percent Sauvignon Blanc. After harvest, the juice ferments in new oak barrels. New oak is used for the additional tannin it provides since the juice gets little or no tannins from the skins or the stems, which are separated after picking. For some 3 ½ years, each barrel is topped off (filled when small amounts of wine evaporate) and then blended and bottled. In poor years, there is no Chateau d'Yquem bottled, other than its lesser and less sweet wine, Ygrec. In the years Yquem is bottled, it is unbelievably luscious. But it must have some age on it—usually at least 6 years to start smoothing out into probably the best dessert wine in the world. And this wine is the exception to the relative inexpensiveness of the Saurternes and Barsac wines.

Following Yquem, the best wines are Suduiraut, Rieussec, Lafaurie-Peyraguey, Climens (a Barsac) and de Fargues (not a classified wine). The 1855 Classification for Sauternes and Barsac appears in Appendix B.

There are several Bordeaux districts of minor importance just north and northeast of Sauternes and Barsac that make lesser-quality, less-sweet and much-less-expensive sweet wines. Following are three such wines and my favorite producer(s) of each:

Cadillac—Chateau Fayau
St. Croix-du-Mont—Chateau Loubens and Chateau du Mont
Loupiac—Chateau Les Roques and Chateau du Cros

THE REST OF BORDEAUX

Bordeaux is significantly larger than the famous districts covered above. While the quality of wines from other Bordeaux districts generally wanes, the lower prices make the best wines great bargains. Following are districts from the right bank of Bordeaux (right side of the Gironde River), with the reds primarily Merlot, and my favorite wines found therein:

Lalande de Pomerol—just next to Pomerol—Chateau Les Cruzelles and Chateau La Fleur de Bouard

Entre du Mers (translation means "between two oceans," but actually is located between two rivers)—produces more reds, but the whites are superior. Chateau Bonnet (white)

Cotes de Castillon—Chateau d'Aiguilhe, Chateau Poupille, Domaine L'A and Chateau de Pitray

Cotes de Francs—Chateau Puygueraud (the latter two districts are just east of Saint Emilion and mostly Merlot and Cabernet Franc)

Bourg—Chateau Roc de Cambes

Blaye—Chateau Les Jonqueyres (the latter two districts are just across the Gironde from the famous chateaux of the Médoc and are mostly Merlot and Cabernet Sauvignon)

Fronsac—Chateau Fontenil (owned by esteemed wine consultant Michel Rolland), Chateau de la Riviere and Chateau Renard Mondésir

Canon-Fronsac—Chateau Canon de Brem, Chateau Roullet and Chateau Moulin Pey-Labrie (the latter two districts are just east of Pomerol)

Premieres Cotes de Bordeaux—just south of the expansive Entre du Mers—Chateau Reynon (red and white), Chateau Carignan and Chateau Suau (reds).

BURGUNDY

Burgundy evokes images of richness in color and texture. One of the never-to-be-solved debates is which region boasts the best wine—Bordeaux or Burgundy? There is, of course, no answer.

Burgundy is a region in the eastern/northeastern part of France. The top Burgundy wines come from an area called the Cote d'Or, which is in turn divided into the Cote de Nuits (nwee) on the north and the Cote de Beaune on the south. The Cote d'Or is about 25 miles long—covering slightly less area than California's Napa Valley. But rather than a valley, Cote d'Or runs flat from the Saône River on the east and meanders for about one-half mile to a range of hills on the west, all burgeoning with gorgeous vines.

The longest-lasting, fullest-bodied Burgundy reds come from the Cote de Nuits. Here, the Pinot Noir grape achieves a certain excellence that, so far, has not been attained elsewhere in the world. The red wines of Cote de Beaune are not as big and powerful, but sometimes are just as charming and pleasing. The Cote de Beaune is also the home of—at least historically—the greatest dry white wines in the world; however, as I will point out in a later chapter, California has made great strides in receiving such accolades.

Let's look at a map of the Cote d'Or:

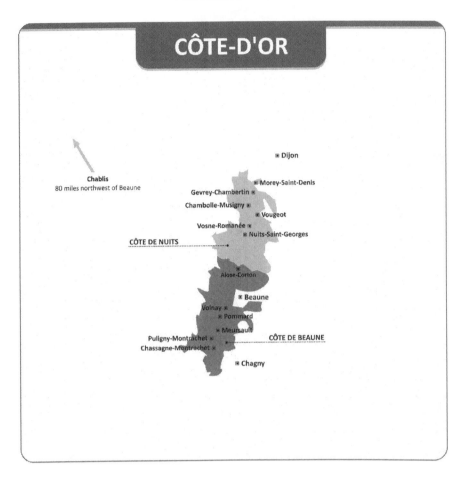

Burgundy the region is not too complicated. Burgundy wines themselves are a whole other topic of contorted facts. If two wine lovers discuss a bottle of 2005 Chateau "X" from Bordeaux, they are talking about one wine and one blend produced from the one estate in Bordeaux. A bottle tasted tonight will taste similar to one tasted a year ago, albeit with an additional year of bottle age. But in Burgundy, under Napoleon, the large land holdings were split up, resulting in extreme fragmentation and sometimes hopeless confusion.

For instance, let's compare two actual famous vineyards: One in Bordeaux and one in Burgundy. The Clos de Vougeot in Burgundy, the largest vineyard in the Cote de Nuits, is comparable in size to Chateau Latour, one of the First Growths in the Médoc in Bordeaux. In Bordeaux, there is one ownership family or group for each chateau, and, for example, the same final blend will go into every bottle of 2005 Chateau Latour. At the 125-acre Clos de Vougeot vineyard, however, there are approximately 75 owners, some with as little as one-third of an acre. Each owner either tends his or her own vines or leases the right for a shipper to tend them, and each owner may produce and/or bottle his or her own wine, or simply sell the crop for someone else to harvest and sell the wine.

Also adding to the complexity of the Clos de Vougeot is the partially sloped terrain. While many vines benefit from excellent drainage, others are disadvantaged by growing near or at the bottom of a hill. Therefore, two bottles of 2005 Clos de Vougeot may present disparate wines: different owners, vineyard managers, winemakers, positions in the vineyard, bottlers and shippers! So how does one sort this out?

Most of the growers in Burgundy sell their grapes or their barrel or two of wine to a négociant (shipper) who either makes or finishes the wine. In Burgundy, the négociant is of primary importance.

When a Burgundy owner does make and bottle his/her own wine, the label will state: "Mis en bouteilles au domaine", "Mis au domaine" or "Mis en bouteilles à la propriéte." Any substitutes, such as "Mis en bouteilles dans nos caves," are usually meaningless.

The most expensive wine in the world is Romanée-Conti, and it hails from the village of Vosne-Romanée. The vineyard, which is only four and one-third acres, is the "superstar" of the holdings of the Domaine de la Romanée-Conti, which owns all of La Tache and has holdings in several other famous vineyards, including Richebourg, Grands-Echezeaux, Echezeaux (eh shay zoe), Romanée-Saint-Vivant and Montrachet (more about Montrachet, a white wine, later). Some of these wines fetch prices that befit museum pieces.

My favorite vineyard in Burgundy that produces almost-affordable wines—at least generally less expensive than Romanée-Conti, La Tache and Richebourg from the Domaine de la Romanée-Conti—is Chambertin. These Burgundies are incredibly sturdy and long-lasting wines. The famous Clos de Vougeot and the Musigny vineyards are in the same class, but produce a somewhat lighter, smoother wine than Chambertin.

COTE DE BEAUNE

One of the best values here is Cote de Beaune-Villages—normally under $20, even from a top shipper. But the Cote de Beaune is more widely praised for its white wines, the greatest which comes from two villages—Puligny-Montrachet (poo lee nyee mon rah shay) and Chassagne-Montrachet (shah sahnyuh mon rah shay)—these pronunciations being two more wine knowledge separators. Here, the Chardonnay performs to its maximum potential. The wines labeled Puligny-Montrachet and Chassagne-Montrachet have outstanding vintages such as 2004, 2005 and 2006. The unrivalled vineyard of Montrachet, or Le Montrachet, which is partly in Puligny and partly in Chassagne, produces the most expensive and greatest dry white wine. A serious competitor for this honor is Corton-Charlemagne, which is in the village of Aloxe-Corton. In general, a wine from a good vintage and shipper, labeled Puligny-Montrachet, Chassagne -Montrachet or Meursault, will be a first-class Chardonnay priced in the $30 to $60 range. If one of these names is followed by a Premier Cru vineyard, like Chassagne-Montrachet La Boudriotte, the wine is at the high end of this range, or more.

CHABLIS

About 70 miles north of Dijon, Chablis is another famous Burgundian village. The wines from Chablis are crisp, assertive and have a classic austerity. The name has been abused by some California vintners who bottled a bland white in a jug and foisted it on the public with the name Chablis. The wine didn't and still doesn't even have to contain any Chardonnay. Fortunately, due to efforts of companies such as Gallo, this inexpensive generic (named after a place) wine improved over the years, and actually encouraged many to try wine and eventually move up to better wines. The same holds true for California Rhine Wine (doesn't necessarily have Rhine-type grapes) and California Burgundy (doesn't have to contain Pinot Noir).

GREAT BURGUNDIES, GREAT VALUES

The best values in white Burgundies are produced south of the Cote de Beaune in areas are called Chalonnaise and Mâconnais. Such wines include Rully, Montagny, Saint-Veran and Macon Blanc. The well-known Pouilly-Fuisse usually is a bit better than these, but perhaps not worth the significantly higher prices, which many think are based purely on the name Pouilly-Fuisse (which almost everyone mispronounces). It's poo yee fwee say!

The greatest wines of the Cote D'Or are classified as either Grands Crus or Premiers Crus. A contextual comparison, although oversimplified, might be that the 30 Grands Crus are comparable to the Médoc First and Second Growths and the Premiers Crus are comparable to the Third and Fourth Growths. The Premiers Crus vineyards are always preceded by their village, such as Vosne-Romanée (village) Les Beaumonts (vineyard).

And now—TRUMPETS—some very important information—the négociant (shipper). There are several who consistently produce top Burgundies. Maison Louis Jadot is one. Bouchard Père & Fils (Sons) and Joseph Drouhin are two others. On the high end with discouraging prices are the Domaine de la Romanée-Conti, Domaine Leroy and Domaine D'Auvenay. In the more affordable range, but still expensive, are Ponsot, Armand Rousseau, Claude Dugat, Jean Grivot, Jaques Prieur, Ghislane Barthod, Henri Gouges, Louis Latour and Remoissinet. Some well-known importers whose wines are generally more affordable, and usually good values, are Kermit Lynch, Neal Rosenthal, Louis-Dresser, Robert Chadderdon, Becky Wasserman and Polaner Selections.

Appendix C contains the Grands Crus and Premiers Crus Burgundies of the Cote D'Or. Although a small sampling of Cote D'Or wines, these are some of the supreme wines of the world. No need to memorize them—the label will state Grand Cru or Premier Cru. The best bargains here—and far more available—are wines with the village name (such as Gevrey-Chambertin or Chambolle-Musigny) from a good shipper without the name of a famous vineyard following.

BEAUJOLAIS

Most people are not aware that Beaujolais, made from the Gamay grape, is actually in the far southern part of Burgundy. There are three types of Beaujolais. The first is simply labeled "Beaujolais" or "Beaujolais Superior," which hails from the southern part of Beaujolais. A significant step up is Beaujolais-Villages, from around 35 villages in central Beaujolais. The top wines from Beaujolais are from the 11 northern villages and are called the "Cru" Beaujolais wines. My favorites are Moulin-a-Vent, Brouilly (especially the fabulous Chateau de la Chaize) and Julienas, but all are superior and more expensive in most cases than other Beaujolais wines.

The "king" of Beaujolais is Georges Duboeuf. Once again, the shipper is of great importance. In a great vintage like 2009, the Beaujolais-Villages wines are excellent and the "Cru" wines are exceptional. But they are not big and rich like their big brothers from Pinot Noir to the north. Complementary foods for Beaujolais range from a ham and cheese sandwich to grilled quail wrapped in bacon.

Chapter 4
THE REST OF FRANCE

Note, in the map below, Bourgogne is the French word for Burgundy.

CHAMPAGNE

A virtually guaranteed way to enliven a gathering is with a bottle of chilled Champagne. And depending on the group, the status of the supplying member increases proportionally to the price and prominence of the label. Everyone perks up at the sight and sound of a cork being popped off a non-vintage Moet & Chandon. Expectations may be heightened further with a vintage Champagne. And if it's Dom Perignon or Cristal, the anticipation, as well as the supplier's reputation as a host, may soar to record levels.

Sparkling wines are made around the world—many by cheap methods, others by the method champenoise (or méthode traditionelle), the true Champagne process. Germany is a large producer of sekt and Spain an even larger producer of cava, their versions of Champagne respectively. Wonderful versions of sparkling wines also hail from the U.S., Australia, Italy and other parts of France. But there is only one Champagne (a few producers outside Champagne call their wine Champagne, as some outside of Burgundy call their wine Burgundy).

Champagne is a region about 90 miles east and a little north of Paris. In the old days, not all of the sugar fermented after the harvest because of the extreme cold. However, in the spring, the rest of the sugar began to ferment, and the wines in barrels became effervescent. In the mid-1600s, Dom Perignon, a Benedictine monk who was a cellarmaster, is reputed to have created a better way for the wine to retain its sparkle (CO_2 bubbles). He is also credited with discovering that a more harmonious sparkling wine could be made from various vineyard blends than from just one vineyard. This early discovery led to today's practice of the consistently excellent non-vintage "house-style cuvées" from so many producers.

The grapes for Champagne are Chardonnay, Pinot Noir and Pinot Meunier, the latter two being black grapes. It is understandably a delicate process to make a light-colored Champagne out of black grapes, but the practice has been perfected over the years. While most are blends, a wine labeled blanc de blancs is 100 percent Chardonnay.

In the early days of Champagne making, with bottles that were not uniform and secondary fermentations in bottles not fully understood, it was not unusual for a third of a Champagne cellar to be involuntary liquidated by bottle explosions. Around 1800, a French chemist devised a way to measure the unfermented sugar and calculate how much sugar to add prior to the secondary fermentation, thus producing the precise amount of CO_2 pressure for safe bottle aging. All the while, the actual bottles were being improved and becoming more stable.

During the second fermentation, dead yeast cells form around and on the corks through a process called riddling—a method which, incidentally, is attributed to the widow Clicqout, whence also cometh the name Veuve Clicquot, one of the most popular Champagnes. When it's time for the final bottling, the corks are frozen and popped out along with the dead yeasts. Each Champagne house then adds its "dosage," which results in an optimal amount of sugar and a proper fill. The exact dollop of "secret syrup" makes the Champagne brut, extra dry, etc. The goal of every Champagne house is to produce a consistent non-vintage blend each year (fans then know what to expect).

Occasionally a "natural" will crop up, meaning that little or no "secret syrup" was added to the dosage. Next is "brut," which is dry with around 1 percent natural residual sugar but never more than 1.5 percent. "Extra dry" actually means slightly sweet and usually contains 1.5 percent to 2 percent. "Demi-sec" stands for medium sweet, containing 3 percent to 5 percent, and can be served as a dessert wine as long as the dessert is not too sweet. A "doux" is a true dessert Champagne.

There are close to a billion bottles of Champagne resting in different stages of development in the cavernous cellars underneath the various Champagne houses. It is truly a sight to behold. Magnums and bottles of Champagne are always fermented in the same bottle that is "disgorged" (cork frozen and popped out). The same is true of some half bottles. This generally is not true with splits, tiny bottles and very large bottles, which do not age nearly as well. I recommend sticking to bottles and magnums.

The non-vintage bruts are the best-quality non-vintage wines. Because sugar masks defaults, slightly lesser-quality juice may be used for extra dry and demi-sec. Some of my favorite non-vintage Champagnes are Deutz Brut Classic, Pommery Brut Royal, Charles Heidseick Brut, Pol Roger Brut, Louis Roederer Brut Premiere and Billecart-Salmon Brut. Except for the more expensive Billecart Salmon, all are in the $30 to $45 range.

Although Champagne is usually reserved for celebrations, there is nothing better with caviar, smoked salmon or paté as hors d'oeuvres. Brut is always best to me, but for those who enjoy a little sweetness, extra dry works well. For a dessert wine, I recommend two relatively new wines from Champagne: Moet & Chandon Imperial Nectar and Imperial Nectar Rosé.

THE RHONE VALLEY

My wine world once primarily revolved around Bordeaux. That changed at Dr. Lou Skinner's 1981 weekend tasting in Coral Gables of the best 50 Bordeaux reds from the fabulous 1961 vintage. During that weekend my eyes were opened to the northern Rhone.

We were Lou's guests at an International Wine and Food Society dinner. One wine served was a Hermitage from the Northern Rhone. It was as good as any wine I've had before or since.

Bordeaux is a region. Burgundy is a region. Hermitage is a large hill with its own appellation along the Rhone River south of Burgundy. With one exception, the greatest wines from the northern Rhone come from that hill. The reds are 100 percent Syrah and among the world's longest-living red wines. Descriptors include deep color and displaying flavors of roasted sirloin, pepper, cassis, minerals, blackberries and black currants. Other adjectives for these very expensive wines include concentrated, intense, bold, pure and rich.

Hermitage from a good producer and an excellent vintage generally needs five years of cellar age after release, and another 10 years will prove the owner thereof brilliant. The most well-known producers besides Jaboulet include Chapoutier, Chave, Tardieu-Laurent, Marc Sorrell, Delas Freres, A. Clape and more recently E. Guigal. Vintages are not as important as they used to be because of severe pruning, crop thinning when necessary, sorting, etc., but avoid the poor 2002 vintage here.

The next great wine of the northern Rhone is Cote Rotie in the far north. There is one world-class producer here, E. Guigal. His La Landonne, La Moulin and La Turque offerings—usually around $200+ a bottle at release—are on par with the greatest Hermitage wines.

Perhaps it's the weather, latitude, soil or the fact that a blend of around 5 percent Viognier (a white grape) is typical, but most Cote Roties do not match up to their more famous Hermitage brethren slightly to the south. After Guigal, the supreme Cote Rotie producers include Rene Rostang, Jaboulet, Delas Freras and Michel Ogier. The best recent vintages for the northern Rhone are 1999, 2003, 2006, 2007 and 2009, with the latter perhaps being the superstar.

The other major appellations of the northern Rhone are, from north to south, Condrieu, St. Joseph, Crozes-Hermitage and Cornas. The extremely expensive Condrieu and its tiny inner appellation Chateau Grillet produce whites from Viognier, which I've never considered good values next to the best California and even Texas Viogniers.

St. Joseph produces primarily reds along with some whites from the Marsanne and Roussanne grapes. With the exception of the top producers, I don't think of St. Joseph as a northern Rhone. The combination of microclimate and soil, along with east-facing vineyards (thus losing critical, late-afternoon sunshine), results in lighter, less-ripe grapes that typically should be consumed early in their lives.

Just to the south is Crozes-Hermitage. There is about 10 times more Crozes-Hermitage produced than big brother Hermitage. Although most of the wines are red from Syrah—the blending of up to 15 percent white grapes are allowed—there is a small production of white from Marsanne supplemented with Roussanne. The wines here are a slight step up from St. Joseph; however, there are no Hermitage look-alikes.

Cornas, in the southern part of the northerern Rhone, is a different story. Here is a challenger to Hermitage made from 100 percent Syrah. Like Hermitage, this wine can be a dense, dark-colored beauty with good aging prospects. Cornas occasionally can be found from top producer A. Clape. Other Cornas winners can be found from some of the winemakers found above, and if you're lucky, you may come across one from Patrick Lesec, Durand, Domaine Courbis, Alan Voge or one of my favorites, Verset.

Following is a general list of what you could expect to pay for a very good vintage from a better producer:

Hermitage—$75-$100

Cote Rotie (except for the top producers) —$60-$75

Condrieu—$50-$60

St. Joseph—$20-$30

Crozes-Hermitage—$30

Cornas—$40

The most famous wine of the southern Rhone is Chateauneuf-du-Pape. Top producers include Chateau La Nerthe, Domaine du Vieux Télégraphe,

Beaucastel, Henri Bonneau, Domaine du Caillou, Clos Saint-Jean, Patric Lesec, Domaine du Pegau, Saint-Cosme and Pierre Usseglio. Possibly the longest run of great vintages in France, disturbed only by the worthless 2002 vintage, is the southern Rhone from 1998 to 2007—all outstanding vintages, with 2007 possibly being the best of all time. The 2009 and 2010 vintages are also excellent.

The principal grapes here are Grenache, Syrah, Mourvèdre and Cinsault. The next top appelations in the southern Rhone are Gigondas and Vacqueyras.

In the area south of Chateauneuf-du-Pape (also southern Rhone) are wines called Cotes-du-Rhone. These wines are less distinguished, but in a year like 2010, can provide very good drinking for between $15 and $20 a bottle. Tavel, known for its rosé wines, is also located in the southern Rhone. My favorites are Domaine Ott and Priéure Montézargues.

THE LOIRE VALLEY

Boasting some of the world's most beautiful wine country, the Loire Valley starts at Nantes on the west coast and stretches several hundred miles to France's interior. Although not as famous or complex as some other wines of France, the white wines, and to a lesser degree the reds, provide some surprises!

The best white is Sancerre followed by Pouilly-Fumé. Both are made with the Sauvignon Blanc grape, have excellent acidity, a smoky, flinty bouquet and more fruit than their cousins in Graves (not really fair since Semillon is primary in Graves). One of the best wine/food matches in my experience was a 1976 Sancerre with Mussels Mouclade at Le Chalet Restaurant in Royan, France, in 1977. The late Dr. Lou Skinner, one of the most knowledgeable experts on French wine and food, told me in the late 1970s that when he dined in France, he always asked to start with the best, most recent Sancerre on the wine list (this cued the sommelier that the American patron knew something about wine).

The Chenin Blanc grape excels in Loire as well. The most recognized wine from this grape is Vouvray. Although the Vouvray winemakers pride themselves in their sweet wines (Moelleux), the fact that sweet wines have never quite caught on caused them to ferment most of their wines until dry. The Chenin Blanc wine garnering the most attention recently from Loire is Savenniéres.

The other famous wine of the Loire is Muscadet, which is a grape varietal. Muscadet is a lighter and less acidic wine than Sauvignon Blanc or Chenin Blanc. All of these whites are splendid with seafood.

Before we leave the Loire Valley, I must mention the two reds that have a following: Chinon and Bourgueil (boor guh'y). Made from the Cabernet Franc grape, they have been known in the past as light, pleasant and, frankly, not too appealing. Modern-day winemaking has changed that. If your local wine merchant touts you on one, it might be worthwhile trying (and it won't break the bank). The largest and most important producer of premium wines in the Loire Valley is Saget La Perriere.

ALSACE

The following description of Alsace was written for me in 1978 by Jack T. Holmes, who was at the time Commandeur of the Fort Worth Chapter of the Confrerie St.-Etienne d'Alsace and a member of its International Grand Council. You can feel his passion for Alsace in his rich and colorful prose.

"The vibrant green vineyards of Alsace are nestled among the broken lower slopes of the Vosges Mountain Range. Across the misty valley of the Rhine River to the east lies Germany's Black Forest. To the south in the swelling foothills of the Alps is Colmar, the ancient capital of Charlemagne. North some 100 kilometers, German turreted Strasbourg guards the northern flank.

"Between these two picturesque, ancient cities runs the Alsatian Route du Vin strung with half-hidden medieval villages like baroque jewels on a precious necklace. This rich land has known Roman legions, Teutonic invaders, crusaders and many a warring expedition over the centuries. Today, its beautifully tended vineyards yield pale golden, crisp and fragrant wines that have few peers in the world."

The primary grapes, in ascending order, are:
Sylvaner—Light and clean. Sometimes one dimensional.
Pinot Blanc—More depth. Refreshing. Aperitif or hors d'oeuvre wine.
Gewurztraminer—Full-bodied with a spicy bouquet and taste. Litchi comes to mind.
Riesling—The classic wine of Alsace. Elegant bouquet and fabulous fruit/acid balance. Pair with seafood.
Pinot Gris—My favorite. Opulent and full-bodied.

> **From Alsace to California – a Perfect Pairing**
>
> In the mid-1980s my friend Bill Rice, food editor for the *Chicago Tribune,* and I attended a luncheon in Houston. The entrée was a ham and corn casserole, and Bill and I were each asked to bring a wine to serve with it. Bill's selection: a Joseph Phelps Gewurztraminer from the Napa Valley with around 2 percent residual sugar; mine: an Alsatian Gewurztraminer Vendange Tardive with around 2 percent residual sugar. And yes, they both were perfect pairings!

Most Alsatian wines are dry—some severely dry. Notable exceptions are some of the wines of Zind-Humbrecht, possibly the best producer in Alsace. A richer, slightly sweet Alsatian wine is called "vendange tardive" or late harvest. Some of these are very slightly sweet and others are moderately sweet.

Some think the oldest vineyard in literature is Chateau Haut-Brion in the Médoc, since it was mentioned in Samuel Peppy's diary in 1663. But the Steinklotz Vineyard in far northern Alsace was reported in 589 AD to belong to Merovingian King Childebert II. And my favorite producer of wines from this extant top vineyard is Helfrich. My favorite producer from the far south is Lucien Albrecht, which was founded in 1425! Other notable producers are Josmeyer, Trimbach, Hugel, Marcel Deiss, Albert Mann, Andre Ostertag and Domaine Weinbach.

PROVENCE AND LANGUEDOC-ROUSSILLON

In far-southeastern France lies the region of Provence. This is the wonderland of Saint-Tropez, Cannes and Antibes. The dry rosé is the wine of choice here. The best wines, including reds and whites, are labeled Cotes de Provence and Coteaux d'Aix en Provence. The most-admired red is Bandol, from the seacoast village of that name, and the top name in Bandol has long been Domaine Tempier. This is one of the world's best examples of what the Mouvédre grape can accomplish, and the wine can age beautifully.

Just west of Provence, Languedoc-Roussillon is the largest wine-growing region in France. Until the late 1980s, almost all of the wine from here was ordinary. But in a frenzy of new winemakers and wine-making techniques, the region is now a treasure trove of wines for under $20 a bottle. The two main appellations are Coteaux du Languedoc and Cotes du Roussillon. Some of the famous names within the Languedoc are Corbiéres, Costières de Nimes, Saint-Chinian and Minervois, and the dessert wines Muscat de Frontignan and Muscat de Rivesaltes (whites) and Banyuls (red).

There are several cooperatives that have successfully marketed Syrah and Mourvèdre (my favorites from this region), Grenache, Cabernet Sauvignon, Chardonnay and others. The best known is Val d'Orbieu and its Reserve St.-Martin. To find a winner from here, ask a trusted retailer (or wine steward) to suggest some of the best wines from the Languedoc area. There are literally hundreds of wines that provide some of the best values on the planet. One of my favorite under-$20 reds comes from Cobières. It is the Blason d'Aussières from Les Domaines Barons de Rothschild (Lafite).

There are two towns in southwest France of some importance. If you can name these towns and the primary grape from each, you will be privy to some facts that are primarily known only by the wine cognoscenti: Cahors—Malbec and Madiran—Tannat. As a matter of interest, there is a nascent wine industry in Uruguay based on Tannat! Cuatro Caballos Tannat from Uruguay won a silver medal at an international wine competition in November 2011.

STOMPING OUT PHYLLOXERA

As the Civil War was coming to a close, a tiny, almost microscopic louse (read, ugly little bug) was accidentally imported by Europe (probably from the eastern United States). The native East Coast vines of the U.S. had become immune to the parasite. However, once the organism landed in Europe, it multiplied and spread to such an extent that the non-immune vinifera vines of Europe—Cabernet Sauvignon, Merlot, Syrah, Chardonnay, Riesling, etc.—were systematically devastated.

Although the nascent problem was noted in the early to mid-1860s, nobody had a clue for years what was causing the death of the vines. It was finally discovered that this louse, the phylloxera, attached itself to the roots of the vines and sucked out their life supply. And since the California vineyards were planted primarily with vinifera grapes brought over from Europe, they eventually began to suffer the same fate.

T.V. Munson, of Denison, Texas, was one of several men who sent hundreds of thousands of native U. S. rootstocks to Europe, where vinifera vines were grafted onto these immune rootstocks. Munson helped save France from the phylloxera. He was awarded the Chevalier du Merite Agricole of the Legion of Honor along with two other Americans—the first Americans to be so honored since Thomas Edison.

It is rumored that many of Munson's cuttings, most of which were from east Texas, were used for grafting in the Champagne area. The next time someone remarks that there is only one real Champagne and that no other sparkling wine is competitive, you can respond, "Well of course that's true now, since so many of the vines there were grafted onto Texas (or U.S.) rootstocks!"

The last year I know of that top-quality pre-phylloxera Bordeaux was produced would be 1878, and I have had the Chateau Mouton-Rothschild from that vintage from a magnum. It looked and tasted like one of the great vintages of the 1920s, 1928 in particular.

I have been fortunate to experience many pre-phylloxera wines. The oldest was Chateau-Gruaud Larose 1819, tasted at a magnificent two-day affair in Fort Worth. The tasting was orchestrated by Dr. Marvin Overton, one of America's great wine connoisseurs and collectors. The bottle was brought from the chateau where it had been recorked and re-filled with more 1819 every 30 years or so for about 170 years. The wine showed good color with a light rim and barely a hint of oxidation. A most remarkable, very drinkable wine, it could easily pass for a wine 100 years younger. It had "astonishing preservation," according to David Peppercorn, M.W. (Master of Wine), who was in attendance from England.

The greatest pre-phylloxera wine I've ever tasted, which is also my favorite wine of all time, is Chateau Lafite-Rothschild 1870 (magnum) from the famous Glamis Castle cellar. In the early 1980s, it had a youthful appearance—still opaque—and was a colossus, drinking more like a 1945 on steroids. It was seemingly from another planet. Maybe it was, and when the aliens left, they took the infected rootstocks with them, zapped the phylloxera and are enjoying pre-phylloxera Lafite on Venus.

Alas, the debate about the differences between pre- and post-phylloxera wines is becoming moot. One thing that concerns me is that, sadly, I find no mention of T.V. Munson in many large tomes about wine. If you're interested in this "Grape Man of Texas," go to www.eakinpress. com, search for T.V. Munson, then click on "Texas Biographies," or call 800-880-8642.

The T. V. Munson Memorial Vineyard and the T. V. Munson Viticulture Enology Center are located on the campus of Grayson County College, Denison, Texas, where degrees in viticulture and enology have been offered for the past 30 years. Contact Dr. Roy Renfro for information: renfror@ grayson.edu or 903-463-8707 or www.grayson.edu.

CALIFORNIA SHAKES UP
THE WINE INDUSTRY

In a very condensed nutshell, some of the big names in California's early wine history are:

- Father Junipero Serra transported Mission grapes from Mexico to southern California in the late 1600s.
- Jean Louis Vignes was the first to bring European wine-grape cuttings to California in the early 1830s and the first well-known winemaker in California.
- "Count" Agoston Haraszthy (a wild and crazy guy) brought some 100,000 cuttings to California from Europe, representing over 300 varietals, in the 1860s. He purportedly was killed by an alligator in South America some time later.
- Finnish sea captain Gustave Niebaum purchased Inglenook Vineyard in 1879 and proceeded to build the leviathan, gothic Inglenook Winery (completed in 1887), the first great winery of California. A descendant, John Daniel, took over shortly after Prohibition. Daniel continued the grand tradition until he sold the winery to United Vintners in 1964.
- The California Wine Institute was established in 1934 and the first real quality standards were adopted.
- Andre Tchelistcheff, a Russian immigrant who had studied wine in Bordeaux, arrived in 1938 as winemaker for Georges de la Tour

at Beaulieu Vineyard. Tchelistcheff was the first truly great wine-maker in California, made the wines at Beaulieu (B.V.) through the 1972 vintage, and consulted for many wineries until his death in 1994 at almost 94 years of age. He smoked like a chimney, and when we became friends in the late 1970s, he told me he tried to quit once, but started again because he could no longer taste the wines!

- James Zellerbach brought the first French oak barrels (as opposed to American oak barrels) to his Sonoma Winery, Hanzell, in 1957.
- Robert Mondavi split off from his family at Charles Krug Winery in 1965 and started the Robert Mondavi Winery in Oakville (Napa Valley). I was fortunate to attend his 80th birthday party at the winery, during which his wife presented him with a llama! Until his recent death at age 94, he traveled the globe as the great ambassador for California wine. Brother Peter Mondavi, who remains at Charles Krug, celebrated his 97th birthday on Nov. 8, 2011.
- Moet Hennessy purchased 700 acres in the Napa Valley in 1973 for its subsidiary Domaine Chandon, the first of the numerous foreign ventures and joint ventures (such as Opus One—first vintage 1979, and Dominus—first vintage 1983).

California has been the leading wine state since around 1870 (when it surpassed Missouri and Ohio in wine production), as well as following Prohibition, when winemaking was reborn in the U.S.

In Ithaca, New York, at the Second Annual Meeting of the Society of Wine Educators, I listened to an amusing first-hand account of post-Prohibition California. In the early 1930s, Ernest Gallo, a Californian, felt certain that Prohibition would soon end. Ernest offered

In the 1960s and early 1970s, the most popular table wines were usually in jugs: Chablis, Pink Chablis, Mountain Rhine Wine, Burgundy and others, made by Gallo, Swiss Colony, Almaden, Inglenook and many others. These wines had the science behind them (not yet the art) and were a good value for the money. Wines from other parts of the world in that relatively cheap price range were inferior by comparison.

The progression of wine drinking in the 1960s, '70s and '80s for Americans usually went something like this: sweet numerous grape growers double the current rate for next year's crop. Sure enough, Prohibition ended. Ernest remarked to his brother Julio, "Now that we will have all these grapes, I think it would be a good idea if we learned to make wine." With that, they went to the local library and studied the art of winemaking from a book written in the 1800s! E&J Gallo later introduced decent, low-cost wines to the country, the most famous probably being Hearty Burgundy.

Portuguese rosés (Mateus and Lancers), sweet Italian whites (Asti Spumanti) and sweet Italian reds (Lambrusco, which by the mid-1980s, accounted for over half the Italian wines sold in the U.S.), sweet German whites (Blue Nun being the most famous), then dry whites (California Chablis, etc.), and finally dry reds (California Burgundy, etc.)—people actually started having wine with food—and then into the better dry whites and reds.

During Andre Tchelistcheff's run at Beaulieu Vineyard through the 1972 vintage, he trained many of the future winemaking stars, and he continued to serve as consulting winemaker at numerous wineries, including Chateau Ste. Michelle in Washington and Jordan in the Alexander Valley. At one point, I lined him up with Ed Auler at Fall Creek Winery in Texas, and Tchelistcheff became Auler's long-distance consultant for several years in the mid-1980s! Tchelistcheff's wines were among less than a handful of great California wines in the 1950s and barely a handful of world-class wines in the 1960s, including Heitz, Ridge, Stony Hill and Mayacamas.

It was not until the early 1970s that a paucity of "those in the know" came forth to proclaim the virtues of California wines, and, of course, these daring souls were flayed mercilessly by anyone who had put French wines on a pedestal. Wine writer Robert Lawrence Balzer organized a comparative tasting in New York of the best California whites and the best French whites. The tasters included, among others, Alexis Lichine (owner of Chateau Prieur-Lichine in Bordeaux), Alexis Bespaloff (author of the *Signet Book of Wine*), Frank Schoonmaker (wine writer and merchant who was the first in the early 1940s to introduce his eponymous selection of wines named after the grapes, like Chardonnay and Pinot Noir), and Gerald Asher (another well-known wine writer). Of the 28 wines present were Corton-Charlemagne and Le Montrachet, the two greatest white wines from Burgundy. The first four places went to California wines: Freemark Abbey, Chalone, Christian Brothers (no longer extant) and Mirassou. The two French whites mentioned above placed seventh and 12th, respectively.

When I cut my teeth (or in this case, stained them) on wine in the mid-1970s, it was on French wines. If anyone was venturesome (or wealthy) enough to order an expensive wine, it was always French. In fact, waiters would routinely don a smile when offering a French wine and a slight sneer when describing the "domestic" counterpart. Of course, nobody desired the latter.

For hundreds of years, no other regions in the world could produce wines that rivaled France. Almost all of the noble grape varieties had originated and reached their apex in France. Since the 1855 Bordeaux Classification, the First Growths were preeminent in the world of Cabernet Sauvignon. For centuries, it was argued, the microorganisms in the soil, the trial and error of finding the perfect microclimates, soils, drainage and locations, and the wisdom of the generations had all culminated in an unrivaled offering. And for white Burgundy, there's a quote about its most famous wine that will suffice for the reputation there—that "Montrachet should be consumed on bended knee with head bowed."

As of 1976, it was virtually unanimous that the greatest Cabernets came from Bordeaux and the greatest Chardonnays from Burgundy. In California, it was not uncommon for a winemaker to wish or even attempt to make a Chateau Lafite-Rothschild or a Chateau Latour from Cabernet grapes or a Corton-Charlemagne, or Le Montrachet from Chardonnay grapes.

In the late 1970s and early 1980s, my favorite pastime was to serve the 1976 Jordan Cabernet Sauvignon blind to fellow oenophiles who professed to abhor California wines. I was never disappointed: they always loved it, but some were visibly depressed when the facts interfered with their preconceived notion that California wines were no good. Later in the 1990s, I pulled the same stunt with J Vineyards Sparkling Wine (owned by Judy Jordan, daughter of Tom Jordan). As one aficionado attempted to guess which of the great Champagnes it might be, he said, "Oh No!" when I revealed it was from California.

AND NOW FOR THE EXCITEMENT! On May 24, 1976, a seminal event took place in Paris. Stephen Spurrier, a Londoner who ran a wine shop in Paris and taught wine classes (mainly about French wines), with the help of employee Patricia Gallagher, an American, organized a tasting of California and French wines. Spurrier knew that if the labels were revealed to the group of French wine experts, the California wines would be relegated to the bottom of the barrel. So he served the wines blind. Spurrier actually knew very little about California wines, so what was he out to prove? Nothing other than to showcase some of the better California wines that he and Patricia had discovered. For starters, he "stacked the deck" in favor of the French by pitting a Batard-Montrachet, Puligny-Montrachet Les Pucelles, Meursault-Charmes and Beaune Clos des Mouches from the most famous and well-regarded French producers against six upstarts from California in the Chardonnay tasting.

Equally lopsided, he thought, he selected two First Growths (Chateau Haut-Brion and Chateau Mouton-Rothschild from the heralded 1970 vintage) and two fabulous Second Growths (a 1970 Chateau Montrose and a 1971 Chateau Léoville-Las-Cases) to go against six upstart reds from California for the Cabernet Sauvignon tasting. Although the event was widely publicized, only one reporter attended: George M. Taber from *Time* magazine. The French press assumed this would be a non-event.

In what has become known as another Waterloo for the French, Chateau Montelena Chardonnay 1973 placed first, Chalone Chardonnay came in third and Spring Mountain Chardonnay ranked fourth in the Chardonnay competition. And even worse for the French, Stag's Leap Wine Cellars 1973 won first place in the Cabernet Sauvignon competition, beating Mouton-Rothschild and Haut-Brion, which came in second and third, respectively.

Taber's article appeared in *Time* buried on page 58 in the Modern Living section. Enough people read the article, however, to decimate in short order the remaining supplies of the winning California wines. That alone galvanized new hope for winemakers in California and worldwide. But at that time, outside of the wine community, people either didn't hear about the tasting or just didn't care.

Taber has sparked a new interest in the controversial event with his book *The Judgment of Paris—California vs. France And The Historic 1976 Paris Tasting That Revolutionized Wine*. It is a fascinating read!

Following the publication of Taber's book, the movie *Bottle Shock* was released. The film is based on the Paris Tasting. The "stars" of the Paris Tasting were the owner and winemaker at Stag's Leap Wine Cellars, Warren Winiarski, and the winemaker at Chateau Montelena, Mike Grgich. The movie is more centered on the Baretts, owners of Chateau Montelena. Winiarski got short shrift, and Grgich is nowhere to be found!

DEMYSTIFYING WINE

Sixty years ago, few people in the United States regularly drank wine with their meals. Conversely, in Italy and France, wine was considered an uncomplicated, civilized and simple pleasure that accompanied every meal.

Changes began to occur here when soldiers returned from World War II and shared their newly acquired knowledge of wine. But it was just a start. Even by the early 1970s, most customers at a good steakhouse preceded dinner with a mixed drink and did not order wine.

Contrast that to today. Oftentimes there is a bottle or a glass of wine on virtually every table. The catalyst for this change can be largely credited to the efforts of French and Italian restaurants.

But the evolution of wine was not fully realized until the early to mid-1980s. By then, Robert Finigan, Robert Parker and Denman Moody, the three favorite wine writers of *Food and Wine* magazine at that time, had been publishing their newsletters for five years or more. And wine columns began appearing in newspapers around the country. At about the same time, a small undertaking called *The Wine Spectator* was purchased by Marvin Shanken and has become a remarkably successful endeavor. More than 300,000 copies are published each issue.

Along the way there have been several well-meaning writers who may have hampered the progress of wine enjoyment rather than enhancing it. For example, one writer insisted on publishing misinformation such as the following (these are not quotes, but you'll get the general idea):

"X" wine—Open 25 minutes prior to drinking and then re-cork between servings so as not to over-aerate.

"Y" wine—Refrigerate for one hour and 40 minutes and then open 12 minutes before serving.

"Z" wine—Open one hour and 15 minutes prior to drinking to let breathe properly, and do not re-cork between servings, as it needs to continue to aerate.

I'm sure that many readers bought into this malarkey, thinking that there must be an exact amount of time for "aerating" and chilling that each wine needed prior to being served. Believing that wine was some enigmatic substance only understood by the cognoscenti, some readers probably just gave up, or worse, pawned off this spurious information to others as wine gospel.

There are, of course, some general rules concerning wine temperature, and there is room enough for an elephant to wander through on the subject of whether "breathing" is necessary.

Finally, the first screw caps that appeared on premium wines were greeted with derision; however, recent studies show that a substantial percentage of wine consumers have accepted them, and for good reason. This simple change and the growing acceptance thereof is part of the education process.

I sincerely believe that with the proliferation of top-notch journalists, improvements in wine quality, and public enthusiasm for wine knowledge and enjoyment, we're on the right path to, as a nation, enjoying a bottle of wine with a meal as an uncomplicated, civilized and simple pleasure.

THE URBAN LEGEND OF SULFITES
by Richard Olsen-Harbich

Richard Olsen-Harbich has worked in the Long Island wine industry since 1981 and is a leader in establishing regional identity and vinification techniques. After graduating from Cornell University in 1983, he worked to establish Long Island's second commercial winery in Bridgehampton, where he was among the first to market Long Island wines to New York City. Over the past 30 years Richard has assisted in implementing pioneering techniques for Long Island vineyards and consulted for wineries throughout the eastern United States. He is the author of all three federally recognized Long Island American Viticultural Areas (AVAs) and in 1996, developed the first Bordeaux/Long Island consultation partnership with M. Paul Pontallier of Chateau Margaux. Since 1995 Richard has been on the advisory board for Cornell University's Wine Grape Research program based in Riverhead, N.Y. In 2004 he helped found the Long Island Merlot Alliance—the first wine quality alliance on Long Island. Today as winemaker at Bedell Cellars, Richard is dedicated to producing delicious handcrafted wines through the exploration and identification of local terroir, the use of sustainable and natural winemaking techniques, and perfecting the fine art of blending.

All of the stories are the same and involve a couple returning from a recent trip to Europe. The couple talks about how they drank wine like crazy and never once had a hangover. They reminisce about meeting local winemakers who told them, "American wines all have sulfites and ours don't." The couple agrees that in the U.S. they cannot drink wine the same way and enjoy it as much. They insist that the sulfites used in American wine gives them a headache and they inevitably want to know why we have to use them. They usually try to stick to white wine because of the sulfites in reds. Sometimes, they vow to never buy another bottle of American wine.

The above statements have been made to me many times to varying degrees. My answer is always the same: "Perhaps it has something to do with you being relaxed and on vacation!" I tell people the reason they feel so good in Europe is simple:

"Being away from home, the kids, the pets, the daily grind of work, sleeping a little later, having lots of "intimate time.""

This explanation usually affords me looks of disbelief. I then attempt to explain that there's nothing in medical literature proving sulfites cause headaches, and that red wines contain lower levels of sulfites compared to whites.

Whatever people may want to believe, one thing is for certain. The problem is not sulfites. It's time for this urban legend to be debunked.

The fact is, some European wine producers are habitual, shameless liars. Many imported wines actually contain higher levels of sulfites than their domestic counterparts. European wineries are allowed to use far more additives than wineries are permitted to use in the U.S. For more than 400 years, European wine producers studied the effects of sulfur in wine. They learned that good wine could not be made without its use. We learned everything we know about it from them and have continued to improve our knowledge.

Let's get one thing straight—all wines contain the preservative sulfur dioxide, whether it's added by the vintner or naturally occurring. Wines without any added sulfur can still contain anywhere from 5-40 milligrams per liter. The same yeasts that convert sugar into alcohol also produce sulfite as a by-product. The human body actually produces about 1 gram per day.

Chances are you will ingest more sulfites in your average restaurant dinner than from a glass of your favorite wine. French fries, scalloped potatoes, shellfish, soy flour, sushi, olives, pizza, cheese, crackers and fish—the list goes on—can contain more sulfites (in milligrams per liter) than most wines. The average bag of dried fruit and nuts contains about 10 times the amount of sulfites found in a bottle of wine.

Sulfite in wine was not an issue until the mid-1980s. A couple of asthma attacks and a few anti-alcohol legislators later and—voilà—U.S. wine producers must include sulfite warning labels on their bottles. Some European producers saw this as an opportunity to set themselves apart from their American competitors. Don't be fooled—all wine is made pretty much the same way, no matter its origin.

Don't get me wrong, the folks who are allergic to sulfites have to be very careful. The most dangerous reaction to sulfites involves anaphylactic shock that constricts the breathing passages and severely lowers blood pressure. This type of reaction only occurs in about 0.4 percent of the total population (about 150,000 people). In comparison, about 4 percent of the population (about 11 million people) suffers from severe food allergies. As an example, peanuts are far more dangerous than sulfites. Since 1990, the FDA has reported 19 sulfite-related deaths—none as a result of wine. Most of the deaths were from prescription drugs containing high levels of sulfites (200ppm and higher). Peanut allergies alone result in at least 100 deaths per year.

So what's my point? As I tell my customers, unless you are one of the few who are truly allergic, you shouldn't worry about sulfites in wine. If you want to worry, there is something else in wine to be very concerned about. Alcohol is a well-documented toxin to the human body and a known carcinogen at high levels of consumption. It typically makes up 10 percent to 16 percent by volume of an average bottle of wine.

According to the National Council on Alcohol and Drug Dependency, about 105,000 people in the U.S. die annually from alcohol-related causes, which include everything from falls to drunken driving accidents to cirrhosis of the liver. Add to this the tens of millions affected by alcohol-related illness and addiction. Sobering stuff, I know, but part of enjoying and appreciating wine must include drinking it in moderation.

As a society, we tend to react negatively to the awful-sounding names that science has given some very ordinary and natural things—many of which have been around far longer than human beings. The ultimate goal of science is to uncover the truth. We need to do a better job of stepping back and understanding the bigger picture. So the next time you're in Europe on vacation, remember to enjoy yourself, drink good wine and set any deceptive winemakers you come across straight.

CALIFORNIA WINES GO CULT

As mentioned earlier, in the 1960s, '70s and '80s, the predominant California wines boasted generic labels—named for a famous place such as Chablis. A wine might appear with half French Colombard and half Chenin Blanc and be called California Chablis, when true Chablis from France is 100 percent Chardonnay! In a fit of poetry in 1978, when I started writing about wine, I took sides in the debate that was raging about this practice, and wrote the following:

Fraud on My European Guest
Before we dine,
Let's have a California Rhine.
Oh! You must have been blinking
And missed the J. Riesling.[1]

With the course from the sea,
Let's have a California Chablis.
Oh! You must have turned away
And missed the Chardonnay.

To wash down the lasagna
Let's try a Chianti from California.
I'm beginning to feel uneasy—

---

[1] At the time, Riesling in the United States was generally referred to as Johannisberg Riesling.

Have you also missed the Sangiovese?[2]

With dessert here you'll learn
Not to have a Sauterne.[3]
But if you insist,
Let's have one with the final "s".

In spite of the myriad generics—some very good, some mediocre—by the early 1970s, there were many excellent wines being made in California. A major shift occurred with the near-perfect 1974 vintage. During a tasting I contributed to in conjunction with the KPHR Public Radio Wine Classic Auction and Tasting in Honolulu in 1988 (which I "had"

---

[2] The primary grape of Chianti

[3] Sauterne from California is usually dry and bears no resemblance to Sauternes from France.

to attend), of the 53 top California Cabernets I had collected, I scored 15 outstanding and 11 very good. Another 13 were good to very good.

But there was still a major problem. Most U.S. producers could name a wine after a grape (called varietal labeling, such as Cabernet Sauvignon), when only 50 percent of the wine was made from that varietal. It's not hard to imagine how little some wines tasted like the one advertised when half of the wine was potentially made from some very inferior grape! In a consumer-friendly act, the feds mandated that beginning in 1983, a varietally labeled wine must contain at least 75 percent of that varietal! This was another huge boost for wine quality.

The golden period for north coast Cabs arrived with a vengeance in the 1990s. Although Bordeaux had marvelous 10-year runs in the 1920s and from 1981 to 1990, the north coast Cabernets (particularly Napa) boasted the most spectacular run of vintages from 1990 to 2008. The 2000 was inferior and the 1998 just good, but the other vintages were either excellent ('06, '04, '03, '99, '96 and '93), outstanding ('08, '95, '92 and '90) or near-perfect ('07, '02, '01 '97, '94 and '91). At this stage, 2009 and 2010 appear to be excellent vintages also.

Stony Hill had started the boutique, mailing-list only trend back in the dark ages. But the wine boutique trend took off in the early 1990s. One of the first to get my attention was Napa's Dalla Valle with its Maya, named after then 77-year-old Gustave Dalla Valle's 6-year-old daughter. The wine was made from a relatively new blend of 50 percent Cabernet Sauvignon and 50 percent Cabernet Franc, and it helped make wine consultant Heidi Barrett famous. Maya was one of the best wines I had ever tasted; in fact, at a dinner I hosted in the late 1990s, the 1992 Maya was on par with the "perfect" 1990 Chateau Montrose from Bordeaux.

Wine pursuits involving Heidi Barrett and several other "cult" winemakers yielded covetous wines in the $100-plus range at release by the mid-1990s. Although Heidi has recently been replaced at Screaming Eagle Winery and Vineyards, Screaming Eagle Cabernet Sauvignon has become one of the most sought-after wines in the world—now bringing $750 a bottle at release.

Other renowned names in the spectacular, high-priced California realm include Colgin, Bryant Family, Harlan Estate, Bond, Marcassin and Araujo. There are so many pricey Cabs from California now that I won't name them all, but some to look out for are Shrader, Hall, Scarecrow, Peter Michael Les Pavots, Dominus and Opus One. The prize for the classiest bottle design, along with a great wine, goes to Buccella.

Another trend began to take shape in the 1990s, even though Chateau St. Jean had produced a Robert Young Vineyard Chardonnay and Joseph Phelps and Heitz had produced Eisele Vineyard Cabernet and Martha's Vineyard Cabernet, respectively. Far Niente owner Gil Nickel created Nickel & Nickel to produce boutique, single-vineyard, single-varietal wines. Today, this winery produces great Cabs from such vineyards as John C. Sullinger, Branding Iron, Rock Cairn, Vogt, etc., and recently other varietals such as Chardonnay, Merlot, Zinfandel and Syrah. The late visionary was right on!

Today, California is known primarily for its Cabernet Sauvignon, Chardonnay, Merlot, Sauvignon Blanc, Zinfandel and, more recently, Pinot Noir. There are over 900 wineries in California, and many make as many as 10 different wines. So how do you sort through such an overwhelming selection?

Another wine knowledge separator is knowing where the best of these wines are produced. Copy this list and keep it handy, and you will be far ahead of the herd when buying from a shop or selecting from a restaurant's wine list:

Cabernet Sauvignon and Merlot—Napa and Sonoma;

Chardonnay and Pinot Noir—Russian River Valley, Sta. Rita Hills, Anderson Valley, Sonoma Coast, Santa Lucia Highlands, Santa Maria Valley and Carneros;

Zinfandel—Dry Creek Valley and Lodi;

Syrah—Paso Robles, Santa Ynez Valley;

Sauvignon Blanc—Napa and Sonoma.

Here are some of my perennial favorites in different price ranges:

$50 to $150

- Chardonnay—Patz & Hall single vineyards, Lynmar Quail Hollow, Freestone, Far Niente;
- Cabernet Sauvignon—Duckhorn, Caymus, Caymus Special Selection, Phelps, Stewart, Constant, Far Niente, Nickel & Nickel, Frank Family Reserve, Winston Hill, Beringer Private Reserve, Joseph Phelps Insignia, Merus, Continuum, Palmaz Gaston Vineyard, Revana, L'Aventure Estate Cuvée;
- Merlot—Jarvis;
- Pinot Noir—Kosta Browne, EnRoute, Patz & Hall, Lynmar Quail Hollow, Sea Smoke, Goldeneye.

$20 to $50

- Sauvignon Blanc—Kunde Magnolia Lane, Duckhorn, Joseph Phelps, Starmont, Dry Creek, Clos la Chance Hummingbird, Chamisal Califa;
- Chardonnay—Frank Family, Ferrari-Carano, Mer Soliel, Beringer Private Reserve, Landmark Overlook, Migration, Talbot Sleepy Hollow, Palmaz, MacRostie, Clos la Chance, Clos du Bois Calcaire, Byron Historic Vines, Talbot Sleepy Hollow, Ojai Clos Pepe, Marimar Dos Lias, Sea Smoke, Kuleto;
- Cabernet Sauvignon—Jordan, Joseph Phelps, Blackstone Rubric, Hess Collection Mountain Cuvée, Tudal Clift Vineyard, Chappellet Mountain Cuvée, Bennet Lane Maximus, Robert Mondavi Napa, Dry Creek, Ehlers Lane, Adobe Road, Summers, Persistence (Reynolds Family Winery);
- Merlot—Duckhorn, SIMI, Thomas Fogarty, Clos la Chance Hummingbird, Ehlers Lane, Starmont, Gargiulo;
- Pinot Noir—J Vineyards, David Bruce, Iron Horse, Alta Maria, Robert Sinskey, Fog Dog, Sebastiani, Decoy, Migration, Rodney Strong, Clos du Val, Presqu'ile, Calera;
- Zinfandel—Ridge, Seghezio, Ravenswood Single Vineyards, Rosenblum Single Vineyards, Paraduxx, Dasche, Earthquake, Starlight, Bella;
- Petite Sirah—Stags' Leap Winery, Earthquake;
- Syrah—L'Aventure Optimus, Beckmen, McRostie Wildcat Mountain, Nickel & Nickel Darien Vineyard, Earthquake, Zaca Mesa.

Under $20

- Chardonnay—Franciscan, Cupcake, Concannon Conservancy, Blackstone Sonoma Reserve, Chateau St. Jean, Fess Parker, Wente River Ranch, Saintsbury, Wente Morning Fog, Clos du Bois North Coast, Jackson Grand Reserve;
- Cabernet Sauvignon—Dry Creek, Bogle, Columbia Crest Horse Heaven, Liberty School;
- Merlot—Columbia Crest Grand Estates, Blackstone Sonoma Reserve;
- Pinot Noir—McMurray Ranch;

- Zinfandel—Ravenswood Vintners Cuvée, 7 Deadly Zins;
- Sauvignon Blanc—Geyser Peak, Dry Creek, Chateau St. Jean;
- Petite Sirah—Petite Petit, Bogle;
- Syrah-- Sixth Sense, R & B Cellars;
- Pinot Gris—J Vineyards;
- Chenin Blanc—Dry Creek;
- Riesling—Firestone;
- Pinot Grigio—Tamás.

There are a number of grapes that have either become fairly well known in California, such as Viognier, or are about to become well known, such as Albariño. My favorite California versions include:
- Viognier, pronounced vee-oh-n'nyay (Rhone Valley)—Fess Parker, Zaca Mesa;
- Roussanne (Rhone Valley)—Qupe Bien Nacido, Alban;
- Marsanne (Rhone Valley)—Krupp Black Bart, J.C.Cellars;
- Semillon (Bordeaux and Australia) —Robert Foley, Ahlgren;
- Albariño (Rias Baixas, Spain)—Bonny Doon, Hendry, Bodegas M Querida;
- Gruner Veltliner (Austria)—Dr. Konstantin Frank (New York);
- Cabernet Franc (Bordeaux)—Chapelette, Jarvis, Constant;
- Malbec (Bordeaux and Argentina)—Arrowood, Crocker & Star;
- Tempranillo (Spain) —Cayuse (Washington State), Bodegas M Tinto de Paso, Booker;
- Sangiovese (Tuscany)— Villa Ragazzi (www.villaragazziwine. com), Altamura, Venge, Frank Family;
- Mourvèdre (France)—Ranch Arroyo Grande Dry Farmed.

THE BIG CONTROVERSY

The 1976 Paris tasting prompted me to stage a number of California vs. French tastings/dinners, primarily in the late 1970s and early 1980s. Some were private and some with 100 or more in attendance. To rival the California wines, I selected slightly more expensive and mature French wines from excellent vintages. The usual pairings would be:

Sancerre from the Loire Valley vs. California Sauvignon Blanc

White Burgundy (usually Puligny-Montrachet) vs. California Chardonnay

Red Burgundy vs. California Pinot Noir

Left bank Bordeaux (mostly Cabernet Sauvignon) vs. California Cabernet Sauvignon.

In almost every instance, the attendees preferred the California wines by a wide margin.

The French vs. California controversy has morphed into a debate over the situation we find ourselves in today, which has been caused in part by the great American wine writer Robert Parker. More about that later. Let's stick to Bordeaux vs. Napa for this discussion. In Bordeaux, the grapes do not always ripen because of the cold temperatures, rain, lack of sunshine, etc. before and/or during the harvest. If the grapes reach 22.5 degrees or 23 degrees brix (natural residual sugar), they are typically considered ripe and ready to pick. This can be tricky, because if the grapes are left to ripen on the vine for (hopefully) an additional week of sunshine, as Chateau Lafite-Rothschild was in 1964, and the weather turns the wrong way (read, rain), a significantly lesser wine is made than, for example, Chateau Latour, which picked before the 1964 rain.

Napa is a horse of a different color—gold, as in sunshine! Many, at least in the early days, thought that 22.5 degrees or 23 degrees brix was the time to pick in Napa (and some still do). The problem is that there is a difference between ripeness and phenolic ripeness. California grapes picked at the sugar levels thought to be ripe in Bordeaux produce wines that, even though containing 13 percent or so alcohol like most of the best Bordeaux wines, often taste "green and acidic." In Napa, almost every year is an excellent vintage. The problem in Napa can be too much sun and heat, causing dehydration of the grapes. But many think that phenolic ripeness occurs in Napa around 26 degrees brix (actually, most winemakers simply pick when the grapes taste ripe, rather than relying on sugar readings). One reason California wins in blind tastings is the fruit is so much riper, and the resulting alcohol after fermentation is higher (14.5 percent vs. 13 percent, for example). Another reason is that the abundance of sunshine lessens acidity. On the other hand, it can be argued that Bordeaux wines are more food friendly due to lower alcohol, more restrained fruit and higher acidity.

Robert Parker has championed the big-fruit, high-alcohol reds. A perfect example is the 1990 Chateau Montrose, which he scored 100. Some in the British press have compared it to a California wine, exhibiting too much fruit and too little acidity. And Parker's high scores on the big, red Rhone wines and many opulent California reds have created a problem for some winemakers. They need a score of 90 or above from Parker to sell all of their wine. Some winemakers have hired consulting winemakers to "up the ante" and make their wines, or even consulted with Enologix, a company that shoots for higher Parker ratings, among other things.

California is, in fact, able to do something that is difficult to do in France—pick extremely ripe grapes in most vintages. But in comparing our wines to those of the French, concluding that their wines go with food and ours don't is an extreme oversimplification.

It all depends on the food you serve with the wine. Bordeaux reds may be perfect with beef tenderloin with Bordelaise sauce; however, that same piece of beef by itself or in sauces with black currants, black cherries, berries, etc. would be a better match, especially for the American palate, with a rich, ripe-fruit, tender-tannin, higher-alcohol California Cabernet. The proof is in the pudding. Have you ever had one glass of your favorite, big, rich California Cab with a steak at your favorite steakhouse and thrown away the rest of the bottle because it didn't go with the steak? NOT!

Another aspect of this discussion is whether the big, bold style is a fad or a trend. Some call these wines "monsters" and only sing praises of elegant, "food-friendly" wines. The answer for me is that there is enough room for both styles. Consumers would not continue beating down the door for the big California Cabs just because Robert Parker or anyone else gives the wines high ratings!

A LITTLE EXTRA CALIFORNIA WINE HISTORY

The end of Prohibition in 1933 found the California wine industry—which was alive and well prior to 1920—in shambles. Fortunately, some wineries had remained open for the legal practice of supplying sacramental or altar wines. And even more fortunate for the future of California wines, a man named Georges de Latour of Beaulieu Vineyards, one of the Napa wineries that had remained open, hired Andre Tchelistcheff, a research enologist at the Institut National Agronomique in Paris, to come to Napa as Beaulieu's winemaker. Born in Moscow, Russia, in 1901, Tchelistcheff arrived in Napa in time for the 1938 harvest.

Demonstrating the immediate impact of Tchelistcheff, a Beaulieu Burgundy, made interestingly enough from Cabernet Sauvignon grapes, received the grand prize for red wines at the Golden Gate International Exposition in 1939.

Tchelistcheff has been quoted as saying that he only made two great wines at Beaulieu: the 1946 and 1947 Pinot Noirs. He told me once that he had made one and one-half great wines: 1946 Pinot Noir was one, but I've forgotten the half, if he even told me. As an aside, my wife and I had dinner with Andre and Dorothy at their Napa home in the early 1980s. I brought him a bottle of the excellent Beaulieu Burgundy 1968, which I thought might be the "half" he had mentioned. He thanked me sincerely and put it in what he called his "cellar"—under the bed! He was a rare, unpretentious, hard-working genius of the wine industry, single-handedly thrusting California perhaps 20 years ahead of where it would have been without him.

Although he made some great Cabernets in the 1940s, the first perfect California wine I consumed was the 1951 Beaulieu Georges de Latour Private Reserve Cabernet Sauvignon, tasted in 1982. Within the same time period, I had tasted the best 1961 Bordeaux wines and the 1955 Grange Hermitage from Australia, and I found the Beaulieu, or B.V., to equal the latter wines in quality. The '51, '58, '59, '60, '68, '69 and '70 vintages were my favorites from the Tchelistcheff reign at B.V. The '71 and '72 were his last true vintages there, but both were off-years.

In the late 1970s, the best Cabernets still available besides the '68, '69 and '70 B.V. Private Reserves were the '68, '69 and '70 Heitz Martha's

Vineyard Cabs. The '71 and '72 were non-events (my favorite inexpensive '72 was a Parducci Cellarmaster Selection from Mendocino County) and '73 produced some very good wines, Joseph Phelps Cabernet (one year prior to the release of Insignia) being one of the most memorable in its price range—about $5 or $6! And of course, the '73 Stag's Leap Wine Cellars Cabernet at about the same price won the 1976 Paris tasting.

During a tasting I contributed to in conjunction with the KPHR Public Radio Wine Classic Auction and Tasting in Honolulu in 1988, SIMI Reserve Vintage and SIMI Special Reserve were in the top tier. How did SIMI, an old-faithful, moderate-quality winery, suddenly catapult from mediocrity to top quality? Guess who became their consultant in 1973? Andre Tchelistcheff!

THE GREAT VINTAGES FOR NORTH COAST CABERNETS

I must mention that in addition to the wines from the 1960s and early 1970s described above, rivaling the best Cabs of the time were the Ridge Cabernets from the Monte Bello Vineyard: '62, '64, '67, '68, '69 and '70.

The next great vintage for north coast Cabernets after 1974 was 1978. The reason I knew this early on is simple. During the 1978 harvest, my wife and I were standing outside the SIMI Winery in Healdsburg with Tchelistcheff, watching some Cabernet juice snake its way through a clear hose near the winery. OK, so my memory isn't perfect, and I don't recall why it was in the hose or where it was headed—probably into the winery. I do remember Andre saying, "This is going to be a great year for Cabernet. It's the best color since 1974."

That's all the nudge I needed to buy all the 1978s I could get my hands on. As I consumed these wines over the next 10 years or so, I kept one bottle of each. This was fortunate because wine buddies Archie McLaren and Dennis Foley asked if I would contribute the wines for a tasting held in conjunction with a charity auction in Washington, D.C. Robert Parker was to lead the tasting—that alone obtained some serious extra money from bidders—and, of course, I "had" to be there also. The tasting was blind and served in tranches of five or six over two days. I donated my collection of 65 different Cabs, and Parker added four Cabs and a ringer Merlot.

He wrote up the tasting in his Wine Advocate Number 66 (Dec. 15, 1989), and the top six were, in descending order: Joseph Phelps Eisele Vineyard (a vineyard now owned by Araujo); Diamond Creek Red Rock

Terrace; Diamond Creek Volcanic Hill; and tied for fourth, Caymus Special Selection, Chateau Montelena and Mayacamas.

I must digress for a moment to discuss the ageability of wine. Even the top wines from great vintages have their peaks and plateaus, and then begin a downward spiral. The best example would be Dr. Louis Skinner's superb tastings in Coral Gables of his perfectly stored, 50-case collection of 1961 Bordeaux wines. At the first tasting, which I attended in 1981, the wines were at the top of their form. I gave perfect scores to Pétrus, Palmer and Margaux. Others were near perfect, and all but a few were still very good. At subsequent tastings some five and 10 years later, from the articles I read, many of the wines were significantly less pleasant-tasting.

After the tasting of 1974s in Honolulu in 1988, I attended another '74 tasting that presented even more Cabs than I had put together. Ironically, it was also in Coral Gables but from the cellar of Dr. Steve Mandy. This took place several years later, and once again, even though most of the top stars were still coruscating, a noticeable number had slipped.

Domaine Chandon had started the French/Napa wine venture business with plantings in 1973. John Wright, a CPA who had been hired by Moet to help them find a perfect winery location, was rewarded for his excellent work by being named president of Domaine Chandon. And the first marketing director was Michaela Rodeno, who has recently retired as CEO of St. Supery Winery.

The 1979 through 1983 vintages were not too exciting, but this is the period when the French/American joint-venture business was engendered. Opus I debuted in 1979, with the label depicting Baron Philippe de Rothschild of Mouton facing west and Robert Mondavi facing east. The gorgeous Opus I winery, an architectural masterpiece, was built years later. The 1983 vintage was the first for Dominus, with Christian Moueix of Pétrus joining the Lail sisters, descendants of John Daniel of Inglenook fame.

The vintage of 1984 was very good, but a fabulous trio of vintages followed: 1985, 1986 and 1987.

After a mediocre '88 and '89, the north coast Cabs entered the golden years with a vengeance, which I have described in detail in chapter 6.

ANDRE TCHELISTCHEFF

The below information was given to me by Mrs. Andre (Dorothy) Tchelistcheff. Since Andre was a great friend, and I had never seen published much of the information herein, I am very happy to pay tribute to the legacy of this extraordinary wine consultant in this book.

Andre Tchelistcheff was born in 1901 in Moscow, Russia, the son of a law professor. After graduation from the military academy of Kiev, and after having served in the White Russian army, he continued his schooling at the Institut of National Agronomy in Brunn, Czechoslovakia, graduating with the technical degree of Engineer-Agronomist.

He began his professional career in Europe, but by 1937 decided to spend more time studying viticulture and enology. He selected the Institut of National Agronomy in Paris, where he completed graduate work as an assistant to the director. At the same time, he took a post-graduate course in wine microbiology at the Insitut Pasteur and also studied horticulture and floriculture at the Trade Aboriculture School at Chateau de Versailles.

Georges de Latour, the founder of Beaulieu Vineyard in Napa Valley, was seeking an enologist and viticulturist, and upon the recommendation of Professor Paul Marsais of the Institut of National Agronomy, Tchelistcheff was hired in 1938 to head the vineyard and winery activities at Beaulieu.

On July 10, 1954, the French government conferred its highest award in agriculture, Chevalier de Merite Agricole, upon Tchelistcheff for his contribution in helping bring French qualitative philosophy of winemaking to the American wine industry. In September 1979 a second award, Officer de Merite Agricole, was conferred on him by the French government.

Tchelistcheff was a charter member of the American Society of Enologists, and in 1970 was awarded the Merit Award by the society and was given the title of Winemaker's Winemaker. He was a charter member of the Technical Advisory Board of the California Wine Institute; charter member of the Napa Valley Technical Group; honorary member of the Pairie des Vins d'Arbois; Honorary Winemaster of Confrerie St. Etienne de Alsace, Fort Worth Chapter; Supreme Knight of the Universal Order of the Knights of the Vine, and in 1981 received the Gold Vine award; Chevalier of the Les Amis du Vin International Society; Award of Merit winner from the American Wine Society; the Junipero Serra Award for Excellence recipient from the California Wine Patrons; member of the Commandeur d'Honneur of the Bontemps de Medoc et Des Graves in Bordeaux; "Man of the Year" in 1974 from the Friends of the Junior Arts Center in Los Angeles; and one of the Grand Award recipients of the Society of Wine Educators in 1983.

During his career at Beaulieu, Tchelistcheff pioneered the cold fermentation process as well as developing and controlling methods in the use of malolactic fermentation of red wines. He also pioneered frost protection techniques in Napa Valley, helping to develop the combination of wind machines and smudge pots that are in use in vineyards today. Additionally, he did significant work in vine disease prevention. He was universally recognized as the leading wine consultant in America, and on par with the leading wine consultants in the world.

While at Beaulieu Vineyard (or B.V.) during the 1940s and 1950s, he maintained his own enological laboratory in St. Helena and served as consultant to many wineries. Not only did he train numerous, now-famous winemakers, he trained his son Dimitri, who is the consultant at Jarvis Winery, among others.

In 1967, Tchelistcheff accepted a new challenge—to aid in building the winegrowing reputation of the state of Washington as a consultant to Chateau Ste. Michelle Winery. I wondered why the 1975 Chateau Ste. Michelle Cabernet Sauvignon was so great (I believe it cost about $6 a bottle) until I found out who made it—Tchelistcheff!

My wonderful, late friend died in 1994 at the age of 93, and he has left behind a glorious legacy!

JORDAN VINEYARD AND WINERY

In 1970, successful Denver geologist and wine lover Tom Jordan was about to purchase a chateau in Bordeaux. However, a light went on when he tasted a 1968 B.V. Private Reserve Cabernet Sauvignon in San Francisco. Tom decided he would pioneer a new wine concept in California.

After conducting exhaustive research, he bought a 275-acre prune orchard in the then little-known Alexander Valley in Sonoma County. Tom hired Andre Tchelistcheff, the winemaker who made the 1968 B.V., as the consultant to his one and only winemaker, Rob Davis.

While Tom oversaw the construction of the most gorgeous Chateau in Sonoma County, as well as the planting of vineyards, Andre and Rob traveled the wine areas of Europe. The two refined their knowledge of the science of winemaking by exploring the European art of winemaking. Actually, Andre had it all, as he had studied in Bordeaux at an early age.

My wife and I visited Jordan around 1980, just as the 1976 Jordan Cabernet was being released. We tasted it from the bottle and the 1977 and 1978 from the barrel. I was overwhelmed! In 1980, most Cabernets were either under $5, thin, bland and forgettable, or, conversely, were excellent—like B.V. Private Reserve Cabernet or Heitz Martha's Vineyard Cabernet—cost $20 or more and needed several years of aging.

The Jordan 1976 Cabernet was a revolutionary wine. It cost about $12 but was in the same league as the very best, without requiring additional bottle age. On the now-ancient scale of 20, I scored it an 18! And the 1978, a year or so from being bottled, was even better—19!

The 1976 was a seminal wine that I gave to friends who shunned domestic wines (the pejorative title given to California wines at that time). Some of those friends told me it was the best wine they'd ever tasted. The 1978 was not only better, but improved for years and was drinking well into the mid-1990s.

Jordan's first Chardonnay was released in the early 1980s. It is a rich and complex wine, similar to Meursault in Burgundy. And because Jordan believes the Russian River Valley is the best growing area for Chardonnay, starting with the 2000 vintage, prime Russian River Valley grapes have been increasingly used in the final blend. The 2001 carried the Sonoma County designation; and from 2002 on the more specific and impressive—Russian River Valley.

Tom Jordan has recently turned over the CEO job to his son John, who has thrown himself full-bore into the business and who knows? It might get even better! www.jordanwinery.com

GREEN VALLEY AND IRON HORSE

Two years prior to George Yount planting the first grapes in Napa Valley in 1838, Russian settlers planted grapes in Green Valley, which lies in the southwestern corner of the well-known Russian River Valley. Over the years, as the Russians returning home abandoned their grapes, and phylloxera and prohibition took root, Green Valley went through a long fallow period. In fact, for many years it was accepted that the area was too cold, too frost-ridden, and too hazy for the noble grapes to survive and ripen properly.

The Dutton family was the first to replant grapes in the 1970s. Audrey and Barry Sterling started Iron Horse in 1976, and even then they were advised to go to Napa instead. Mainly because of the Duttons and the Sterlings, Green Valley received its own AVA designation in 1983.

Situated between Sebastopol, Forrestville and Occidental, the diminutive Green Valley is about an hour north of the Golden Gate Bridge. It is the only AVA with 60 percent one soil type, Gold Ridge Fine Sandy Loam. There are over 100 growers in the area and eight key wineries: Dutton Estate, Dutton-Goldfield, Goldridgepoint, Hartford Family Winery, Iron Horse Vineyards, Marimar Estate, Orogeny and Tandem.

Green Valley is the first place where fog settles in and the last place where it burns off. In summary, Green Valley is the coolest, foggiest part of the Russian River Valley. Guess what loves cool and fog? Chardonnay and Pinot Noir. In fact, according to Daniel Roberts, known as "Dr. Dirt" since his mother laid that moniker on him when he was 7 years old, it is actually perfect weather for Pinot Noir—around 55 degrees at night and in the low 80s by mid-day. The region cools off quickly—also great for Chardonnay. As an aside, Dr. Dirt grew up and obtained a PhD in dirt!

As cool as Santa Barbara County is, Dr. Roberts says Green Valley is even cooler. The soil is particularly valuable for high-quality Chardonnay and Pinot Noir production because of its excellent drainage and low fertility. (Grapes like to struggle a bit—gives them character!)

Although Chardonnay and Pinot Noir thrive here, I've also had some respectable Zinfandels and Syrahs from this area. An interesting fact: Prime, raw vineyard land here that sold for $6,000 an acre 25 years ago now brings in $60,000 per acre. I predict huge land value increases for similar acreages in other AVAs around the country over the next 10 years.

The No. 1 ambassador for Green Valley is Joy Sterling from Iron Horse. She is seemingly ubiquitous and always bubbling with excitement about what's new at Iron Horse and Green Valley. Her wonderful parents, whom I have known for 30 years, are the pioneers with the vision, capital and know-how; Joy and her brother Laurence are the second generation with the skills and enthusiasm, which is paying off in terms of publicity for Iron Horse and its ever-evolving wines.

And I haven't even mentioned the most well-known product of Chardonnay and Pinot Noir from this great estate—its sparkling wines. According to Ed McCarthy, Certified Wine Educator and America's leading authority on Champagne, Iron Horse is one of the top two sparkling wine producers in California! www.ironhorsevineyards.com

THE WINES OF SANTA BARBARA COUNTY

We have friends who lived in Santa Barbara County many years ago. After my brief visit there in October 2005, I wonder how they ever brought themselves to leave. The weather is perfect, the views spectacular, and then there are the endless pursuits: great ocean views, mountains, valleys, museums, scuba, yachting, fishing, gardens, parks, fish market, walking tours, "101 Free Things to do in the American Riviera" (www. santabarbaraCA.com), jeep tours, and the many wineries in the area.

It is so easy to get to wine country from Santa Barbara. I recommend taking highway 101 north for several miles and then jumping on highway 154, which branches off to the right. It's about 35 miles and 45 minutes to Los Olivos, and the drive on 154 through the mountain range is well worth the effort. After one turn back to the left on your descent, you'll be greeted by a lake scene that would befit the cover page of "Paradise Regained."

While Solvang is an interesting, nearby Dutch town, it is relatively spread out and was terribly crowded the day I visited. The perfect place to stop is Los Olivos, a tiny, condensed place of 1,000 residents. There are many winery tasting rooms, as well as one that boasted the wines of about 10 wineries. Unfortunately, it displayed a sign that said, "back in 5 minutes," but nobody ever appeared.

The best tasting room was that of Andrew Murray Vineyards. Every wine served was an excellent value.

There are two American Viticultural areas I tried to taste through: Sta. Rita Hills and Santa Ynez Valley. Among the best Pinot Noirs in the cool Sta. Rita Hills is Sea Smoke. Melville also makes some really marvelous wines: 2 Chardonnays, a Pinot Noir and a Syrah—all exceptional values. Sanford makes superior Pinot Noir and Babcock gets kudos for its wines, including Syrah Black Label and the Pinot Gris "Naughty Little Hillsides."

Of the wines that hail from the Santa Ynez Valley, Andrew Murray and Zaca Mesa knocked my socks off. In addition, the Daniel Gehrs Syrahs are world-class and Au Bon Climat, Qupe and Consilience are favorites. Lastly, Fiddlehead Cellars makes a Sauvignon Blanc from Santa Ynez Valley grapes called Honeysuckle that is expensive but luscious.

Traveling home from the wine country entails a little more distance, but it's faster and easier to hop on 101 south and head back.

My trip was made more pleasant by my stay at the Simpson House Inn (www.simpsonhouseinn.com), built in 1874 and located two blocks from State Street, the main street for just about everything in Santa Barbara. Wear your tennies and take advantage of the perfect weather. The best restaurant in the area is the very expensive Citronelle, which affords an ocean view and necessitates a cab ride. The Wine Cask and Olio e Limone are both a block off State Street and absolutely top-notch!

After Napa, Sonoma and the Finger Lakes in New York, Santa Barbara is the place for your next long weekend. If you have an extra day, drive north to San Luis Obispo (about an hour north of Los Olivos) to check out the wineries as well as the restaurants, Pismo Beach, etc. And there are even better winery selections just another hour north around Paso Robles—and to the north of that...

KUNDE ESTATE WINERY

In 1904, Louis Kunde acquired the historical Wildwood Vineyard about 15 miles north of Sonoma and shortly thereafter built a winery. His son Arthur took over at Louis' death in 1922, and Arthur's two sons greatly expanded the estate. In the 1960s and 1970s, the fourth generation continued the expansion, planting additional vineyards. Today there are 1,850 acres, about 800 of which are vineyards.

The striking views leading up to the winery, which has the most impressive trellising system I've observed, made me wish I could get a bird's-eye view. After driving to the top of a hill later with Jeff Kunde in his pickup and viewing about 600 or more of the finest-looking vineyards imaginable as well as 1,000 or so acres of woodlands, lakes and pastures, I thought this might be a dream.

Although their operations aren't nearly to such a large scale, many second- and third-generation farmers, ranchers and vineyard owners abound in the area. Many of them incorporate sustainable farming, organic farming, certified organic farming and biodynamic farming. Although each practice is a vast subject in itself, Jeff explained that true sustainable farming, which includes many of the practices of the others, expands from farming techniques into a way of life. For example, not only have the Kundes utilized bird boxes high above the vineyards for owls and hawks to control moles and other rodents harmful to vines, but they've also gone to great lengths to decrease energy consumption, use natural composting materials, control erosion, etc. Furthermore, they've involved every employee in the winery and vineyards in the project.

One unique practice for the Kundes involves fourth- and fifth-graders who visit on school fieldtrips to help plant trees along the streams on the property. This project aids in erosion control and shades the creeks, thus creating a cooler environment for the fish eggs deposited during the annual steelhead migration. The children are encouraged to come back over the years and see how the trees are doing—then someday bring their own children to see a firsthand account of environmental stewardship!

Kunde has even assembled a green committee with at least one person from each department of this large operation (they still run cattle, too). Interestingly, one of the tasting-room employees has a degree in environmental sciences and has joined the committee. Everyone is very pleased about this!

Jeff is very passionate about sustainable farming, but in a very practical way. Kunde will do anything it can within reason and budget to safeguard its property and to improve its farming, ranching and winemaking practices. The goal is to maintain the natural beauty and sustainability of the operation for future generations—hopefully including lots of Kundes!

Kunde's next step is the sponsorship of green tours for hiking and wine enthusiasts. Such tours enhance public education and awareness of sustainable winegrowing practices.

One green tour is the sustainable walking tour 1,400 feet up, which is moderately strenuous. The hike and taste tour is less arduous and a little more horizontal. Hikers on this tour wind through a range of sustainable ecosystems and native habitats, stopping for an occasional tasting along the way. The tours are $30, and one should pack a lunch and wear appropriate shoes. Reservations are required; call 707-833-5501. If you're not a candidate for a tour, do not miss visiting this gorgeous place next time you're in Sonoma County. It is comforting to know there is someone working passionately to make sure when you visit—as well as the next generation—everything will be even more beautiful and productive with less energy usage, less waste and more environmentally friendly practices. And of course, they're always pursuing ways to improve their wonderful wines.

STAGS LEAP DISTRICT WINEGROWERS

Once I returned from Napa Valley—my teeth purple—where I had sampled the wines of the famous Stags Leap District. There are no "under $10 wines" to be found in this renowned district.

About 30 years ago, some of the favorite Napa wines were Charles Krug Chenin Blanc, Robert Mondavi Napa Gamay, etc. As time charged on, people figured out that Chenin Blanc, Gamay and grapes such as French Colombard were not necessarily the optimal grapes for one of the most famous wine areas in the world. Even if the wines tasted good, they would never bring the big bucks that the top varietals would.

When a wine won the famous 1976 Paris Tasting, it became apparent that the top varietal in the Stags Leap area might be Cabernet Sauvignon. After a court battle between Warren Winiarski and Carl Doumani regarding their wineries named Stags Leap—part of the battle's outcome is the positioning of the apostrophe (in some cases none)—the two came to a truce and jointly released a wine named Accord.

Although Stag's Leap Wine Cellars (Warren Winiarski's) is not part of the Stags Leap District Winegrowers Association, Stags' Leap Winery (notice the apostrophe), which was sold to Beringer in 1977, is a member. The other members are Chimney Rock, Cliff Lede, Clos du Val, Hartwell, Ilsley, Pine Ridge, Regusci, Shafer, Silverado, Robert Sinskey and Steltzner. There are also 14 members who are vineyard owners, some of whom, such as Taylor, have started small wineries recently.

Each of these wineries has an interesting and sometimes historically important story to tell. For example, the original Stags' Leap Winery was established in 1893 and maintains the 19th-century home on the property for tastings and tours. One morning when we stayed in a guest house there, we were awakened by a huge Tom turkey gobbling about an inch from our floor-to-ceiling window. He peered in at us as if he wanted to come in for breakfast. My favorite Stags' Leap Winery offering is the Ne Cede Malis from an ancient estate vineyard field blend, and its Petite Sirah and Merlot. Actually, the Cabernet Sauvignon is great as well.

Chimney Rock has the most unusual and visually striking winery with a lengthy, white, South African-style, Cape-Dutch edifice. Its winemaker is a former president of the association, and all of the wines there are very palatable. Another, newer winery to the north, Cliff Lede has already stamped its signature on the area with a small contemporary art museum next to the winery, possibly the top wine consultant in the world—Michel Rolland—and the recent opening of its fabulous Poetry Inn.

Clos du Val was started by an American, John Goelet, and Bernard Portet, son of a former regisseur at Chateau Lafite-Rothschild. Bernard's brother Dominique was one of the founders of Taltarni in Australia. Although the 1973 Stag's Leap Wine Cellars Cabernet won the 1976 Paris tasting, Clos du Val's 1972 Cabernet won a re-creation of the event 10 years later in California! Under the leadership of John Clews, a native of Rhodesia with top credentials and experience, the wines have greatly improved—especially the Chardonnay and Pinot Noir.

Regusci sold its grapes for many years, but now produces its own wines. I particularly enjoy the Chardonnay and Zinfandel. The tasting room is ensconced in the former Grigsby-Occidental Winery, which was built in 1878 on the property!

Down the road, Shafer, one of the area's best-known properties, uses sustainable agricultural practices and is one of the few that opted for big-time solar power. The cost was around $800,000; however, governmental reimbursements and electricity savings have allowed Shafer to break even after seven years. For about the next 15 years, the power will be virtually free until the original panels wear out and are replaced. This is a pretty big deal considering that the monthly utility bills are in the thousands. Shafer's Firebreak, a lovely Sangiovese blend, has been discontinued, but the Hillside Select Cabernet remains one of Napa's best-known big hitters.

Robert Sinskey, which had its first crush in 1986, is certified organic and is now run by Robert's son, Rob Sinskey. The stunning redwood and stone winery, with its 18,000 square feet of caves (another huge electricity bill saver in the future), was completed in 1988. Sinskey's Pinot Noirs from its Carneros property are wonderful.

Across the street is Hartwell, which was established in 1986. It is a fine-looking property that produces some massive and excellent Merlots and Cabernets.

The last one I'll mention is Baldacci. Although this was a new name to me, all the wines tasted there were excellent: Gewurztraminer; Pinot Noir; Cabernet Sauvignon IV Sons; and Cabernet Sauvignon Stags Leap District.

DRY CREEK VALLEY

Every year, the Winegrowers of Dry Creek Valley (next to Alexander Valley, except running north to south just west/northwest of Healdsburg) invite a select group of people from the wine media and wine trade for an educational event. The event I attended focused on the workhorse grape of Dry Creek Valley, Zinfandel.

The seminar on day one addressed the subject, "Is Bigger Better?" The impressive panel consisted of winemakers Eric Cinnamon of Rancho Zabaco and Phyllis Zouzounis of Duex Amis, as well as owners Ted Seghesio and Dave Rafanelli from their respective wineries.

Rafanelli presented a concise history of Zinfandel from the 1960s to the present (with a few additions from the writer):

1. In the 1960s, Zinfandel was primarily a blending grape. The price per ton to growers was in the $125-$175 range.

2. In the 1970s, with the boom of varietal sales (vs. Hearty Burgundy, Rhine Wine, etc.), the price per ton for Cabernet, Pinot Noir, etc. topped $1,000 for the first time. Zinfandel barely reached $400 a ton by the late 1970s, and to maximize their income, growers produced five to six tons per acre with little or no pruning or thinning, resulting in large-quantity/low-quality Zinfandel.

3. By the end of the 1970s, a bottle of Zinfandel sold for around $3.50 to $4.25. And with the vast array of Zins, this varietal fell out of favor.

4. Sweet, white Zinfandel picked up the slack for a while in the 1980s.

5. Producers of high-quality red Zins were praised by wine writers for instituting such vineyard practices as clonal selections, pruning and crop thinning, drip irrigation, etc., resulting in less-quantity/higher-quality wines.

6. Today, Dry Creek Valley Zin brings $2,700 a ton and is the top varietal there! Eric Cinnamon unabashedly stated that he is looking for "rich, blue and black fruit and big chewy wines."

The other panelists then presented their thoughts, which, in a nutshell, consisted of Zouzounis and Seghesio discussing their attempts to make consistent, well-balanced Zins from year to year.

Just as I thought Seghesio was on one side—elegance and lower alcohol—and Cinnamon on the other—richness, boldness and high alcohol (this is true, to some extent)—Seghesio agreed that high alcohol was not necessarily a problem as long as the wine was balanced. Everyone seemed to agree that a recently released Zin at 16.7 percent alcohol was just too much to handle.

As a matter of fact, with all the recent innovations in vineyard management, Zin is no longer such an early ripener, and it's actually difficult for some of the Dry Creek Valley vintners to pick ripe Zin grapes that don't ferment out to at least 14 percent.

But as far as many of the critics are concerned, primarily Robert Parker, big, bold, dark-colored, high-alcohol Zins are in. Eric Cinnamon focuses on ripe tannins, green dropping, leaving "raisins" behind—Zins ripen unevenly, as I once observed. The first six grapes on a vine cluster at Ridge Lytton Springs were black, blue, light red, red, pink and green—uneven likeness to the max.

Almost all Dry Creek Valley vintners add Petite Sirah, Alicante Bouchet and/or Carignane for extra tannin and color. This practice also "fills in the middle taste of Zinfandel," which by itself has a wonderful front end of strawberries, blueberries, raspberries, blackberries, etc., and on the finish has a beneficial "bracing acidity."

Petite Sirah is apparently the very best; it infuses viscosity and complexity, as well as color and tannin, but does not change the basic character of Zinfandel, whereas certain other varietals do.

Although some Dry Creek Valley producers would prefer a more consistent style for their Zins vis-à-vis the consumer, this probably will never happen. The 20-mile-long valley is warmer and sunnier to the north and cooler to the south. The vineyards face both east and west—in the north, central and south. The soils vary in each area. And then there are vineyard managers and winemakers with varying ideas on how to make a Zinfandel. Personally, I find this marvelous.

My recommendation is to taste a number of Dry Creek Valley Zins and find one that suits you. Zins are easy to pair with food, from burgers to roast beef sandwiches to Italian foods with tomato sauce and olive oil; and from steaks to pork loin stuffed with your favorite fruit. Pittsburg wine writer Bruce May loves it with lamb.

My favorite wines from Dry Creek Valley come from the wineries listed below, and just about any one is worth a try:

Amphora Winery
Bella Vineyards
Dry Creek Vineyards
Duchamp Estate Winery
Frick Winery
Gallo of Sonoma
Gopfrich Winery
Nalle Winery
Preston Winery
Quivira Estate Vineyards
A. Rafanelli Vineyards
Rancho Zabaco
Ridge Lytton Springs
Seghesio Family Vineyards
Talty Vineyards
Unti Vineyards

The Winegrowers of Dry Creek Valley website is www.wdcv.com.

TOURING CALIFORNIA WINE COUNTRY

On the afternoon of July 22, 2006, as I emerged from the caves at Robert Sinskey Vineyards, a tasting room employee informed me that it was 117 degrees on the porch. The 10-second walk from the cave door to the tasting room was akin to passing through a sauna.

The official high in Napa Valley was a record 113 degrees, but the winery and vineyard owners were not too concerned. Winemaker Todd Graff of Frank Family explained why. Because veraison had not yet occurred (the red grape varietals are still green but about to change colors) and the grapes were not close to ripening, they would just shut down and go into survival mode. The foliage also provided relief by shading the clusters. However, if this heat wave were to encroach later in September, the grapes would start dehydrating and burning before phenolic ripeness, and that would be a cause for alarm.

On the route from the Golden Gate to Napa, an easy and highly recommended "Welcome to California" stop can be experienced at Gloria Ferrer Winery, which is actually in Sonoma County. All of the sparkling wines are excellent. I reveled in the Brut Sonoma County non-vintage ($18), Royal Cuvée Sonoma County ($28) and Carneros Cuvée Sonoma County ($48.95). Of the still wines, the Pinot Noir Cuvée Jose Ferrer is the best.

One of the "hottest" wineries in Napa Valley today is Frank Family Vineyards on Larkmeade Lane in Calistoga. Legendary winemaker Koerner Rombauer assisted former legendary Disney exec Rich Frank in locating and purchasing the former Hans Kornell Winery. The tasting room resembles a beehive with wine—not honey—being the attraction. More than 90 percent of the entire production is sold at retail prices in the tasting room!

One of the best-known tasting-room figures, Dennis Zablosky presides there, as does the entertaining and knowledgeable Pat Cline and others. From the land of Disney, Frank obviously learned a thing or two about entertaining.

I'm not sure whether it's Frank, winemaker Todd Graff, the vineyards, the location, the superb wines or a combination thereof, but the place gets an A+. My favorites are the Chardonnay Napa Valley ($35), Zinfandel Napa Valley ($40), Sangiovese ($40), Cabernet Sauvignon

Napa Valley ($50) and Cabernet Sauvignon Rutherford Reserve Napa Valley ($80), which was voted best of 1,700 wines at a recent Orange County Fair tasting.

Only minutes away from Frank Family is Bennett Lane. My favorite is the outrageously underpriced Maximus Red Feasting Wine Napa Valley at $35.

To round out your tour of Napa Valley, consider these winners (call in advance; most of the winery tastings are by appointment only):

Clos Pegase—In conjunction with the San Francisco Museum of Modern Art, Clos Pegase owner Jan Shrem hosted a competition in which the winning architect was commissioned to design a winery facility. Architect Michael Graves won, and today his "Temple to Art and Wine" houses Shrem's incredible art collection, as well as many excellent wines, mostly from estate vineyards in Carneros. My favorites at Clos Pegase are any of the wines labeled "Hommage," the Sauvignon Blanc Los Carneros Mitsuko's Vineyard and the Chardonnay Los Carneros Mitsuko's Vineyard.

Far Niente—If you can wrangle a tour and tasting at Far Niente (Chardonnay, Cabernet Sauvignon and Dolce—a Chateau d'Yquem look-alike), as well as the sister winery Nickel & Nickel, you will have accomplished much.

Far Niente does not make a reserve, but the wines are already first-rate with the Chardonnay being a true Corton-Charlemagne look-alike, and since 2001, the Cabernet tasting somewhat like a First Growth Bordeaux. The estate vineyards are nestled among the greatest in Napa: Robert Mondavi Reserve, Opus I, Heitz Martha's Vineyard and others. All three of the wines are spectacular: Chardonnay Napa Valley; Cabernet Sauvignon Napa Valley; and Dolce Napa Valley.

The best blend of Bordeaux varietals from the estate vineyards produces a Cabernet of class and distinction every year. At Nickel & Nickel, just the opposite philosophy is extant. Each wine is a single vineyard, single varietal, produced to gain the best of the terroir of that particular piece of "dirt." While the Stelling is my favorite Nickel & Nickel Cab, if you spy someone with any bottle of Nickel & Nickel at a BYOB restaurant, he or she probably has a clue about wine.

Patz and Hall—If you like Chardonnay and Pinot Noir, this is another "must." All six Patz and Hall Chardonnays recently scored an unprecedented 90 or above in a major publication. Although the winery is in Sonoma, the offices and tasting room are located about five minutes south of the city of Napa. Patz and Hall is a Nickel & Nickel look-alike, but producing mostly single vineyard, single varietal Chardonnays and Pinot Noirs.

Darioush—Started by a California grocery magnate who was born near Shiraz, Iran, Darioush is a unique stop, for both the architecture and the wines. My favorites are Signature Viognier Napa Valley ($40), Signature Chardonnay Napa Valley ($45) and Signature Merlot Napa Valley ($50).

Jarvis—Touring the caves at Jarvis Winery, one expects James Bond to jump out with a bottle of 1952 Krug at any moment. It is said that during construction of the winery, Mr. Jarvis quit counting after the cost reached $20 million. The winemaker is Dimitri Tchelistcheff, son of Andre Tchelistcheff, late dean of California winemakers. Although the Cabernet is the primary wine at Jarvis, all of the wines are well-made, and Jarvis fans abound. My favorite is the powerful, spirited, black stallion-like Merlot.

The ultimate in underground wineries is the recently completed Palmaz, founded by a cardiologist, Dr. Palmaz, who invented the stint. The winery must be at least 14 stories underground!

Duckhorn Winery has grown from an embryonic vineyard to a sizable presence. Accompanying Duckhorn Winery in Napa Valley, there is now Paraduxx in Napa Valley, where a highly regarded Zinfandel/Cabernet blend is made, and Goldeneye in Anderson Valley along with its little sister (both Pinot Noirs) Migration.

With the highest-quality vineyard locations, wineries and winemakers, and off-the-charts Sauvignon Blanc, Zinfandel, Pinot Noirs, Merlots and Cabernets, Duckhorn has become one of the world's premier wineries. And Migration has just added a Russian River Valley Chardonnay to complete Duckhorn's offering of great wines.

Constant, which requires an appointment (as do most of the wineries in this article), is the best-kept secret in the Napa Valley. Mary and Freddie Constant's show-stopping home was featured in *Architectural Digest*. Since bringing Paul Hobbs on board as consulting winemaker, Constant has boasted some of the best wines anywhere!

Finally, following are my favorite Sonoma spots (call ahead for reservations at each):

Iron Horse—Most gorgeous vineyards and top sparkling wines, Chardonnays and Pinot Noirs, not to mention the wonderful Sterling family.

Lynmar—Fabulous Chardonnays and Pinot Noirs, and the best, most underpriced picnic lunch served with the wines.

J Wine Company—Tastings of the winery's outstanding sparkling wine, Pinot Gris, Chardonnay and Pinot Noir, accompanied by a perfect hors d'oeuvre, are conducted with the winemaker in the Bubble Room. Pricey, but worth it. Or visitors can drop by to just taste the wines.

Jordan—Beautiful European Chateau in the midst of hundreds of acres in the Alexander Valley. Fabulous Russian River Chardonnay and Napa Cabernet Sauvignon that has been listed as one of the top three or so Cabernets sold almost every year in fine restaurants. Very classy private tastings.

Kunde—Approaching Kunde, you'll be greeted by a breathtaking scene of the hill, streams and vineyards behind the winery. And excellent wines.

THOUGHTS WHILE SIPPING A CALIFORNIA CABERNET SAUVIGNON

In the aftermath of the 1976 Paris Tasting, some of the French judges claimed that the organizers fixed the competition so the California wines would win. Many of these judges were understandably taken aback, to say the least; moreover, they were embarrassed beyond the pale at having participated. But the wines were chosen, in the opinion of Stephen Spurrier, to give the French selections the upper hand.

From the judges, two of the primary excuses/pouting/revisionism, etc., were:

1. Our great French wines were not ready to drink. Since California wines don't age well, ours will eventually surpass them.
2. OK, so these young, fruity California wines did well in a blind tasting. So what? Wine is meant to be consumed with food. French wines are the best in the world with food, whereas California wines are not ideal for food/wine pairings.

Now I'll counter those arguments. First I'll address the "readiness for drinking theory." The winning California Cabernet was a 1973 (three years old) and three of the four French wines it defeated were from the fabled 1970 vintage (six years old). Which of the French First Growths should have been in the tasting? 1961? 1945?

At that time, the ability of California wines to age was seriously questioned. The French disdained our young wines and heaped insult upon injury by predicting the wines had no future either. Ah, but this was before the Paris Tasting. Afterward, everything changed, right? At least now the French had to acknowledge that some of our wines might be decent when young. Wrong! It was a fluke, rigged, a one-time anomaly. Actually, this was a disaster for the French; however, the long-term effect was positive, serving as a wake-up call for the French to increase their efforts (which they did) to improve their wines (which they have)!

I attended a scaled-down, "recent vintage" version of the Paris Tasting at a wineandfoodweek.com event in July 2006. For me, of the four whites—which I fortunately guessed blind—the 2003 Grgich Hills Chardonnay (made by the same Grgich who made the winning Chateau Montelena Chardonnay at the Paris Tasting) was the best, followed by the 2004 Chalone Estate Chardonnay. The two great French white

Burgundies, although very good wines, were third and fourth. And of the Cabernets, a California Cab and a Bordeaux were neck and neck for first.

Ten years later, if California wines win once again, the writers and experts across the ocean will muse, "Now in 2016, the California Cabernets have more Cabernet Franc (or Syrah, Zinfandel or whatever) and global warming has made it even hotter, decreasing the wines' acidity levels; therefore, even though the California wines have won yet again, will they age?" Ha! Ha! Ha!

Now I'll dissect argument number two. For decades, those across the ocean have repeated ad nauseam that our wines don't go with food. In the early 1980s, I read about a big, voluptuous California Chardonnay that some writer said didn't go with food. I've mentioned this before, but I tried to dislike it with hors d'oeuvres. I tried to dislike it with fish. I tried to dislike it with chicken. Pretty soon, I had devoured a case of it trying to dislike it with anything, to no avail!

Fast-forward 25 years. Some "experts" are still trying to tell us California wines win blind tastings but don't go with food. I have two comments:

1. If you're just having a glass of wine with no food, as several million people across America do daily or weekly—not everyone sits around dreaming up perfect food/wine matches—guess what? The French are correct. Our wines are the best! Think about that one for a moment.

2. Next, when someone is on the subject of wine and food, what type of food is it? I'll concede that one of my favorite matches is a First Growth Bordeaux from a great year with a steak and Bordelais sauce. And how about roasted duck with a Grand Cru Burgundy from the Cote de Nuit? Or roasted chicken with a mango salsa? Ah-ha! A fruity California white. How about duck with black Bing cherries? A big, rich, fruity California Pinot Noir. And a pork loin stuffed with prunes or your favorite fruit? A big California Zin. Or a simple chilled chicken salad al fresco on a hot day? I'll take a nice unoaked or very lightly oaked sprightly California Chardonnay.

Even if blind tastings are conducted from here to eternity, regardless of which wines win, each country has something to offer—especially with the foods of that country. There's no need to defend any particular country's wines if they don't stand out in a blind tasting. It's almost irrelevant.

PHOTO GALLERY 1

Some people are photographers. I'm not one of them. There are thousands of wonderful pictures I could have taken, but it was not to be—and still isn't. The photos presented here and later in the book were taken by my wife and friends over the years. I'm really thankful that I was smart enough to save these. One of my most egregious errors is having never had a picture taken with my longtime wine-country friend, Tom Jordan. After realizing I had no picture of us prior to publishing this book (when I finally got around to hunting up some pictures), I immediately thought of flying to San Francisco, renting a car and driving to his winery in the Alexander Valley. Tom, being the modest and soft-spoken man that he is (and one of the most brilliant businessmen I've ever met), would have just laughed and said he was too busy working at his oil company, the winery or heading back home for one of his early dinners.

Michael Mondavi and I at the Robert Mondavi Winery in 1978. Michael and his dad used to unabashedly serve La Tache side by side with their Pinot Noir Reserve, and Chateau Haut Brion next to their Cabernet Sauvignon Reserve to show that they were in the same league as the very best. They were!

Another of my first close California wine buddies, John Parducci (left), whose Mendocino County Cellarmaster's Selection Petite Sirah was one of the best values of any red wine in the world at the time this photo was taken (1979).

Talking wine with me in 1980 is Andre Tchelistcheff (left), winemaker at Beaulieu Vineyard and architect of B.V. Private Reserve Cabernet Sauvignon, which put the world on notice about Napa Valley. He trained generations of winemakers and consulted for numerous wineries, including Jordan in Sonoma County and Chateau Ste. Michelle in Washington. Andre quit smoking once, but told me he could no longer taste the wine, so he resumed the habit. He lived to age 93, working almost to the very end.

Having fun at the Third Triennial International Wine and Food Society Convention in 1980 are (left to right) Dr. Lou Skinner of Coral Gables Fla., host of the 1961 claret tasting held a year later; Len Evans, the "father" of Australian wine writers and wine promoters; and yours truly. Len was possibly the greatest wine character on the face of the earth.

Robert Mondavi (left), visionary and ambassador for California wines, and the author at Robert Mondavi Winery in March 1983. I apologize for the quality of the picture, but I couldn't leave this one out.

I was honored to attend an incredible dinner with Corinne Mentzelopoulos (center), owner of Chateau Margaux, and the brilliant wine consultant Emile Peynaud (right), in 1983 in Houston.

Visiting Rex Hill Winery in Oregon in 1989.

Totally contented. Wouldn't you be if you had just finished a course prepared by Charlie Trotter, and were in the process of consuming 59 of the greatest 1959 wines produced? This leviathan effort that took place in 1994 was thanks to my friend Stephen Kaplan, the host of the event and one of the only people in the world who could pull such a collection from his own cellar. The equally happy attendees on my left are Paula Kaplan Scott, Stephen's sister, and Scott Heiman, Stephen's niece's husband.

This was the wine weekend for the ages. 1959 has been mentioned as being in the same class with 1982, 1961 and 1945 as being one of the great vintages of the 20th century. I previously wrote an article that includes my experiences at this incredible event with a dose of humor, which appears below.

After a flight consisting of Chateau Rouget, Vieux Chateau Certan, Trotanoy and Chateau Petrus, I wrote:

"At this point I must digress. There is a Proverb that states something like, "Pride goeth before a fall." As I was admiring the most expensive sport coat I have ever owned, and thinking how very handsome I must look, out of the corner of my eye, it appeared that the waitress threw a glass of wine on my left sleeve. Of course, it was actually an accident. Had it been the Petrus, I might have started sucking on my coat sleeve, but I believe it was the Rouget.

"One morning while in college, I was having a cup of coffee and a sweet roll with a friend. It was one of those sinfully sweet things with concentric rings surrounding one small circular glob in the middle, which was covered with a double dose of goo, sugar, honey and pecans. I had eaten meticulously around the outside, saving this last, luscious bite and saving one large gulp of coffee to ultimize (new word?) my breakfast. Before I could comprehend what was happening, my friend stabbed the gooey orb, plopped it into his mouth, and it was over.

"My response to both this culinary malfeasance of the '60s and the wine on my sleeve in the '90s was the same. I said nothing and did nothing. I was in shock! Fortunately Linda Lutz was sitting next to me. She leaped up, snatched my coat off and marched to whomever was in charge of the room with instructions as to what to do with my coat. It was back in an hour in perfect shape."

After five gorgeous Saint-Juliens, I wrote the following:

"Three wines from Margaux followed. Stephen had asked me to speak. As an attorney, Chartered Life Underwriter, Chartered Financial Consultant and former bank trust officer, I have given approximately 200 talks in the last 20 years to groups ranging from 10 to 1,000 about estate planning. Additionally, I have spoken to many groups about wine and conducted myriad wine seminars/tastings/dinners with the purpose being fun first and education second.

"As may be the case with other writers, my magic pen engenders words and thoughts that could never come out of my mouth. To sniff and drink with the imminent threat of having to stand and speak to a group such as this one, many of whom know as much or more about wine as myself, I normally render poor service to the wines. There's always the chance that as I mention "cedar and roses" in the bouquet of the '59 Chateau Margaux, some confident and powerful orator with an M.W. behind his name will stand up, point at me and roar, "Cedar and roses, Ha! This wine does not have cedar and roses. Anyone who knows anything about wine can tell from one sniff that this wine has overtones of coffee and tobacco and hints of ripe mulberries!"

Our dear friends Susan and Ed Auler (far left and left), owners of Fall Creek Winery and founders of the modern Texas wine industry, with my wife and me after a delightful meal in 1995 at the Auberge du Vignes outside of Beaune, Burgundy.

My late friend and the visionary Gil Nickel (left), who had a penchant for race car driving and unique, antique car collecting, started Far Niente Winery, Dolce and Nickel & Nickel, among the superstars of wineries worldwide. We are shown here in 2002.

OREGON AND WASHINGTON WINES – FRESH FLAVORS OF THE PACIFIC NORTHWEST

by Patricia G. Chapman, J.D. L.L.M.

Prior to 1994, Patricia Chapman practiced law for a large law firm in Houston, Texas, and enjoyed wine as a semi-educated consumer. That changed in 1994, when she moved to Portland, Ore., to pursue a graduate law degree. Chapman met other students whose knowledge of Oregon and Washington wines piqued her latent interest in things "wine" and "winemaking." During frequent trips to the Willamette Valley and to the wine areas of Eastern Washington, Chapman tasted, critiqued and enjoyed the local wines. Chapman found the winemakers congenial and willing to educate a wine novice. Returning to Texas, Chapman started her own wine distribution business in 2005 that sold only wines from Oregon and Washington. Although she sold her business in 2008 to return to practicing law, Chapman continues to conduct wine tastings, educating the public on the wines and winemakers of Oregon and Washington.

When I conducted public wine tastings promoting the wines of Oregon and Washington, I was always astonished when I was asked questions such as—"Do they make wine in Oregon (Washington)?" "Isn't it too cold there to produce wine?"

Unfortunately, while some sophisticated wine lovers are aware of the quality of the wines from Oregon and Washington, most of the general public is not. Washington is the second-largest producer of wines in the U.S. (California is the first) and Oregon is the third. Some of the growing areas in both states are on the same latitude as France's Bordeaux region. Additionally, the geographical diversity, good soil and available water sources in Oregon and Washington's growing regions allow for the culture of a large variety of grapes. Washington and Oregon wines tend to be "fruit forward," emphasizing the characteristics of the wine that come from the grapes (as opposed to characteristics resulting from wine aging or the winemaker's art). The wines are also balanced and eminently drinkable both when they are young and when they have been cellared.

Washington is best known for its "big reds"—particularly Cabernet Sauvignon, although the rising star is Washington Syrah. Washington wineries also produce fine Rieslings and Sauvignon Blancs. As for Oregon, say "Oregon" to any oenophile and the spontaneous reply would be "Pinot Noir." Oregon is also known for its fine "second wine" Pinot Gris.

WASHINGTON WINES

Washington's first wine grapes were planted at Fort Vancouver, Hudson's Bay Company in 1825. Additional plantings followed in other areas of the state as early settlers moved in. By the 1960s, the first commercial-scale plantings were planted by Chateau St. Michelle and the predecessors to today's Columbia Winery. The wine industry rapidly expanded through the efforts of these two pioneers (and others) in the mid-1970s. Fast-forward to the 21st century, where the industry is growing at light speed. According to the Washington Wine Commission, a new winery opens in Washington nearly every 15 days. There are currently 700+ wineries throughout the state.

CLIMATE/AVAS

Washington's growing region averages 17.4 daily sunlight hours during the growing season (two more than California's prime growing region). That additional sunshine allows the wine grapes to fully ripen. Plentiful sunshine in the summer, coupled with an abundant water supply from aquifers, rivers and snow melt, creates an ideal climate for grapes.

There are 11 American Viticultural Areas (AVAs) in Washington. While those areas are located principally east of the Cascade Mountains, there is one AVA just outside of the Seattle area. The AVAs (in order of their date of recognition) are: 1. Yakima Valley (1983); 2. Walla Walla Valley (1984); 3. Columbia Valley (1984); 4. Puget Sound (1995); 5. Red Mountain (2001); 6. Columbia Gorge (2004); 7. Horse Heaven Hills (2005); 8. Wahluke Slope (2006); 9. Rattlesnake Hills (2006); 10. Snipes Mountain (2009); 11. Lake Chelan.

Two new AVAs that are currently part of the Columbia Valley, Ancient Lake and Naches Heights are pending recognition. Naches Heights has the distinction of being the first 100 percent AVA in the United States.

VARIETALS

Washington's vineyards grow approximately 30 wine grape varieties. The top white varietal is Riesling, followed by Chardonnay, but Washington's crisp Sauvignon Blancs are not to be dismissed. The top red varietal is Cabernet Sauvignon, closely followed by Merlot, but the Washington Syrah wines are the rising stars.

RIESLING

Riesling is the number-one white grape grown in Washington. Generally, the Washington Rieslings are floral in the nose with vivid fruit flavors on the palate balancing the wine's acidity. My favorite Washington Rieslings are crisp and typically crafted by the winemaker in a dry to off-dry style, although sweet, fruity Washington Rieslings are also available. If the conditions are right, Washington vintners also make some phenomenal ice wines from Rieslings and other white varietals.

CABERNET SAUVIGNON/SYRAH

Cabernet Sauvignon is the number-one red grape produced throughout Washington for a good reason—it grows magnificently! Washington's Cabernet Sauvignon wines tend to be heady and fruit forward, but they always pair magnificently with food, such as beef, pork roast and even mushrooms. Drinkable while young, the wine is subtle and smooth, but when aged, the wine's true characteristics shine. Full bodied, lush and flavorful in the nose and on the palate, the aged Washington Cabernet Sauvignon is superb.

While Cabernet Sauvignon may be the most popular, the rising star of the red varietal wines is Syrah. A relatively newcomer to Washington State (most vines were planted less than 15 years ago), the Syrah grape has increased exponentially in acreage and popularity in the past couple of years.

Washington Syrah is a big, dark, intensely concentrated wine with aromas and flavors of berries, currants, roasted coffee, tobacco and leather, rich on the palate and long on the finish. Like Cabernet Sauvignon, the wine is drinkable young—but the impact that aging has on the wine's growth in character and depth is worth the wait. My personal favorite Syrahs come from Walla Walla, Red Mountain and the Columbia Valley, but all are drinkable.

OREGON WINES

Although wine grapes were planted in Oregon as early as the mid-19th century, the industry didn't really begin to develop until the mid-1960s. In 1961, Richard Sommers, with the help of Adolph Doerner (whose family first planted wine grapes in the Umpqua Valley in 1888), moved to the Umpqua Valley and planted Riesling grapes and other varietal grapes. After Sommers' Hillcrest Vineyards was well established, more winemakers migrated to Oregon to take advantage of the favorable climate and abundant water.

Further north in the Willamette Valley, three winemakers arrived to grow cool-climate wine varieties. David Lett, Charles Coury and Dick Erath and their families established vineyards in the North Willamette Valley. They were the first in the Willamette Valley to plant Pinot Noir, Pinot Gris and Chardonnay. In fact, this effort was the first recorded plantings of Pinot Gris commercially in the New World. Other winemaker adventurers soon followed, with each believing that Oregon would/could become an important wine-growing region.

In 1979, David Lett (Eyrie Vineyards) entered his 1975 South Block Pinot Noir in the 1979 Gault-Millau French Wine Olympiads and won the top Pinot Noir honors against some of France's best labels. This achievement (like the 1976 event that first established California wines) was seminal in announcing that a new, legitimate winemaking region was effectively taking its place in the world. The Oregon wine industry has continued to grow; today, according to the Oregon Wine Advisory Board, there are 419 wineries in the state located throughout 16 different AVAs.

CLIMATE/AVA

Like Washington, Oregon's wine-growing regions exhibit a wide diversity of climates, from the mild climate of the Willamette Valley with cool, wet winters and warm, dry summers to The Rogue Valley AVA, with its warm and dry growing seasons. The AVAs east of the Cascade Mountains have climates that are similar to those of Eastern Washington with very hot days and cooler nights. However, each AVA exhibits its own characteristics and each is capable of growing a variety of wine grapes.

There are 16 American Viticultural Areas (AVAs) throughout the state of Oregon. Some of those are located along the Washington/Oregon border or in the eastern part of the state; however, most are in the Northwest portion of the state between the Cascade and Coastal mountain ranges. The AVAs (in order of their recognition) are 1. Columbia Valley (1984); 2. Umpqua Valley (1984); 3. Walla Walla Valley (1984); 4. Willamette Valley (1984); 5. Applegate Valley (2000); 6. Rogue Valley (2000); 7. Columbia Gorge (2004); 8. Dundee Hills (2004); 9. Southern Oregon (2004); 10. Yamhill Carlton District (2004); 11. McMinnville (2005); 12. Red Hills Douglas County (2005); 13. Ribbon Ridge (2005); 14. Chehalem Mountains (2006); 15. Eola Amity Hills (2006); 16. Snake River Valley (2007).

VARIETALS

With Oregon's varying climates and microclimates, the Oregon vineyards successfully grow dozens of grape varieties. Those varieties are utilized by Oregon winemakers to blend with named varietals to produce unique flavors in the wine. Oregon state law requires that a varietal wine's content be at least 90 percent of the grape variety that gives the wine its name (unlike most other states, which require only 75 percent of the varietal grape). The other 10 percent of the content comes from blending other grapes in the wine (the exception is Cabernet Sauvignon, which may contain up to 25 percent of another varietal). Of the 72 grape varieties planted, 15 varietals comprise 97 percent of Oregon's acreage. The top two varietals produced in Oregon are Pinot Noir and Pinot Gris. Like Washington state wines, Oregon's wines are fruit forward.

PINOT GRIS

Pinot Gris' presence in Oregon has an interesting history. In 1965, when David Lett first arrived in Oregon, he had with him 160 Pinot Gris cuttings from four "mother vines" cut from the UC/Davis ampelography collection. While getting his start as a winemaker (and starting Eyrie Vineyards), David sold college textbooks throughout the Northwest; another source of income was selling these Pinot Gris cuttings to other fledgling winemakers, although he gave away as many Pinot Gris cuttings as he sold. This effort was the first substantive planting of Pinot Gris in America.

Pinot Gris is made from the same grape known as Pinot Grigio. However, there is a marked difference between an Italian Pinot Grigio or Alsatian Pinot Gris and Oregon Pinot Gris. The Oregon Pinot Gris grapes ripen slowly in the long, mild summers, creating a distinct Oregon grape. The resulting wines are crisp and medium bodied with a definite minerality and good acidity balanced by the fruit. Pinot Gris is a good "food wine" whose flexibility promotes serving it with almost any cuisine. Oregon Pinot Gris is best consumed young when the wine is fresh and full of flavor, although it cellars well for three to five years. My favorite Pinot Gris, Dundee Hills, comes from the Willamette Valley.

PINOT NOIR

Oregon and Pinot Noir are synonymous. A Pinot Noir grape is difficult to grow, but Oregon's soil and climate create the almost-perfect growing conditions for this sometimes stubborn grape. Oregon's Pinot Noir vineyards (located mainly in the northern part of the state) take advantage of the terroir and climate to produce luscious Pinot Noir grapes that are almost perfectly ripened. Oregon's Pinot Noirs are characterized by intense fruit and complex fragrances of red and black fruit, with sometimes more than a touch of minerality; the wine's finish is long and frequently accented by a spiciness that suggests cinnamon, nutmeg or mint. Typically, although the wines are full bodied with a long, silky finish, the texture is not heavy. Oregon Pinots are usually fresher than California Pinot Noirs, with a higher acidity and crispness. My favorite Pinot Noir is, again, from the Willamette Valley, Dundee Hills.

FINGER LAKES, NEW YORK

If you haven't been to the Finger Lakes wine country in New York, make this destination a priority on your travel list. The best time to visit is mid-June through September. October is great for the foliage, but I've been warned that October weekends, particularly around Columbus Day, draw large crowds. The wines are good—sometimes outstanding—the people are friendly and the scenery for wine country is unrivaled in the United States.

My wife and I visited this region in June 2005, tasting the wines we thought would be the best in the area based on my research and personal knowledge.

KEUKA LAKE

There are merely eight wineries on the Keuka Lake Wine Trail. We stayed at a bed-and-breakfast called Keuka Overlook, which is also a small winery. It was practically worth the trip just to meet the owners, Bob and Terry Barrett, and to hear their stories about going from home winemaking in Cleveland to owning and operating a winery and bed-and-breakfast in Wayne, New York.

Bob shared one of his last bottles of his fabulous Triumph 2001, but mentioned that his 2003, soon to be released, would be just as good.

We still speak of the opulent breakfast that featured Amish-prepared sausage and pineapple pancakes with a homemade mixture of melted butter and maple syrup.

The three wineries we visited on the southwestern side of the lake are the most well known. Dr. Konstantin Frank's Vinifera Wine Cellars is the apogee of all Finger Lakes wines. The winery was established in 1962 by Dr. Konstantin Frank, a Russian immigrant with a Ph.D. in plant sciences. After several years of washing dishes and working as a janitor—English was not one of the five languages he was fluent in—he convinced the president of the formidable Gold Seal Winery to employ him.

At that time, nobody thought the great vinifera grapes—Riesling, Chardonnay, Cabernet Sauvignon, Pinot Noir, etc.—could grow in that cold climate; however, Gold Seal allowed him to experiment with vinifera right up until the time he opened his Vinifera Cellars.

Although Frank died in 1985, his legacy continues. Now run by his grandson, Fred, the winery was the first to be honored by the New York Wine and Grape Foundation. The number of gold medals Dr. Frank's wines have won in international competitions, especially the Riesling "Dry" and "Semi-Dry," is unparalleled among New York wineries. One of the most recent and memorable medals was a double gold, best of class at the Houston Livestock Show and Rodeo International Wine Competition. In addition, Dr. Frank's 2008 Bunch Select Late Harvest Riesling was named Top Sweet Wine at the competition. This recognition landed Dr. Frank's an outrageously expensive pair of hand-tooled leather chaps with sterling silver medallions for a tasting room showpiece. A 9-liter bottle of the Riesling sold at the Rodeo auction for $35,000!

While not as historically important, Walter S. Taylor's story at Bully Hill Vineyards is just as interesting and even scandalous! Fired from the gargantuan family business, the Taylor Wine Company, Walter S. Taylor, with the help of his father, started Bully Hill. After Coca-Cola purchased Taylor Wine Company, the corporate giant took Walter S. to court and won an injunction mandating him to remove the name "Taylor" from all of his labels. As a descendant of P.T. Barnum, he quickly got his promotional juices flowing.

It's a long story, but with a legion of supporters, he led a large group through the streets with a wagonload of all his unused "Walter S. Taylor" labels to deliver to the Taylor Wine Company. But that's not all. He also tried to drop off a goat upon which he had written, "Walter S. Taylor." Apparently the corporation didn't accept the goat, but the press and the people loved it! Even today, on his Bully Hill Love My Goat Red Wine, this quote appears: "They have my name and heritage, but they didn't get my goat."

On other labels, his name still appears as Walter S _____. A fan of French-American hybrids, Taylor died in 2001. His wife now runs the restaurant at Bully Hill and maintains their sterling reputation for great food and service. This is the place to have dinner!

While Heron Hill Winery does not have the same historical or hysterical past, the establishment boasts a stunning winery, tasting room and restaurant high on a hill. It is unique among wineries we visited. Heron Hill has a grand tasting hall, a quality gift shop and the Blue Heron Café. One can also picnic on the grounds.

A perfect wine day would begin with a tasting and lunch at Heron Hill, followed by a stroll around the quaint town of Hammondsport, a tasting at Dr. Frank's from 3 p.m. to 5 p.m., and end with a tasting and dinner at Bully Hill.

I optimistically predicted that within five years—and it is now six years later—because of the beauty of the area and the high quality of many of the wines, the name recognition of the Finger Lakes area would grow exponentially. I also foresee, with just as much enthusiasm, a dramatic rise in the appreciation of Riesling in this country—especially Finger Lakes Riesling!

As a matter of fact, the wine with the highest percentage growth in the U.S. in 2009 was Riesling, with Sauvignon Blanc and Pinot Noir close behind.

SENECA LAKE

The exceptional Glenora Wine Cellars was the first winery to open here, established in 1977 by Gene Pierce and three partners. Since then, Glenora has purchased Knapp Winery on Cayuga Lake (the largest lake) and Logan Ridge Wine Cellars on Seneca Lake, as well as building the Glenora Inn, one of the best lodging and dining facilities in the Finger Lakes.

Ten of the 30 rooms at Glenora Inn, on the western side of the lake, have large Jacuzzis and fireplaces. All afford a spectacular view of the vineyards and lake. The dining experience, also with a dazzling lake view, is a combination of attentive, professional service and top-quality food.

There are now some 36 wineries on the Seneca Lake Wine Trail. Some of our favorites include Herman Wiemer (famous for Rieslings), Miles (several "certified" ghosts and excellent Rieslings) and Fulkerson (Vidal Ice Wine). At all of our stops along the way, we found good wines, especially the Rieslings.

The very best wines we tasted, other than from Glenora, are:

Red Newt Cellars—Run by affable owner/winemaker Dave Whiting and his charming, sprightly, talented wife, Deb, the chef at Red Newt Bistro, this stop is a must for enjoying dinner and their wines. In a fit of disarming honesty, Dave told me that after 17 years, he will no longer make a Chardonnay and will use Chardonnay in his Salamander White, which also has approximately one-third Seyval Blanc and one-third Vidal.

Fox Run Vineyards—Owned and operated by Scott Osborn, with the assistance of Australian-trained winemaker Peter Bell, as well as an excellent vineyard manager who has been there since day one and a Culinary Institute-trained chef. Fox Run is a choice stop for lunch and a wine tasting. Fabulous soups, sandwiches and pastas are showcased deli-style, with the shrimp wrap being the most popular menu item.

Incredibly, there were more than 70,000 customers at Fox Run in 2004, mostly from Rochester and Syracuse, but many from Buffalo, three hours away, as well as from surrounding states and Canada.

Chateau Lafayette Reneau—Owned and operated by Dick Reno, a likeable, successful businessman who has created something special on the southeastern side of the lake.

Attention to every detail is supervised by Reno and executed by his very able winemaker, Tim Miller. Reno explained that his Proprietor's Reserve Chardonnay 2002 was aged in all-new French oak for 10 months with biweekly stirring of the lees. No malolactic was done because of the abundance of natural malic acid, which couldn't be improved upon. This is a necessary visit not only for the wines, but just to chat with Reno, a fascinating individual!

AMERICAN WINE FRONTIERS
by Wes Marshall

Wes Marshall started collecting wine when he was 17 years old and the legal drinking age was 21. He later discovered the salutary effect of taking girls to his college dormitory room to show them his ill-gotten wine collection ("You drink wine? How interesting!"). Once embarked on a career, he was able to wangle a job with a newspaper covering wine. His editor asked him to cover the local Texas wines. Under duress, he went to a couple of wineries and was shocked to discover good wines! Shortly thereafter, Wes wrote *The Wine Roads of Texas*, which went on to win the Wine Press Award from the Texas Wine and Grape Growers, and is currently in its fourth printing of the second edition. Wes also served as the Executive Producer for the three-part PBS documentary based on his book. That sparked another book, *What's a Wine lover To Do?* (Artisan), a well-reviewed guide to 343 questions such as how to read a German wine label, which foods go with Sangiovese, and how to saber a bottle of Champagne. Wes now has a column in the *Austin Chronicle*, he is a special contributor to the Dallas Morning News, and also writes for *Wine & Spirits*, *The Wine Enthusiast*, *Imbibe*, and *Wines & Vines*.

A quick check of your local wine shop might lead you to believe that all American wine comes from states that touch the Pacific Ocean. Of course, in volume terms, you wouldn't be far off. In the most recent report from the Tax and Trade Bureau, California, Washington and Oregon account for 89 percent of the wine produced in the United States. Add in the burgeoning powerhouse of New York and the number climbs to 97.5 percent.

These numbers are as fluid as the wine. Every state defines wine production differently. The Tax and Trade Bureau of the Treasury Department only cares about how much fermented grape juice you made, how much you had in stock, and what you ended the month with. Cooking wine, plonk that's exported to third world countries and Screaming Eagle are all lumped into the same category. Wine America, the national association of wineries says just California, New York and Washington account for 97.5 percent of the nation's wine production.

Still, all 50 states produce wine, and there is a lot of action in that 2.5 percent remainder. We decided to pick four states from around the U.S. to get an idea of what's happening in wine's hinterlands. You'll probably notice that I don't rank the states' wine production. The first four are easy: California, Washington, New York and Oregon. From there, it gets a little complicated.

COLORADO

Winery owners are generally tough, opinionated and out-spoken. Most are generous to a fault; many are inclined to the "ready-fire-aim" school of public relations; a few are irascible and tend to be touchy when they feel pushed around. All have outsized personalities. Trying to gather all these characters and aim them at a single cause, no matter how benign, is like trying to herd cats.

Doug Caskey, Executive Director of the Colorado Wine Industry Development Board, was a wine lover before becoming an official. He's done a better job than most at focusing the industry so that it now resembles a team working toward a common goal. He's also an indefatigable cheerleader for Colorado wine. His view on his state's wines: "We're really seeing some strong quality improvement. The good wines are getting even better and new wineries are coming on line with a real commitment to make great wine."

Norm Christianson at Canyon Wind Cellars agrees. "I think the growth of licensed wineries will continue to grow at a pretty wild pace," he told me. "Some of these are serious, and some are hobbyists that will wash out. But the competition for consumers is causing the wines to get better and better."

Colorado is a big state with nearly every weather pattern from deserts to mountains to plains. The best wine growing areas tend to be just west of Grand Junction in the Grand Valley AVA and 200 miles south around Cortez. Skyrocketing land prices in and around Grand Junction will likely force more wineries to the south. Already, one of the biggest wineries in Grand Junction has gone on the auction block. Whether it remains vineyard or becomes condominiums will probably tell a lot about the AVA's future as a wine growing force in the state.

In the meantime, you can use a few rules of thumb when you spot a Colorado wine. If it has a Grand Valley AVA on the bottle, Cabernets (Sauvignon and Franc) are adapting well to the hot summers and freezing winters. At a higher and cooler elevation, the West Elks AVA grows Riesling, Gewurztraminer and Pinot Gris that develop crispy acidity and intense aromas.

Down toward Cortez, late spring frosts make early-developing grapes like Chardonnay risky, but their higher elevations create much cooler summers that allow longer hang times. The benefit is delicious natural acidity in wines like Riesling, Viognier and Cabernet Franc. Winemaker Guy Drew has been championing the area for quite a while, offering a delicious Alsatian-styled Dry Riesling. Like most Colorado winery owners, he sees a bright future: "So many of our wines are on young vines, and as they get older, I think the wines should get better and better," he said. "Plus, as we develop more history, we'll have the opportunities to try new winemaking techniques with different grapes."

Mike Thompson of Boulder Creek Winery doesn't grow grapes, he buys them. From his viewpoint, the best of Colorado is the Cabernet Franc, Cabernet Sauvignon, Syrah and Viognier grown in the Grand Valley AVA. "We're now at a point where we are beginning to get the attention—and capture the interest—of wine judges, writers and enthusiasts throughout the country," he said. "I see the next five years bringing us national recognition for our wines."

MICHIGAN

When it comes to wine, Michigan is really two states. The Old Mission Peninsula and Leelanau AVAs are the coldest areas with just 145 days for a growing season. The Lake Michigan Shore and Fennville AVAs are down in the southwestern quarter of the state and have a substantially longer growing season.

Doug Welsch has 33 years of experience with Michigan wines. His Fenn Valley Vineyard produces nearly 30,000 cases per year, making it one of Michigan's largest wineries. Like a lot of other winemakers, he thinks Michigan will become famous for its Riesling.

"Riesling expresses itself very well here," he told me. "Michigan should be able to develop and capitalize on it. We grow it well, and there's been a resurgence of its popularity. We'll be riding on that one." Like most Michigan wineries, he sells the majority of his wine from the tasting room, and he knows he'll have a lot of different folks walking through the door. "We produce 35 to 40 different wines per year. I have something for everyone, from sophisticated dry wines to wines aimed at the blue-hairs who like sweet wines." They even use the areas' raspberries and blueberries to make wines.

At the other end of the state, white wines do best. Again, Riesling is king, but other varieties are catching up fast. Bryan Ulbrich, the winemaker at Peninsula Cellars in the Old Mission Peninsula AVA, said: "Our Gewurztraminer, Riesling, and Pinot Blanc develop a really intense aroma that surprises people. They are always surprised we can grow grapes here, but we're moderated by Lake Michigan. We're in a fruit growing area with apples, cherries and peaches all around us. People think we're a frozen tundra, but we're really a great grape growing area."

While the three dependable Alsatian varietals (Gewurztraminer, Riesling, and Pinot Blanc) provide a convenient recommendation, Michigan makes good wines of every type. The southern appellations are also creating rich, elegant Pinot Noirs and Bordeaux blends.

Doug Welsch sees a bright future for Michigan wines: "About seven or eight years ago, 3 percent of wines consumed in Michigan were Michigan wines. Now it's just over 5 percent so we've barely even scratched the surface."

TEXAS

You should know that I live in Texas, write about Texas wines for several newspapers and have a book out on Texas wines. I'm also a fifth-generation Texan, and we are occasionally derided for our supposed lack of humility (untrue) when it comes to things Texan. So you'll understand when I say that Texas makes the best wines on earth.

Just kidding. What I can tell you is that, just like every other wine area, whether it's California or France or Australia, there are good to great wines and there is a lot of plonk. Most of the state's grapes come from either the Texas High Plains AVA, which is around the city of Lubbock in west Texas or the Hill Country AVA close to Austin (where I live).

Like many states, Texas has had an explosion of wineries in the last decade. Four years ago, there were less than 50; today, the number is rapidly approaching 150. Also like other states, a lot of the action is occurring where the doctors, lawyers, and capitalists like to have their second home. Nothing like having a little vineyard to call your own.

The one grape you can depend on in Texas, the one that makes great wine no matter who touches it, is Viognier. It started when Richard Becker of Becker Vineyards in Stonewall bought Viognier grapes from Gary Elliott at Driftwood Vineyards (both operations are in the Texas Hill Country AVA) and made a fragrant, spicy and rich wine that amazed everyone. Since then, there has been a deluge of Viognier planting, and, believe me, I've been trying to find a bad one. They are all good. My pick is still Becker's, but good examples also come from Llano Estacado, Fall Creek, Driftwood Vineyards and Alamosa Winery. Prices are under $20 for all except Driftwood, who charges a gulp-inspiring $35. Condrieu, anyone?

Other white wines do well both in the Hill Country and in the High Plains. Sauvignon Blanc generally tastes more like Sancerre than New Zealand or California versions; Pinot Grigio has a light but fragrant character similar to what you get in Friuli; and Orange Muscat, which most of the world makes into a dense dessert wine, but here in Texas arrives as a light, incredibly aromatic, dry to semi-sweet wine.

Red wines do well all over the state. While no one will be rushing in to plant Pinot Noir, hot weather varietals thrive. Sangiovese, Syrah, Grenache and Touriga National all flourish. Vineyards in the High Plains and a select few north of Dallas do a great job with Bordeaux grapes.

One interesting point that generally surprises people: Texas has one of the 25 largest wineries in the United States, and you've probably never heard of it. The name is Mesa Vineyards and their main imprint is Ste. Genevieve. The reason you've never heard of it is they sell every single drop they make inside the state borders.

As for that pesky No. 5 ranking, Dr. Tim Dodd, head of the Texas Wine Marketing Research Institute at Texas Tech University explains it this way: "Texas is fifth based on net production. According to the TTB, some other states have more production, but in most cases it's from bringing in juice from other states and bottling it."

VIRGINIA

Virginia has a long tradition with grapes, stretching back to Jamestown and later, through its wine aficionado President, Thomas Jefferson. During the 1990s, Virginia developed a reputation for its rich Chardonnays. Shortly after, wineries like Horton Vineyard hit the national stage with some of the best Viognier made in the U.S.

Kluge Estate Wines is one of the new breed of wineries in the state. They have made the not insubstantial investment of hiring one of the planet's most in-demand wine consultants, Michel Rolland. For those who only know Rolland from the hatchet job done on him in *Mondovino,* be aware that critics as diverse as Jancis Robinson and Robert Parker feel that Rolland has been a powerful force in earning newer wine areas a seat on the world stage. He ain't cheap, either.

"We're thrilled to work with him," said Kristin Moses Murray, part of the family that owns Kluge wines. "We feel like he can help put Virginia on the map." Launched in 2003, the winery features the wealth, connections and business acumen of Patricia Kluge (ex-wife of media mogul John Kluge) and her husband, dot-com boomer William Moses. Kluge has everything in line to jump to the front of the Virginian wine business.

Dennis Horton qualifies as a Virginia trailblazer. His Rhone varietals—Marsanne, Grenache, Mourvèdre, Syrah and the aforementioned Viognier—were the first wines in the state to get positive mentions from Robert Parker. Since then, he's spent his hours searching for the right grapes for Virginia, and thinks he may have found three.

"We do really well with a grape called Norton," he told me. "Lots of states make it, but it was created in the 1830s in Richmond. I was the first to replant Norton in Virginia after Prohibition. It's a grape that's bullet proof in the vineyard." He's also a big fan of Petiit Manseng and Tannat, which he says get more intense fruit flavors than anywhere else in the world (points if you can name two other countries making either of these wines).

Horton is an unapologetic explorer. After all, he says, "People gave the Bordeaux folks 350 years to get it right. You'd think they'd give us 25 years."

Most content originally published by *Imbibe Magazine*

Chapter 8
ITALIAN WINE IDOLS

For immediate release:
1. Italy is the largest wine producer in the world.
2. Italians drink more wine than anyone in the world.
3. Italy produces more types of wine than any other country.
4. The U.S. imports more wine from Italy than from any other country (wine valued at $711 million imported from Italy in 2010, with France and Australia ranking second and third, respectively. The three countries combined equaled 54 percent of all U.S. wine imports).

As mentioned earlier in this book, many Americans first experimented with Italian wines such as the sweet red, Lambrusco, or the sweet, slightly sparkling white, Asti Spumanti. Believe it or not, one of the most popular Italian whites today, Pinot Grigio, was unheard of in those days.

Then Santa Margherita produced a lovely Pinot Grigio (the same grape as the then more-famous Pinot Gris from Alsace) at less than $10, which piqued Americans' interest. At the current price of over $20 a bottle, the wine is no longer a great value. I think some Texans tried it because they were enamored with something that sounded like a Margarita!

Italy's modern wine law, which took effect in 1967, is one of the strictest in the world. Denominazione di Origine on an Italian wine label only means wines identified by the name of a grape by itself or in combination with the name of a region in which the grapes are grown. There is no government approval process to secure this designation.

Conversely, Denominazione di Origine Controllata (DOC) is controlled by the government, and is roughly commensurate with Appellation
Controlee in France. Effective with the 1978 vintage, this quality control
system was carried one step further with the government guaranteeing
the highest possible quality for Barolo and Barbaresco. Since then, other
wines have been added. This designation is Denominazione di Origine
Controllata e Guarantita (DOCG). The quality control is so strict, the
wines so designated will even be sampled by Italian wine officials in
American retail stores to ascertain that the wines have maintained their
quality. Should the U.S. ever institute such wine laws, I will volunteer to
travel the world to taste our best wines and verify they have traveled well.
Someone will have to do it. May as well be me.

TUSCANY

Tuscany, the "loveliest and most inspiring of all the wine-producing
areas of Italy," is home to one of the most famous wines in the world, Chianti. There are different kinds of Chianti produced from the Chianti area
of Central Italy (just below Florence), which can basically be categorized
into two types: Regular Chianti and Chianti Classico.

Regular Chianti is generally meant to be consumed young. Sometimes a second fermentation is induced by the addition of dried, concentrated grapes to the already fermented wine, which gives it a light,
lively body. It is an inexpensive dry red in chubby bottles that range from
delightful to dreadful. It is best served at or near release, in carafes, and
while in Italy! However, a DOC Chianti, up to 3 years old and from a
good vintage, can be surprisingly good anywhere.

Chianti Classico is for those who are less inclined to trust Lady Luck,
and not opposed to spending a little more. Chianti Classico is an area
inside Chianti comprising around 15 percent of all Chianti. These wines
are bottled in Bordeaux-style bottles (also used for California Cabernet
Sauvignon and Merlot), and, if a member of the Chianti Classico Consor-
zio, carry neck labels showing a black rooster. Chianti Classico Riserva
is generally a step up in quality (and expense), with an additional third
year of age.

Although one Baron Ricasole originally designated the makeup of
the allowed grapes for Chianti in the late 19th century (85 percent Sangiovese, 10 percent to 15 percent Canaiolo—another red grape—and 5
percent Malvasia, a white grape), the 1967 law changed this to 50 per-

cent to 80 percent Sangiovese, 10 percent to 30 percent Canaiolo, and 10 percent to 30 percent Trebbiano and Malvasia (both whites). When Chianti was granted DOCG status in 1984, many decried the mandatory use of white grapes for their red wine. The result was a new blend of 75 percent to 90 percent Sangiovese, as little as 5 percent whites in Chianti and 2 percent whites in Chianti Classico, and as much as 10 percent non-traditional grapes, such as Cabernet Sauvignon!

My favorites from Chianti Classico include Peppoli (a single-vineyard wine from Antinori), San Felice, Badia a Coltibuono, Brolio (owned by the famous Ricasole family), Fontodi, Monsanto, Gabbiano, Nozzole and Castello di Quercito.

The very best wines of Tuscany are Brunello di Montalcino and the Super-Tuscans. Brunello is made from a clone of the Sangiovese grape, and is an expensive, very long-lived wine. The wines of the first famous producer, Biondi-Santi, are well-known, long-lived, sell at auctions and are terribly overpriced. Other producers make excellent Brunellos, and the prices of a good vintage are usually $40 to $90. These include Casanova di Neri, Caparzo, Altesino, Argiano, Silvio Nardi, Il Poggione, Fuligni, Banfi, Castelgiocondo, Siro Pacenti and Col D'Orcia. A number are also very good to excellent and selling for over $100 a bottle, but why go there?

To get a hint of what Brunello tastes like for a fraction of the price, try a Rosso di Montalcino. This is the same grape, but without the required wood aging of Brunello (or the additional year of aging for Brunello di Montalcino Riserva).

The Super-Tuscan movement came from the aversion by some to the mandatory use of the grapes mentioned above for Chianti. The 600-year-old firm Antinori, headed by 25th-generation Piero Antinori, made an oak-aged red wine in 1971 from approximately 80 percent Sangiovese and 20 percent Cabernet Sauvignon and called it Tignanello (teen nyah nello). The first commercially viable and quickly renowned Tignanello was produced in 1975. When I had lunch with Alessia Antinori (26th generation) in Houston in October 2009, she was surprised I even knew about the 1971, and said she had never tasted it herself!

Some of the first Super-Tuscans produced were Solaia from Antinori (approximately 80 percent Cabernet Sauvignon and 20 percent Sangiovese), Sassicaia and Ornellaia from Bolgheri near the Tuscan coast, Monte Vertine La Pergola Torte, Flaccionello from Fontodi and many others.

PIEDMONT

Whereas Sangiovese is king in Tuscany, in Piedmont, Nebbiolo is king, Barbera is queen, Dolcetto is prince and Moscato Canelli, a white, is princess. The greatest wine of Piedmont is Barolo—no kin whatsoever to Brolio from Tuscany—from the Nebbiolo grape, and its little brother, also from Nebbiolo, is Barbaresco. Barolo is a deep-red, full-bodied wine bottled Burgundy style. Barolo almost has the aging potential of a Bordeaux and the characteristics of a great Burgundy. Several "almosts" add up to an exceptional wine that, to me, has a unique bouquet of tar and faded roses. Like Brunello di Montalcino, many of the best ones are over $100, but it is not necessary to pay that much.

With due deference to those who love Barolo, the Nebbiolo, with very few exceptions, even in Piedmont, does not pass the "over $100" value test to me. Some of the following vintners produce several Barolos that are over $100; however, they each produce at least one that is between $40 and $70. I recommend the following as values, if you can find them: Renato Ratti, Villa Lanata, Guido Porro, Prunotto, Pio Cesare, Icardi, Aldo Clerico, Giovanni Rosso, Schiavenza, G.D. Vajra, M. Marengo, Michel Chiarlo and Ceretto.

Barbaresco, also from Nebbiolo, is ready after three years of age instead of the five required for Barolo. Attractive but less robust, the current release of Barbaresco is a sneak preview of an unreleased Barolo vintage. The other best-known wine from Nebbiolo in Piedmont is Gattinara, which is allowed 10 percent Bonarda grape and requires four years of age, two of which are in wood.

The most widely planted red in Piedmont is Barbera—ha!—another wine knowledge separator. Barbera wines are among the best values in Italy. The best-known are Barbera d'Asti and Barbera d'Alba (from Asti and Alba respectively), found in the $20 range. Vintners that provide top-quality, rich, full-flavored, all-purpose Barberas include Michel Chiarlo, Pio Cesare, Fontanafreda, Marchesi di Barolo and Paitin.

Dolcetto is a fruiter, less-complex grape. It is more along the lines of Cotes-du-Rhone, Beaujolais-Villages and South Africa's Pinotage—a very pleasant, uncomplicated, satisfying red wine for between $10 and $20 a bottle. The Moscato Canelli, a white grape, is responsible for Asti Spumante, a relatively inexpensive sparkling wine (not made by the Champagne method but the inexpensive

Charmat method), with around 9 percent alcohol and 9 percent residual sugar. It is not considered a "serious" wine by connoisseurs, but is surprisingly nice as a dessert or with cake, cookies (especially Italian cookies) and not-too-sweet desserts. A step up is wine labeled Moscato d'Asti. It is a bit more expensive and only slightly sparkling (frizzante). Fermentation is stopped at around 5 percent alcohol and the wine is also sweet, but more attractive as a dessert wine. Saracco is my favorite at around $15.

Before we continue, let's locate Tuscany and Piedmont on the map. These regions produce some of the best red wines in the world, and by far the greatest of Italy. While I'm at it, I'll throw in the Three Venices in the far northeast, Lombardy and Emilia-Romagna, which I'll discuss next.

THE THREE VENICES (THAT'S WHAT THEY'RE CALLED):

Venice is in the Veneto Region. The other two nearest regions are Friuli-Venezia Giulia and Trentino-Alto Adige. I call these last two Friuli and Trentino. Of importance to note:

- Some of the best Pinot Grigios come from the Veneto.
- Many of the best Chardonnays, Pinot Blancs and Sauvignon Blancs, as well as the local favorite, Tocai Friulani, come from Friuli.
- Very good Cabernet Sauvignon, Merlot and Cabernet Franc come from the Veneto and Friuli.
- Prosecco is a well-known sparkling wine, made by the Charmat method, where the secondary fermentation takes place in pressurized tanks; Soave (Garganega grape blended with Trebbiano) is historically the best-known white and Valpolicella (Corvina grape blended with Rondinella and Molinara) is the best-known red. All hail from the Veneto. Like the progression from Chianti to Chianti Classico to Chianti Classic Riserva, there is Valpolicella, Valpolicella Classico, Valpolicella Classico Superiore and Valpolicella Ripasso. A Recioto della Valpolicella is a slightly sweet but opulently decadent red.
- The most serious, big-time red is Amarone, a late harvest, Corvina-based red, the grapes being laid out on mats for months to dry, taking on a raisin-like quality and culminating as a big, Port-like red without the residual sugar. Also from the Veneto.
- My favorite producer in Friuli is Jermann.
- My favorite producer in Trentino is Alois Lageder.
- My favorite producers in the Veneto are Anselmi (Soave), Pieropan (Soave), Allegrini (Valpolicella), Masi (Amarone), Tommasi (Amarone) and Zenato (Pinot Grigio).

LOMBARDY AND EMILIA-ROMAGNA

The wines in the industrial region of Lombardy are mostly locally known and quaffed. The one true Champagne-method sparkling wine from Italy is made here—Franciacorta. Probably the best-known winery in Lombardy is Ca' del Bosco.

Emilia-Romagna is the food capital of Italy and home of one of the world's great cheeses. This region sadly boasts a dearth of great wines.

The most popular Italian wine in the U.S., similar to Sutter Home White Zinfandel with a sparkle, is this region's Lambrusco, a fizzy, sweet red. As you might imagine, the wine is extremely popular in Emilia-Romagna!

Now we will replicate the map, adding Umbria, Campania, Apulia, Sicily, The Marches and Sardinia.

UMBRIA

Francis of Assisi was born in the region of Umbria, where the well-known white wine Orvieto is made. The primary grape is Trebbiano, blended with Verdello (Verdejo in Spain) and several others. A step up in quality and price is Orvieto Classico.

The "hottest" red here today is Sagrantino di Montefalco. Made from the Sagrantino grape, and relatively unknown in the U.S. until recently, this is a big, Amarone-style red. The other top red of Umbria is Torgiano Rosso Riserva, which, being made from Sangiovese, Canaiolo and Trebbiano, resembles a Chianti Classico. My favotite is Lungarotti's "Super" Togiano Rosso Riserva called Rubesco.

CAMPANIA AND APULIA

Campania boasts such destinations as Naples and the Amalfi Coast. It also lays claim to at least one legendary winery, Mastroberardino. The leading wines of Campania are Aglianico, a big red-black wine (Mastroberardino's is called Taurasi), and two whites, Fiano di Avellino and Greco di Tufo—all indigenous grapes.

The two leading grapes of Apulia are the fairly well-known Primitivo and the not-so-well-known Negroamaro. An affordable wine found in Italian restaurants in the U.S., Salice Salentino comes from the Negroamaro grape. The best producer of this wine is Cosimo Taurino.

SICILY AND SARDINIA

Sicily's leading wine is Marsala, which will be discussed in the chapter entitled "Sherry and Other Fortified Wines." As for table wines, the only exciting red is from the Nero D'Avola grape, the best of which exhibit red-black color, bold fruit and excellent structure. The best-known whites and reds are labeled "Corvo."

The island of Sardinia is known primarily for two whites—Vernaccia and Vermentino, and a red, Cannonau.

THE MARCHES

The Marches is the region just east of Umbria. I mention it only because of the famous white wine Verdicchio, which is sold in an amphora-shaped bottle. My favorite producer of this wine since the 1970s has been Fazi-Battaglia.

A DAY IN THE LIFE OF A MAJOR WINE AUCTION

The first major wine auction I attended was in Houston at an upscale store called Sakowitz. It was the early 1970s, and a young Robert Sakowitz hired Michael Broadbent, then head of Christie's Wine Department in London, to conduct the event. In retrospect, some of the lots went at amazingly low prices.

Next, Hublein Inc. hired Broadbent to conduct wine auctions around the United States. Several of my wine buddies and I attended the auctions in Chicago, New Orleans and one or two others. There were some real bargains during those times, primarily because there weren't very many sophisticated buyers—actually, compared to the present, there weren't that many buyers of any type.

Meanwhile, longtime friend and entrepreneur John Hart had started the Chicago Wine Company out of his home in 1973. It became the wine sales organization of choice for thousands of consumers around the country. The main obstacle to the wine business in those days was the laws that prohibited shipping bottles across state lines. In Houston, a group of us had made significant purchases. One friend in the bunch, a car dealer, flew to Detroit, picked up a large van, drove to Chicago and retrieved all of our wines. Technically, he broke the law each time he crossed a state line on the way back to Texas.

In 1989, John Hart sold his half of the Chicago Wine Company to his partner. He then served as senior wine consultant for Christie's for a while, and in 1993, formed the John Hart Wine Company. When his friends Michael Davis and Paul Hart, both seasoned, successful wine professionals, left Sotheby's (Christie's archrival) in 2003, the formation of Hart Davis Hart was inevitable.

On Sept. 17, 2005, I attended a Hart Davis Hart auction in Chicago, featuring "the most important collection offered in Chicago wine auction history." It was very exciting.

First of all, Hart Davis Hart makes it easy to bid on the Internet. If a certain lot does not receive a high enough price—the "reserve" price unknown to the bidders—the auctioneer will pass. By the evening of September 16, 90 percent of the items had confirmed bids higher than the reserve prices, thus proving the event was a success before the live auction had begun!

However, with the rapid-fire, skillful auctioneering shared by Michael Davis, Paul Hart, Ben Ferdinand and several others, many of the acceptable pre-bids were vastly overridden by bidders in the audience and by real-time telephone bidders.

There are many bargains to be found at these auctions. For some reason, a high-quality lot occasionally will get overlooked. The exact opposite occurs when two bidders are dead set on an item. This can occur between two phone bidders, two audience bidders or one of each. The prime example of the latter was lot # 25, a magnum of Chambertin 1964 from Armand Rousseau, which carried the written comment in the program, "Level 4.5 cm below cork; very slight signs of seepage; slightly wine stained vintage label." The estimated price range for this lot was $2,200-$3,000. One of the two voracious bidders came away with the prize at $6,500.

A similar activity—perhaps the same two bidders—occurred with lot # 526, in which the gavel came down for two bottles of Musigny Comte Georges de Vogue 1949 at $11,000!

A seemingly high bid of $35,100 won the "gem" of the day, a double magnum of Chateau Pétrus 1961, certainly one of the best wines I've ever tasted. I say "seemingly high" because a mere magnum of that wine sold for $13,000 at auction almost 25 years ago.

At a more reasonable and affordable level, many good buys were realized, particularly when considering the extreme professional analysis regarding the condition and provenance of the lots offered. To mention just a few: one case Mouton-Rothschild 1999 — drinking fabulously now—$1,400; one case Ducru-Beaucaillou 1995 — $1,200; six magnums Léoville-Las-Cases 1995—$1,500; and one case of the famous 1998 Lafite-Rothschild—$2,400. And a number of the greatest wines of the world from France, California, Italy and other regions were scattered among the 1,380 lots, including numerous fortified wines from the 19th century.

Magnums are preferable to regular-size bottles in terms of ageability. In lots 249 and 250, two bottles of Chateau Pétrus 1970 went for $1,000 each, but one magnum sold for $4,000. However, with lots 254 and 255, six bottles of Chateau Pétrus 1988 and three magnums of the same wine went for the same price. Go figure.

Another great benefit was the tasting that was held an hour prior to the event. The cost was only $65. Where else could one go to taste prime samples such as Lafite 1990, Léoville-Las-Cases 1986, La Mission-Haut-Brion 1985, Latour 1982 (unbelievably great), Clos de la Roche Vieilles Vignes Ponsot 1999, Echezeaux Anne et Francoise Gros 1993, Montrachet Marquis de Laguiche Drouhin 1995, Ornellaia 1997, Masseto (the Pétrus of Tuscany) 1999, Dominus 1991, Araujo Cabernet Sauvignon Eisele Vineyard 1999 and others?

Hart Davis Hart can be found online at www.hdhwine.com.

BLIND TASTING

Although it is much more constructive to taste a young wine and be able to predict its future evolvement, blind tasting – albeit occasionally humiliating – is great fun.

In the mid-1970s, several of us would gather regularly for blind tastings and take turns guessing the country, grape varietal, vintage and/or winemaker. After several months, some of us could come close and even nail one every once in a while.

Following is a good way to conduct your own blind tasting:

1. Select wines of approximately the same price to taste against each other. Meet every week with another person or persons before or during dinner and try the following blind (designate one person to pour and keep track of the wines):

    Week 1—California Sauvignon Blanc vs. Pouilly-Fume or Sancerre from the Loire Valley and made from Sauvignon Blanc

    Week 2—California Chardonnay vs. Macon-Villages or Rully from Burgundy at the lower end, or Puligny-Montrachet or Chassagne-Montrachet in a higher range, all made from Chardonnay

    Week 3—California or Oregon Pinot Noir vs. Red Burgundy

    Week 4—California Cabernet Sauvignon vs. red Bordeaux from the Médoc

    Week 5—California Merlot vs. red Bordeaux from Saint-Emilion or Pomerol

    Week 6—California Syrah vs. Cornas from the Rhone Valley and made from Syrah

2. Compared to their French counterparts, the California wines generally are made from riper grapes, have somewhat less tannin, and don't age as well. Try a 2010 Chardonnay against a 2008 white Burgundy, an '07 California Cabernet against an '03 or '05 Bordeaux, or even an '04 California Cabernet against a '00 Bordeaux.

3. Serve appropriate hors d'oeuvres that complement the wines. Something as simple as Danish Havarti with Chardonnay or brie or aged cheddar with reds will work. For a simple dinner, try turkey sandwiches with whites and roast beef sandwiches with reds (with or without cheese). If no meal is in sight, plain crackers will do.

4. Make notes on each wine; eventually something will gel. For example, if a red has flavors of chocolate, bell peppers, eucalyptus and/or black currants, odds are it's a Cabernet Sauvignon. If in comparison with a Bordeaux, one has a darker, more purplish color and more ripe fruit in the nose, it's probably the California wine. If a red smells of dirt, leather, tobacco and/or mushrooms, then it's more likely to be Pinot Noir, with the California version having more color and obvious fruit. And if it smells like tar and faded roses, it's Barolo from Piedmont (tough to find a Nebbiolo from anywhere else to taste blind with a Barolo!).

5. If none of this helps, try one match four or five times in a row. Eventually, you'll discover which is which, and even more importantly, why.

Wines made from ripe grapes in California typically have more fruit than their French counterparts. But the sunshine, which ripens the fruit, also dampens the acidity (making the PH higher). This is why in a blind tasting without food, the California wine sometimes far surpasses the French, whereas with food, the French wine sometimes tastes better because it has more acidity. Knowing this can help when blind tasting.

Although I have missed so many times as to be almost depressed, there have been some notable exceptions. One of my favorites occurred in the mid-1990s when I was a guest at the Board luncheon at Christie's in London. Several took a guess at the dessert wine. One guessed it was a 1945 Sauternes. Another speculated it was a Barsac, possibly from 1937. I suggested that it was most reminiscent of an unknown Chateau from the 1921 vintage in Sauternes that I had tasted some 15 years before. It was an unknown Chateau from the 1923 vintage in Sauternes. I wasn't particularly proud of myself, but it was nice that the guest from Texas knew the time of day in some pretty exceptional company.

IS WINE BREATHING NECESSARY?

In May 1977, my late friend Alexis Bespaloff published "A Corking New Wine Theory" in *New York Magazine.* In blind tastings with Robert Mondavi, Paul Draper of Ridge Winery, Alexis Lichine of Bordeaux Chateau Prieuré-Lichine, Kevin Zraly, then cellarmaster at Windows on the World Restaurant and author of *Windows on the World Complete Wine Course,* and John Sheldon, then wine consultant at Tavern-on-the-Green, Bespaloff uncovered an embarrassing fact.

The wine used for the blind tasting with Draper was his 1974 Geyserville Zinfandel. For Mondavi, his 1973 Cabernet Sauvignon; and for Lichine, his 1967 Chateau Prieuré-Lichine. In each case, for each taster, one bottle was decanted one hour before serving. One was simply uncorked an hour before serving. A third was decanted and served minutes before the tasting and the fourth was just uncorked and served minutes before the tasting. Mondavi and Lichine tasted each other's wine also. Don't shoot the messenger, but in every case, including a 1973 Chateau Pichon-Lalande with Zraly and Sheldon, the bottle that was just uncorked and served at the time of the tasting was preferred!

Bespaloff queried both the famous French wine consultant Emile Peynaud and the prominent U.C. Davis enology professor Vernon Singleton on the subject, and each just uncorked the wines and poured them with similar thoughts about non-breathing.

Bespaloff went even further and opened two bottles of 1967 Chateau Figeac on one occasion and two bottles of 1967 Chateau Latour on another occasion, one decanted an hour before and one uncorked minutes before serving. In each case, four other wine drinkers "...discovered, to their astonishment, that the bottle just opened and poured had more flavor and a bigger bouquet than the one decanted an hour before..."

This experiment serves as serious evidence that "letting wine breathe," at least for red wines, is unnecessary. But even though this article appeared 34 years ago from one of the most prolific and knowledgeable wine writers in the world, the custom of opening a bottle to let it breathe and decanting wine to let it breathe remains firmly entrenched.

In the past, I had been convinced that wine breathing, especially in the glass, could be beneficial; however, being a skeptic myself, I decided to test the theory. I asked Bill Floyd at Reef Restaurant in Houston if he would round up some serious wine professionals for a blind tasting conducted by myself. The wine was a 2005 (outstanding year for Bordeaux) Chateau Lynch- Moussas (a very good Classified Growth Bordeaux, at least since 2002). I decanted one bottle two hours before the tasting, decanted one bottle one hour before the tasting, and opened one bottle just before the "judges" arrived. I then poured the three offerings, two from decanters and one from bottle, separated the tasters, and served the wines blind.

The attending tasters were: renowned *Houston Chronicle* sports and wine writer Dale Robertson; one wine-savvy restaurateur; one well-known wine wholesaler; and several well-known Houston sommeliers. All but one attendee agreed: The wine that had been opened and poured just prior to the tasting was the most flavorful!

In late 2010, Tim Mondavi's sons (and Robert Mondavi's grandsons) came to Houston and invited me to dinner to taste their super-premium wine, Continuum. Robert Mondavi spent his last several years helping Tim and his daughter Marci develop this wine. It displays an amazing depth of flavors and is a culmination of everything Robert and Tim had learned over the years. Carlo and Dante, Tim's sons who work at the family winery, mentioned that they struggled with when to open the wine. Recommendations they had received included the morning of the day the wine would be served for dinner, three hours before serving, etc. I told them about Alexis Bespaloff's tests and my own recent test. Carlo said, "We just opened this one right before we sat down and it's tasting better than usual! We'll check this out." In April of 2011, Carlo invited me to another tasting, which I was unable to attend, but I took the opportunity to ask him about when he decanted or opened the wine these days. He replied that they no longer worry about "breathing" with Continuum; they just open it and serve!

SPANISH WINES IN THE SPOTLIGHT

Some of the most heralded Spanish wines of today come from regions that were previously unknown to most Americans. Yecla, Campo de Borja, Bierzo, Rueda, Calatayud, Montsant, Rueda and Jumilla produce widely sought-after wines. Don't worry about remembering these, as I will provide a list of some superlative wines from each region at the end of the chapter. The white wines Albariño and Verdejo are all the rage in the U.S., with plantings even taking place in Texas. And now there's a blast from the white Godello grape, which was unheard of just a year or so ago.

Similar to the Appellation Controllée laws of France, Spain created the Denominación de Origin (DO) law, but didn't seriously enforce it until 1970. In 1991, an even higher and more rigid appellation, DOCA, was granted for Rioja and later for Priorato (DOCA is roughly equivalent to Italy's DOCG). DO and DOCA are enforced by government boards called the Consejo Regulador.

Spain has more vines than any country, but in grape tonnage ranks third

> Spain produces more sparkling wine than any other country. It's called cava. And the city of Jerez is the center for the production of Sherry. These two wines will be discussed in the article titled "Other Sparkling Wines" and the chapter "Sherry and Other Fortified Wines," respectively.

behind Italy and France. Vast plantings, especially in middle Spain, comprise older vines planted on dry plains at very high altitudes, with production closer to one ton per acre versus two or three times the production per acre in Italy and France.

Let's explore the five regions that were well known—OK, Rias Baixas wasn't that well known—around the year 2000.

First, it's important to know that in Rioja and Ribera del Duero, there are three primary wine classifications: crianza, reserva and gran reserva. Although not nearly as pricey, this hierarchy can be compared in ascending quality to the following Tuscans: Rosso di Montalcino, Brunello di Montalcino and Brunello di Montalcino Riserva (notice, it's riserva in Italy and reserva in Spain). Crianza is the least expensive and by far the most prevalent. It is generally young, of good quality, and ready to drink at release. Reservas are aged longer and from the better sections of superior vineyards.

Gran Reservas derive from the very best vineyards and vintages, are the most complex and are aged for a minimum of five years before release.

As more producers lean toward fruitier international styles, Joven and Cosecha—wines less than 6 months old—are seen on more bottles. And gran reserva is fading in popularity because of the holding costs and the fact that many reservas are sufficiently oak aged.

RIOJA

The celebrated Spanish wine region of Rioja was isolated for centuries due to its small population and sizable distance from any major markets. But change came to Rioja following two unexpected cataclysmic events in France: Powdery mildew in the 1840s and the phylloxera epidemic that started in the late 1860s. French wine merchants and growers rushed across the border to northern Spain both to purchase wine and to start new vineyards. Until phylloxera reached Rioja shortly after 1900, the region thrived. Just as quickly as the good times came, they left, and Rioja suffered for decades. By the late 1970s, Rioja once again was producing sufficient quantities of fairly decent wines, such as the ubiquitous Marques de Cáceres.

The primary white grape in Rioja is the Viura (called Macabeo in Penedés). Starting around 2000, some white Riojas, usually blended with Malvasia and Garnacha Blanca, have become interesting, if not spectacular.

Up until the late 1970s, and even throughout the '80s, many Riojas, like the wines of Piedmont, were allowed to age in barrels for too long. Many Riojas came across as oxidized and flat. By the mid-1990s, with the wine-learning boom, new viticultural practices, and innovations in winemaking, everything changed in Rioja and throughout Spain.

The primary red grape of Rioja is the Tempranillo (often described as tasting like a cross between Cabernet Sauvignon and Pinot Noir) followed by the Garnacha (Grenache in France), Graciano and Mazuelo (or Cariñena—Carignane in France). My favorite "old school" producer is Montecillo, and my favorite producers are Cune, Remelluri, Muga, Marques de Murrieta, Conde de Valdemar and Marques de Riscal.

RIBERA DEL DUERO

Located about 90 miles north of Madrid on the Duero River is the Ribera del Duero. In the 1860s, a winemaker who had studied in Bordeaux brought Bordeaux varietals (mainly Cabernet Sauvignon) and planted them at Vega Sicilia along with the local clone of Tempranillo, Tinto Fino. Over the years, this region remained in obscurity. That changed when the first Vega Sicilia Unicos were released in the 1970s and '80s. And when the 1968 was released in the early 1990s, oenophiles worldwide took note. Another wine from Vega Sicilia is Valbuena, which is released at five years of age. Today a newly released Unico brings up to $350, and a Valbuena around $150. An occasional multi-vintage Reserva Especial might bring $450. Other top producers here are Alion, Pesquera, Condado de Haza, Abadia Retuerta, Creta, Vizcarra Ramos, J.C. Conde, O. Fournier and Ismael Arroyo.

PRIORAT (PRIORATO IN CATALÁN)

Priorat's reputation was practically nil until around 15 years ago. Instead of Tempranillo, the wines here are mainly produced from Cariñena and Garnacha, and many are aged in new French oak. With daunting slopes, Priorato has some of the steepest, most labor-intensive vineyards in the world. The black slate soil that lends distinction to the wines is called Licorella. While pioneer Alvaro Palacios is primarily responsible for the new wave of production of these massively structured wines—his wines are L'Ermita and Finca Dofi—there are other fabled and expensive wines such as Clos Erasmus, Clos Mogador and Clos L'Obac. At the "value" end of the spectrum, I enjoy Mas Igneus (white, Macabeo; red, Garnacha), Nita (Garnacha and Cariñena), Pasanau (Garnacha) and Finca Mirador.

PENEDÉS

The first inkling I had that Spain was up to something big in winedom was in 1979. After the 1976 Paris Tasting, France received its next big shock when Guide Gault-Millau staged a Wine Olympics. Going up against the best reds of the world, including First Growths from the Médoc in Bordeaux, Torres Gran Coronas Black Label 1970 from Penedés won the blue ribbon! This wine was a blend primarily of Cabernet Sauvignon with Tempranillo and Monastrell (the Mourvèdre from southern Rhone). Now called Mas La Plana, it is one of the top red values on the market at $40-$60 a bottle. Excellent producers besides Torres here include Masia Bach, Jean Leon and Rene Barbier.

RIAS BAIXAS

Pronounced Rias Bye Jhahs, this area became known only recently. It is sometimes referred to as "Green Spain" because of the lush vegetation. Albariño, the now-famous grape from there, was not so famous when known only as the primary grape for Vinho Verde in Portugal. Because of a unique pergola-style trellising system and new winemaking techniques, combined with the perfect Atlantic influence, soils, etc., by the year 2007, Albariños were popping up on wine lists all over the U.S. This grape is thought to be the best white of Spain by many. It pairs nicely with seafood and displays a beautiful fragrance of flavors, including honey, peach and lime. Similar to Riesling, the wine is not aged in oak so that the flavors remain bright, bold and vibrant. One of my favorites is Burgans, both for taste and price (around $13). Some more expensive and impressive beauties are Morgadio, Lisco, Martin Codax and Pazo de Galegos.

Now let's add some more regions to our map. To find your favorite, secure a good bottle from each area and taste a different wine with your meal on consecutive nights. At least one or two will jump out and grab you like El Albar from Toro did for me.

As promised, here are some excellent producers and/or wines from each region, along with the primary grape:

- Toro: Bodegas Sabor Real (Tinta de Toro—Toro's name for Tempranillo), Vetus (Tinta de Toro), El Albar (Tinto de Toro);
- Yecla: Bodegas Castaño (Monastrell), Señorio de Barahonda (Monastrell);
- La Mancha (World's largest area of vine plantings and home to the most planted grape, Arien): Bodegas Volver (Tempranillo);
- Campo de Borja: Borsao (Garnacha), Alto Moncayo (Garnacha);
- Calatayud: Albado (Garnacha), Bodegas San Alejandro (Garnacha), Bodegas Ateca (Garnacha);
- Montsant: Baronia del Montsant, Flor de Englora (Garnacha and Cariñena), Can Blau (Garnacha), Masroig (Garnacha and Cariñena);
- Jumilla: Sylvano Garcia (Monastrell), Hijos de Juan Gil (Monastrell), San Isidro (Monastrell), Casa Castillo, Las Gravas (Monastrell and Cabernet Sauvignon), Valtosca (Syrah);
- Rueda: Nieva Blanco (Verdejo), Trascampanas (Verdejo);
- Bierzo: Castro Ventosa (Mencia), Luna Beberide (Mencia),Finca Luzon (Monastrell), Bodegas Peique (Mencia), Arganza La Mana Roble (Mencia), Casar de Burbia TEBAiDA (Mencia).

THE JOY OF WINE

Several years ago, I witnessed what may have seemed like a common-place occurrence, but it inspired this article. My wife and I were at a popular neighborhood restaurant that allows customers to bring their own wine for a $7 corkage fee. This particular restaurant has about as many outdoor diners as indoor patrons. We were waiting for a table inside, even though it was pleasant enough outdoors with shade and fans.

Outside, there was a smiling woman, possibly in her late 20s, joy-ously approaching another woman of about the same age. Each held a bottle of wine. Although I could only see the design and color of the labels, I knew one bottle was a Blackstone in a Bordeaux-style bottle; the other a Smooking Loon in a Burgundy-style bottle. Shortly thereafter, a young man carrying a bottle of wine joined the two. Then some more friends arrived, each bearing a bottle of wine. For this group, the wine seemed like a natural part of the evening. This is a vast cultural shift from 30 years ago that I believe signals a wonderful, new era.

Everyone in the group was smiling, chatting and obviously looking forward to a fun evening. I just had to wonder how that picture might have differed in the absence of wine.

I don't think it mattered whether anyone knew much about wine or whether one spent more on a bottle than the others. As a matter of fact, a quick glimpse told me that one person had an Artesa Cabernet or Merlot, which probably cost twice as much as the other two bottles I had spied.

In my imagination, at least one or two members of the group were thoroughly knowledgeable about wine, and perhaps everyone picked up some new information on the subject. If they shared their selections, then everyone experienced some new tastes. Whether the wine was a predomi-nant part of the meal or just brought to enhance the dining experience, I would bet it added a bushel of joy to the evening.

There are such different levels of enjoyment in drinking alcoholic beverages. There is a deep chasm of difference between a bar full of peo-ple on their fourth beer with chips and dips, or their fourth scotch with little or no food at all, and a group at a wine bar sharing wine with hors d'oeuvres and trying new wine/food pairings. (By the way, I enjoy beer, nachos and chili-cheese dogs as much as anyone—I just relish trying a new wine and discovering new wine/food combinations).

Wine is so civilized—there are extra dimensions to the enjoyment of wine that no other beverage can match. And the food/wine pairings that create synergisms are endless. Gone are the days when goat cheese and Sauvignon Blanc, fish with Chardonnay, pizza with Zinfandel, fowl with Pinot Noir and steak with Cabernet were the only solid matches known.

Now I hear people confidently ordering grilled salmon with Pinot Noir, shellfish with Albarino (Spain), fish with Gruner Veltliner (Austria), chocolate cake with Cabernet Sauvignon, pork with dry Riesling, etc. Those who know very little about wine may have the most fun of all. They sometimes show no fear with regard to wine/food matches and may come up with peculiar pairings that they and they alone relish.

One of my favorite new matches occurred with a Dr. Konstantin Frank's Vinifera Cellars Pinot Noir (Finger Lakes, NY) with veal Marsala and a side of spaghetti marinara! Another was a Moet & Chandon Imperial Nectar Rosé (non-vintage) with strawberry cake. It made the traditional dry Champagne with cake seem clumsy and outdated by comparison.

No matter the pairings, the cost or the venue, when evening comes there can be great joy and anticipation with a glass or two of a new wine, or an old favorite, along with a friend with whom to share! Mark Twain said it best: "To get the full value of joy, you must have someone to divide it with."

SOME PRACTICAL HINTS ABOUT WINE— FROM EXPERIENCE

In Europe, wine has been part of a meal for hundreds of years. I sat down to meals in Italy, France and Spain when I was in my 20s, and I don't remember anyone discussing the wines. After every bite or so of food, people would simply pick up their glass and drink.

Professional tasters will swirl the wine around in the glass vigorously in an attempt to release the aroma or bouquet. Serious oenophiles do the same thing, as well as sticking their noses deep into the glass to harvest some fruit or floral components of the wine, and every once in a while, grin knowingly and say something like "blackberries" or "figs." There is absolutely nothing wrong with this. It's akin to a symphony lover sighing with delight during a perfectly played melody or new arrangement.

Following are some hints on how to optimally enjoy wine:

1. If possible, select a proper wine glass without a "lip" around the top inside of the glass. This "lip" spreads out the wine along the glass before it can be consumed and negatively affects the taste profile.

2. Only fill the glass one-third to a half full. A 10- or 12-ounce glass should be just right in most instances, which will allow you to experience a nice bouquet if you take a whiff.

3. Don't worry about wine "breathing." Pour it in the glass and drink it.

4. Abstain from thinking you must hold the glass by the stem so you won't heat up the wine. Think about it—if a glass of white wine is 40-45 degrees, and you pick it up occasionally between bites of food, but hold it by the bowl, will it shoot up to some untenable temperature? And if you do hold it long enough to really affect the temperature, by that time the glass will be empty, so who cares?

5. Don't be so anxious about wine and food pairings. White wine with seafood, white or a light- or medium-red wine with chicken, and bigger reds, like Cabernet Sauvignon or Shiraz, with beef or lamb is a general rule. But there are exceptions. One is that if you like Chardonnay with your steak, it's really nobody's business but yours. Your palate is the best palate in the world for you!

Finally, how to avoid hangovers (at least bad ones):

- Don't drink so much—Duh!
- If you're going to have several glasses of wine with dinner, avoid mixed drinks or beer before dinner.
- As soon as you start drinking, start eating. Having two glasses of wine on an empty stomach prior to a wine dinner is a recipe for a hangover.
- If you will be drinking a dessert wine like Port or Sauternes, have less wine with your meal. The combination of the high alcohol (Sauternes around 15 percent and Port around 18 percent), and the substantial, natural residual sugar can exacerbate the effects of too much wine and food. For meals that include dessert wine, a recommended regimen would be no more than 6 ounces of white wine or sparkling wine with the hors d'oeuvres or appetizer, 6 ounces of red with the entrée and 4 ounces of dessert wine. As long as I don't exceed this, I don't think about the words Tums, Rolaids, Prylosec, Alka-Seltzer or Advil.

Chapter 10
AUSTRALIA AND NEW ZEALAND
BRIM WITH WINE VALUE

Australia is the most arid continent in the world, with the oldest and most depleted soil on the planet. Some would even classify the soil as a fossil. Australia had no indigenous grape vines, and aboriginal Australia is one of the few world cultures that never developed a tradition of fermented drink.

In spite of the lack of early irrigation, Australia contains the majority of the oldest vineyards in the world, which were spared the disease suffered by European vineyards in the 1800s.

Australia's exportation of massive amounts of cheap bulk wines to the U.S. has somewhat tarnished the wine reputation of the land Down Under. Nonetheless, some of the world's best wines, particularly from Shiraz and Shiraz/Grenache/Mourvèdre blends, can be found here.

In the spring of 1980, my wife and I attended the Third Triennial Convention of the International Wine and Food Society in Australia. After three days in Sydney, three days in Melbourne and four days in Adelaide, I had a good handle on the wines of Australia.

It didn't hurt matters that our three main hosts were Len Evans, Australia's leading wine authority and author of the 500-page tome *The Complete Book of Australian Wine*, first published in 1973; Hunter Valley icon Murray Tyrell, whom we had previously met in London in 1977 and were captivated by his 1976 Chardonnay; and Dr. Max Lake, The wine-loving surgeon who planted the first Cabernet vineyard in Hunter Valley in 1961.

Australia's wine history can be traced back to the country's settlement. Eleven small ships with just over 1,000 people—men, women, children and convicts—sailed from England and arrived in New South Wales in early 1788. Vine cuttings were brought over—early records mention the claret grape—and the first plantings occurred shortly thereafter.

The first "grape rush" occurred in the Hunter Valley region of New South Wales in the 1840s, and by 1850 there were 30 growers and over 500 acres under vine. Wine growing then became popular in Victoria, and by 1870 there were some 3,000 acres of vineyards there.

South Australia, specifically in and around Adelaide, is the home of McLaren Vale and Barossa Valley—the equivalent of Napa and Sonoma in California. The famous Penfold's Winery traces its roots in this area back to 1844!

In Western Australia, viticulture enjoys a beneficial maritime influence. The vineyards are situated in the southwestern portion of the state. In contrast to the rest of Oz, where Chardonnay and Shiraz dominate grape growing, here zesty Sauvignon Blanc, superlative Cabernet Sauvignon and bold Zinfandel are the leaders. Western Australia is anchored primarily by the Margaret River District and its famous wineries of Leeuwin Estate, Vasse Felix, Cullen and Howard Park; however, other areas are rapidly emerging, especially the Great Southern area of Frankland River, with Goundry and Plantagenet wineries leading the way.

If you put a map outline of Australia over a map of the U.S., as was done for us in 1980, you'll notice the countries are comparable in size. In 1980, the U.S. had a population of around 240 million, whereas Australia's population was 14 million! Australian wine production predominantly takes place in the southern half of Australia due to a more moderate climate.

When we returned from this trip, I wrote an article about Australian and New Zealand wines—we spent about five days in New Zealand on the way home—in the June 1980 issue of *Moody's Wine Review*. The piece was touted later by one source as one of the first comprehensive Australia/New Zealand wine articles written in the U.S. with some 80 wine recommendations.

While the New Zealand Wine Industry was in its embryonic stage—only nine of the recommended wines were from New Zealand—the Australian wine scene was up and running, especially for Australians. Virtually every oenophile in the U.S. has heard of Robert Mondavi, the late ambassador of California wines. Likewise, everyone I met in Australia, from cab drivers to shop keepers to doormen, was well aware of Australian wine ambassador Len Evans.

The real shocker for me was virtually the same "aha" moment I experienced tasting my first great Bordeaux wine. The 1955 Grange Hermitage wine was served at an other-worldly dinner at the University of Sydney, hosted by Sir Roden Cutler, Governor of the state of New South Wales. Now simply called Grange, the wine remains one of the top reds of the world. It is mostly Shiraz, and Shiraz is the king of Australia wines.

Excellent wineries that produce value wines include Little Penguin (my favorite "critter" wines), Gemtree, Frankland Estates, Marquis Phillips, D'Arenburg, Thorn-Clark, "R" Winery, Fetish, Hewitson, Reilly's, Tyrell's and Morambo Creek. Some special value wines are Schild Barossa Cabernet Sauvignon, Shingleback McLaren Vale Cabernet Sauvignon, Peter Lehman Barossa Shiraz, Oxford Landing Viognier and Sauvignon Blanc, Torbreck Woodcutter Semillon, Water Wheel Shiraz, Henry's Drive Pillar Box Red, Andrew Hardy Little Ox Shiraz, Binder-Mitchell Shiraz, and Leeuwin Estate Margaret River Siblings Sauvignon Blanc and Shiraz.

Excellent wineries in the higher price ranges include Magpie Estate, Rolf Binder, Langmeil, Kilakanoon, Oliver Hill, John Duval, Yalumba, Elderton, Clarendon Hills and Balgownie Estate. Some special wines in the higher ranges, excluding the over $100 crowd, include Trevor Jones Shiraz, Penfolds St. Henri Shiraz and Shiraz Bin 28, Henschke Barossa Shiraz, Grosset Riesling, Wynn's Cabernet Sauvignon John Riddock and Shiraz Michael, and Jasper Hill Occam's Razor Shiraz.

Visit www.australianwineregions.com for a comprehensive overview of Australia's wine regions.

MAJOR WINE AREAS OF
NEW ZEALAND

NORTHLAND

AUCKLAND

Auckland

WAIKATO / BAY OF PLENTY

GISBORNE

HAWKES BAY

NELSON

WELLINGTON

MARLBOROUGH

Christchurch

CANTERBURY / WAIPARA

CENTRAL OTAGO

As mentioned earlier in this chapter, in 1980, New Zealand had little to offer with respect to quality wines. Until the early 1970s, New Zealand wine was primarily fortified and from the North Island. In 1973, Sauvignon Blanc was planted in Marlborough on the South Island. This was the beginning of the modern age of New Zealand winemaking.

New Zealand is a viticultural technology leader for at least two reasons. First, because about 90 percent of all its wines are now bottled with screw caps—thus, almost no cork-tainted wines. Second, Australian viticulturalist Dr. Richard Smart developed the widely recognized balanced vine theory. Prior to his studies, it was believed that all vines had to struggle to produce a wine with character, but Smart's theory is that to produce great fruit, a vine simply needs to be balanced.

With the later introduction of Cloudy Bay Sauvignon Blanc from Marlborough and the show-stopping Pinot Noirs from Central Otago, New Zealand has become a formidable force in the wine industry.

Prominent New Zealand value wineries include Seresin, Pegasus Bay, Babich and Mt. Difficulty. Some special value wines are Palliser Estate Matinborough Pinot Noir, Milton Vineyard Chardonnay, Saint Clair Marlborough Sauvignon Blanc, Oyster Bay Sauvignon Blanc and Chardonnay, Mud House Marlborough Pinot Noir, Nobilo Marlborough Sauvignon Blanc Icon, Kim Crawford Marlborough Sauvignon Blanc, The Crossings Marlborough Sauvignon Blanc and Wild Rock Central Otago Pinot Noir.

Excellent wineries in the higher price ranges include Felton Road and Kumeu River. A special Sauvignon Blanc in the higher range is called TENZ.

SOUTH AUSTRALIA AND THE SOUTHERN OCEAN LODGE

Designed to blend seamlessly with the ruggedly beautiful landscape, the Southern Ocean Lodge appears to float along its secluded cliff-top setting.

My visit to South Australia in late June/early July 2011 cemented my view that the region is one of the premier trips of the world for sampling food and wine. This includes Kangaroo Island, the home of Southern Ocean Lodge. Before discussing this unique, to-die-for travel destination, I'll restate a position I've held since my first visit to South Australia: There's so much to see and do, lining up a driver and a tour is a must. In my case, on Kangaroo Island, about a 25-minute hop by plane from Adelaide, Tim Harris with www.exceptionalkangarooisland.com showed me more in two days (before and after a lunch he cooked "in the bush" each day) than I could have seen in a week on my own. On the way to each scenic wonder we strayed to tour some impressive wineries.

NATURAL WONDERS

While meandering up a walkway from the ocean at the famous Seal Bay Conservation Park, I met my first bull seal. He appeared to weigh about 400 pounds, so I gave him the right of way. The majestic animal

133

was attempting to become acquainted with one of the many female seals taking cover in the bush to keep the cold wind away (it was wintertime, but not too cold). Other sights, such as Remarkable Rocks, a huge geological structure with a cluster of precariously balanced boulders, are must-visits. However, virtually none of the scenes could rival the coastal vista views beyond the floor-to-ceiling windows of the Southern Ocean Lodge. In some ways, this is my favorite lodging facility in the world.

For openers, every member of the staff knew my name when I arrived on the property—not sure how! Next, from the lobby, as far as the eye can see are miles of gorgeous, unadulterated coastline, synergistically paired with the pristine 250 acres of natural bush in which the lodge is ensconced.

There is one small walkway that winds its way from the lodge toward the middle of the bush and then snakes its way back to the ocean. While exploring one of the paths off the walkway, I encountered a large kangaroo. The native animal stood up less than 6 feet away from me, did a double-take and hopped about 10 feet the other way in one bound, before lazily bounding off. On the way back to the lodge, I spied another kangaroo about 40 yards away and whistled at it. It turned toward me, and we were momentarily transfixed. I estimated that he matched my frame at about 6 feet 2 inches, weighing in around 200 pounds. He never moved as I eased down the trail, almost tripping over a small wallaby!

In the lodge, from 6 p.m. to 7 p.m., there is an open bar. Around 40 of the best wines of South Australia are lined up, along with a plethora of mixed drinks. And the meal that followed, with a glass of my favorite wines with each course, was more than memorable. For those who desire first class all the way (everything is included in the room price), this is it! www.southernoceanlodge.com

ADELAIDE

Adelaide is the epicenter of the great wines in Australia. Barossa Valley, McLaren Vale and Adelaide Hills are Napa, Sonoma and Russian River Valley look-alikes, respectively. My driver/tour guide here was fellow Texan Ralf Hadzic of www.lifeisacabernet.com.au. Ralf is a multi-talented "mate" who has escorted everyone from Tom Jones and Roy Orbison to Willy Nelson throughout Australia—partly owning to his days in the entertainment industry and his business association with Jimmy Buffet.

Focusing on Barossa during this trip, I uncovered the following notable wineries: Hentley Farms, Langmeil (where the oldest commercially producing Shiraz vineyard in the world resides), Rusden and The Willows. The top winery I visited in Adelaide Hills is Shaw+Smith. And although I didn't go there, my favorite winery in McLaren Vale is Molly Dooker. A good starting point to plan a wine trip here is www.southaustralia.com.

McLaren Vale is about 45 minutes south of Adelaide, Adelaide Hills just a few minutes away and Barossa about an hour north. The restaurant scene has changed dramatically since I visited years ago, making it problematic for me to decide during this trip where to dine! Some highlights from my Barossa trip included:

Kabminye Winery and Krondorf Road Café—A must-stop for lunch at this winery/café, located in a small valley with a lovely pastoral view from the all-glass dining area, to experience substantial portions of traditional settlers' foods from the mid-1800s. The owner-chef should know, since her family owned the property in the mid-1800s! And her husband, the winemaker, is the ultimate experimenter—excellent wines from grapes such as Kerner and White Frontenac, along with the ubiquitous fabulous Shiraz. www.Kabminye.com

Rest, dinner and overnight at Jacob's Creek Retreat in the midst of Moorooroo Park—An exclusive property offering opulent accommodations, boutique wines and intimate weddings. In the dining room, looking out upon the gorgeous landscaping and trees gives one a sense of animated beauty—it's almost too beautiful to be real. www.jacobscreekretreat.com.au

Seppeltsfield Vineyard Cottage—The slogan here is Heritage-Luxury-Privacy. Perfect for several days to experience an ecologically and painstakingly-restored 1860s cottage with a wine cellar below and a vineyard right outside the back door. Pricey but unique! www.Seppeltsfieldvineyardcottage.com.au.

The most important visits for oenophiles include the great wineries, which abound in Barossa Valley, McLaren Vale, Adelaide Hills and Clare Valley, all within an hour of Adelaide. While in Barossa, the one wine stop that is mandated is Artisans of Barossa, where seven of the top winemaking families in Australia have teamed up to produce seven outstanding wines. The most famous of these is John Duval, former wine-maker at Grange (www.artisansofbarossa.com). Other stops recommended in Adelaide include the Vintner's Bar and Grill, where local winemakers gather (www.vintners.com.au); Ferment Asian, excellent food; and inter-nationally famous Maggie's Beer Farm Shop (www.maggiebeer.com.au).

Back in Adelaide, plan to have dinner at the Penfold's Magill Estate Winery and Restaurant. This is the home of the "whacking" (as they say in Australia) best wine in the world—OK, maybe just Australia—Grange (formerly Grange Hermitage). Almost any of the top Penfold's wines made—even Grange back to the 1950s—can be ordered with din-ner. My meal began with Krug Grand Cuvée Champagne with paté, and along the way, Grange 2006 and Grange 2002! In the world-class barrel room, just four barrels of one recent vintage (400 bottles in each bar-rel worth $600 a bottle) equated to almost $1 million worth of wine at retail. Unbelievable!

Other recommended stops in Adelaide include the reasonably priced Rendevouz Allegra Hotel and a jaunt through the Central Market nearby, as well as La Trattoria, an immensely popular Italian restaurant. The most important websites to explore are www.barossa.com and www.southaus-tralia.com.

WHAT'S UP WITH SCREW CAPS?

The accepted wine bottle closure for nearly 300 years has been the cork. While some think that the cork has a substantial bearing on the way a great wine ages in the bottle, nobody really knows.

More and more, when a cork is popped, the smell of the wine is not the bright, fresh fruit that emanated from the last bottle of the same wine. The naturally occurring compound 2,4,6-trichloroanisole (TCA), present in only tiny amounts, can cause a wine to smell "corked" or "corky." The malodor is similar to moldy cardboard.

Even though this is not the fault of the restaurant or retailer, such a bottle may be sent back. It is just a problem that is dealt with, in some instances, by sending the offending wine back to the supplier.

One of the deleterious effects of these occurrences is that people purchase a bottle of X (which is corked), never buy another bottle, and tell everyone that X wine tastes like dirty dishrags. A problem that used to be minimal in the 1980s and early 1990s has become much more prevalent.

Recently, those who produce and sell corks have taken steps to prevent TCA, and some tests have shown a drop in the number of tainted corks. Depending on the information source, as few as 2 percent or as many as 4 percent of wines with corks have this taint. My experience is around 1 percent, and I taste several thousand wines a year.

What about using artificial corks and screw caps? Artificial corks have certainly cut down on TCA, but they present other complications. And the biggest problem with screw caps is their image. I can't tell you the number of times I've heard, "I only buy wines with screw caps." Ha! Ha! And nobody knows exactly how the wine will age for 10, 15 or 25 years with a screw cap.

On June 30, 2004, Hogue Cellars in Washington announced the results of a four-year study that examined the effect of five different closures on its Genesis Chardonnay and Merlot. Screw caps proved to hold fruit and maintain freshness more effectively than natural and synthetic corks. And of the two screw caps used, the Stelvin screw cap with Saranex liners was the best.

As a result of this study, Hogue bottled 70 percent of its 2004 production with screw caps. After analyzing the study, a Hogue spokesman said, "Bottling our wines with screw caps will yield tremendous benefits:

elimination of cork taint, as well as consistent and appropriate ageing, lower SO2 levels at bottling, and greater ease in opening bottles."

Over 90 percent of New Zealand wines are now bottled with screw caps. It is being reported in the press that most consumers have finally accepted screw caps. I myself love this bottling method. Screw caps are easy to open, don't cause cork taint and, thus far, have proven to store well.

In 2007, George M. Taber (author of *Judgment of Paris*, a book about the 1976 Paris tasting) wrote in depth on the cork vs. no cork controversy. Taber published *To Cork Or Not To Cork, Tradition, Romance, Science, And the Battle For The Wine Bottle*. It's a fascinating read!

STORING WINE

Let's start with the difference between a wine rack and a wine cellar. Assuming you purchase a rack with any number of slots for wine—in this case, let's say 25 bottles—you will probably fill it with a variety of wines to accompany the different foods you serve. Then, when preparing dinner, you won't have to go out and try to find a wine or wines that complement the food.

A cellar carries the implication that you at least have temperature control, not to mention humidity control. There is no substitute for this if you intend to age wines. If you're going to consume your 25-bottle collection within three to six months and restock occasionally, there is really no need for a cellar (albeit for decorative appeal, prestige or other reasons). The best "other reason" is that you can pull cool red wines from your cellar and serve them at cooler temperatures. Some people like their reds served at 55-60 degrees—others prefer 60-65. My preference is around 65 degrees, which allows the wine to evolve as it slowly warms up (it's usually gone by the time it warms up very much)!

To seriously age wines, storing bottles at around 55 degrees is optimal.

Assuming you have a rack or cellar that holds 25 bottles or more, following is a plan for stocking it, and some complementary foods for your collection:

SPARKLING WINE

2 bottles California Sparkling wine—sushi, pate`, smoked salmon canapés, other hors d'oeuvres

WHITE WINE

2 bottles Chenin Blanc, slightly sweet—alone or with spicy Asian or Southwestern cuisine

1 bottle German Riesling Spatlese—cold chicken salad with grapes, al fresco on a hot day

2 bottles California Sauvignon Blanc—goat cheese, salads, shellfish, hors d'oeuvres

2 bottles California Chardonnay (one from Sonoma or Napa and one from Monterey

County)—fish, chicken

1 bottle Macon-Villages or Macon-Blanc (white Burgundy)—fish, chicken

1 bottle Italian Pinot Grigio—by itself or with hors d'oeuvres

RED WINE

2 bottles California or Oregon Pinot Noir—grilled salmon, fowl

1 bottle Cote de Beaune-Villages or Cote de Nuits-Villages (red Burgundy)—fowl or lake trout, using this wine in your sauce

2 bottles California Zinfandel (one from Dry Creek Valley)—burgers, pizza, pork loin with fruit sauce

1 bottle California Merlot—duck or all-purpose red

2 bottles California Cabernet Sauvignon (one Napa and one Sonoma)—roast beef sandwiches, steak, lamb, brie (after the entrée)

1 bottle red Bordeaux—tenderloin medallions with Bordelaise sauce, rack of lamb (no mint jelly)

2 bottles Australian Shiraz (one from McLaren Vale and one from Barossa Valley)—grilled meat, prime rib

1 bottle Chianti Classico—Italian food with tomato sauce and olive oil

1 bottle Barbera d'Asti or Barbera d'Alba—braised beef or veal Marsala

1 bottle Argentinean Malbec—grilled meats

This collection could be assembled, with great values, for anywhere from $250 and up. Now, with almost any food you might serve, you have a complementary wine at your fingertips.

Assuming you go for a refrigeration unit with humidity controls, the traditional wines to cellar are the better Bordeaux wines and vintage Ports, some of which can improve every year for 10, 20 or even 30 years and beyond. This holds true to some extent for the top Burgundies, Rhones, California Cabernets, Super Tuscans, Barolos, some Spanish reds and Australian Shirazes.

As the tannins in the great reds from an excellent vintage combine with coloring and other materials over the years, and fall to the bottom as sediment, the resulting wine can be extremely smooth, complex and even ethereal. A perfect example of the benefits of cellaring for me was the 1964 Chateau Latour. As one of my favorite, barely affordable wines in the mid-1970s, it was still fairly rich, but had smoothed out as the tannins had resolved. I thought it had a good future, even though it probably wouldn't get any better. In 1977, I tasted a 1964 Chateau Latour at Chateau Latour, brought up from the cellars where it had been resting since bottling. Unlike the same wine in the United States, which nobody could tell where the bottles had been stored, much less how many hours they may have sat on a hot dock, non-refrigerated truck, etc., the properly stored wine was still very dark in color, young, closed up and slightly unyielding. In fact, it would have continued to improve for another 10 years or so. Proper cellaring produced a truly different and substantially more valuable wine. (Today the better wines are shipped under refrigeration.) Other reasons to cellar special, big reds include:

1. a highly sought-after wine that soars in value. I purchased some 1989 Chateau Haut-Brion at release, around 1992, for less than $100 a bottle, and within five years it was worth $350 a bottle. When you serve a wine like that, nobody asks what you paid for it—you just get credit for serving an amazingly expensive and, in this case, fabulous wine.

2. wine that is on any kind of allocation, and the only way you will have some in four to five years is if you had purchased it at release and cellared it.

3. cellaring a properly purchased wine that cost "x" dollars, and five years later it is worth "3x" dollars. You can sell it at auction; or, if the wine doesn't appeal to you, trade it to a fellow collector for something you do like. You could also donate it to a "use-related" charity and possibly write off the market value rather than just your cost (discuss with your CPA).

BOTTLE SIZE—IS BIGGER ALWAYS BETTER?

In a *Wine Spectator* column some years ago, Jancis Robinson, M.W., compared regular-size bottles of a wine to the same wine in imperials (eight-bottle size). The conclusion? In most instances, the wines from individual bottles were better.

The first lavish big-bottle event I attended was some 30 years ago in San Francisco. At one unforgettable dinner, we enjoyed Chateau Léoville-Barton 1929 (imperial), Chateau Ducru-Beaucaillou 1929 (imperial), Chateau La Lagune 1929 (jeroboam) and Chateau Ducru-Beaucaillou 1928 (jeroboam).

In the mid-1970s to early 1980s, wine auctions were few and far between, and almost unknown except to devoted oenophiles. We regularly purchased and drank Bordeaux wines from 1945, 1947, 1949, 1959 and 1961. Sometimes wines from the great vintages of the 1920s would surface on the block. On the rare occasion, wines from the great twin years of 1899 and 1900, as well as some pre-phylloxera wines, would emerge—and at ridiculously low prices.

At the San Francisco dinner, I remember thinking that although the large-format bottles created great enthusiasm and an almost surreal ambiance, the wines did not seem to taste significantly better or worse than the same or similar wines from 1928 and 1929 from a bottle.

In 1986, the cellar-master from Chateau Lafite-Rothschild visited several major cities in the United States, re-corking any Lafites 25 years or older and re-filling them with bottles of 1961 brought for the occasion. At the Houston location—owned by one of Houston's most respected entrepreneurs/oenophiles, Bill Sharman—I took a bottle, a magnum and a double magnum of 1961. The cellar-master and I tasted each as it was opened. There is no question that the wine in the magnum was superior to the wine in the bottle or double magnum!

I had been presented with considerable evidence that the magnum is the optimal container for aging red Bordeaux wines. This occasion, and many more since, has convinced me that it is the truth.

For those who cellar Bordeaux wines to serve years later at dinner parties for six or more, magnums are highly recommended for optimal aging and heightened visual enjoyment. Although the wines may taste no different than those from a regular-size bottle, for large dinner parties, the "WOW" factor is exponentially increased with the appearance of a huge bottle.

Chapter 11
CHILE AND ARGENTINA
EXPORT WORLD-CLASS WINES

Winemaking was introduced to both Chile and Argentina in the 1500s by Spanish monks. It wasn't until the late 1800s that both countries began thinking about improving wine quality. Chile got a head start by seeking the advice of French winemakers—certainly the best in the world at that time. Argentina, on the other hand, had little indigenous population by comparison, but was flooded with immigrants from Europe bringing their vines to carry on their native traditions. The strong European mindset of wine with each meal resulted in mass production of low-quality wine to satisfy the local market, with Bonarda being the primary varietal.

Due to a surge in popularity of spirits and cocktails in the 1940s, wine consumption in Argentina plummeted until the 1970s, at which time Argentinian winemakers set a path for higher quality and expanded exports—even bottling by varietals. Blessed by an unrivaled amount of sun days within a growing season, varietals such as the late-ripening Malbec flourished—even more so than in its native Europe. Argentina now accounts for 70 percent of the world's Malbec production!

The best overall wine values now hail from Chile. Top Malbecs and Malbec values are from Argentina. The cost of prime vineyard land and wine production in each country is a fraction for such ventures in the U.S.

Not long ago, the Maipo Valley near Santiago was the only important name to know in Chile. Of the many regions there, the most notable today are cool-climate areas such as Leyda, Bio-Bio, Limari, Elqui and Casablanca, and the renowned Rapel Valley (Cachapoal and Colchagua), Maule Valley and Aconcagua Valley.

It's hard to keep pace with Chile's burgeoning wine scene, as Europeans and Americans have flooded the wine scene in these two countries to get a piece of the action. Paul Hobbs, America's "flying winemaker," has his Viña Cobos in Chile, and famous Europeans such as Paul Pontallier from Chateau Margaux and the Lurton brothers have been in both countries for some time. European "flying winemaker" Michel Rolland produces his excellent Val de Flores in Argentina. The list goes on and on, including the Mondavis from Napa Valley and the Rothschilds from Lafite in Bordeaux. The two best-known joint ventures are Almaviva in Chile (Rothschilds from Mouton and Concha y Toro from Chile) and Cheval des Andes (Chateau Cheval Blanc and Terrazas de los Andes from Argentina). Each of these two is an outstanding wine at about one-fourth the cost of its Bordeaux counterpart. Probably the best value of the famous joint ventures is Caro, from Les Domaines de Barons de Rothschild (Lafite) and Catena Zapata in Mendoza.

In October 2010, I toured the wine country in Chile and Argentina. In Chile, I was impressed with the following wineries, and herein I mention specific world-class wines that are also good values:

Cousiño Macul—Finis Terra

Leyda—Sauvignon Blanc, Classic Chardonnay and Classic Pinot Noir

Chile and Argentina wine knowledge separators

Since phylloxera has never plagued the country, there has been no need to graft the vines onto immune rootstocks. Chile, and to a great extent Argentina, still have pre-phylloxera wines! Another largely unknown fact: There are actually six red grapes of Bordeaux. In addition to the familiar five—Cabernet Sauvignon, Merlot, Cabernet Franc, Petit Verdot and Malbec—there is Carmenére. This grape is gaining prestige in Chile by leaps and bounds, and it is the all-but-forgotten grape of Bordeaux! It may be a stretch, but Carmenére could one day be to Chile what Malbec is to Argentina.

TerraNoble—Pinot Noir and Carmenére
Valdivieso—All sparkling wines, Sauvignon Blanc, Chardonnay and Cabernet Sauvignon Reserve
Ventisquero—Chardonnay and Root 1 Carmenére
Veramonte—Sauvignon Blanc, Pinot Noir and Primus

Other excellent wines to search out:
Maipo—Perez Cruz, Vina William Fevre, De Martino
Cachapoal—Morande
Colchagua— Los Vascos (unrivaled $10 Cabernet Sauvignon), Chateau Los Boldos
Maule—Apaltagua, Botalcura
Aconcagua—Errazuriz

Bio Bio—Agustinos, Canata
Limari—Tabali
Casablanca— Los Vascos (Chardonnay), Quintay

Argentina is an immense country and the fifth-largest wine producer in the world. While Chile quickly started exporting wines, Argentina produced mostly table wine and kept it all for itself. In the past 15 years, this has changed.

Argentina has embraced the idea of making great wines (and wine values) and exporting them. While there is still a plethora of plonk retained in Argentina for Argentinians—actually, that is even improving—Malbec from Argentina is becoming coveted like Shiraz from Australia!

During my 2010 visit to the Argentinian wine country, the coruscating jewel was the Catena Zapata Winery. Nicolas Catena taught economics in San Francisco in the early 1980s. While there, he and Robert Mondavi became close friends, and Mondavi inspired him to create something special at his winery in Argentina. Utilizing Mondavi's recommendations, and later experimenting with higher altitudes, Catena has found the optimal growing seasons to perfectly ripen his grapes. This is evident in his Chardonnay and Malbec, two of the finest wines in the world for around $20. And his Catena Zapata Alta, a Cabernet blend, has won blind tastings against all the First Growth Bordeaux wines. In fact, the 2006 Catena Zapata Alta was the wine Georg Riedel and I had with lunch shortly after I returned from Mendoza. It was fabulous!

The visit to the magnificent Catena Zapata Winery, including the views of the never-ending vineyards, plains, trees and magnificent Andes Mountains, is still vibrant in my memory. Following are impressive wineries I visited, along with my favorite wine(s) at each:

Alta Vista—Torrontes and Premium Cabernet Sauvignon
Renacer—Punto Final Malbec
Rutini—Malbec
Trumpeter—Chardonnay
Zuccardi—Serie A Bonarda and Serie A Malbec
Alma Negra—Sparkling Malbec

Some of my other favorite wineries (and I recommend all the wines) include: Luca (the winery of Laura Catena, daughter of Nicolas); Tikal (the winery of Ernesto Catena, son of Nicolas); Achaval Ferrer; Susana Balbo, Crios de Susana Balbo; Luigi Bosca; Viña Cobos; Finca Decero; Doña Paula; Niete Sentiner; Finca Sophinia; Pascal Toso; Terrazas de los Andes; and Trapiche.

For an in-depth study of Argentinian wines, read Laura Catena's brilliant book *Vino Argentino*. None other than Baron Eric de Rothschild said, "Nobody knows more about the Argentinian wine business than Laura Catena (except maybe her father Nicolas). Laura's new book will certainly be the bible on this subject."

THE MANY PLEASURES OF WINE

For a wine lover, some of life's most pleasurable memories can be attached to a particular vintage, tasting or meal. I was 25 when I experienced my first eye-opening wine/food pairing—a Rioja with a paella at the Madrid Hilton. Prior to that, it was rum and coke by itself or beer met with snacks, burgers or Mexican food.

At age 31, I indulged in a Chinese luncheon in Macao, then a Portuguese City on the Chinese mainland, an hour hydrofoil ride from Hong Kong. The $1.99 sweet Mateus Rosé was the perfect foil for the spicy meal.

From there it just got better, culminating in the "Dinner of the Century" (see final article under Narratives of Momentous Wine Tastings/Dinners).

After "the" dinner, it's hard to say, "The best is yet to come," but who knows?

Throughout the ages, writers have penned the pleasures of indulging in the fruit of the vine. James Howell wrote the following in *Logic*. "…That good wine makes good blood, good blood causeth good humors, good humors cause good thoughts, good thoughts bring forth good works, good works carry a man to heaven, ergo good wine carrieth a man to heaven."

Approximately 2,000 years earlier, Aristophanes wrote in *The Knights*, "Demosthenes: Without question. Go, ninny, blow yourself out with water; do you dare to accuse wine of clouding the reason? Quote me more marvelous effects than those of wine. Look! When a man drinks, he is rich, everything he touches succeeds, he gains (wins) lawsuits, is happy and helps his friends. Come, bring hither quick a flagon of wine, that I may soak my brain and get an ingenious idea."

An evening spent tasting wines with hors d'oeuvres or pairing wines with different dishes in a multi-course dinner with friends can be more entertaining than a movie, sports event or an evening at the symphony. As I've mentioned before, one uses all of the senses while enjoying the experience. Perhaps that's one reason it's so pleasurable.

Finally and pertinently, a quote from Maurice Healy in *Claret* captures the essence of indulging in wine. "…Never bring up your better bottles if you are entertaining a man who cannot talk. Keep your treasures for a night when those few nearest to your heart can gather round your table, free from care, with latchkeys in their pockets and no last train to catch."

HOW TO THROW A CASUAL (AND ECONOMICAL) WINE AND FOOD PARTY

First, let's discuss the senses: sight, hearing, touch, smell and taste. If you can use more of your senses in an enjoyable endeavor, it is reasonable to conclude that, all things being equal, the enjoyment can be multiplied. Just think of all the events that merely involve sight and hearing. But envision a small, simple and inexpensive wine and food party where you and your guests can utilize all of the God-given senses for an enjoyable evening.

It doesn't have to be a gourmet dinner with a $100 wine accompanying each course. The most simple and inexpensive gathering is a wine and cheese party. For six people, an entirely adequate function can be put together for about $90. Try these pairings (served with crackers or a baguette):

- Friexenet Cordon Negro Cava (sparkling wine—Spain) or St. Supery Sauvignon Blanc with goat cheese;
- Columbia Crest Chardonnay Grand Estates (Washington State) with Danish Havarti (no dill or other additives);
- Concha Y Toro Casillero del Diablo Cabernet Sauvignon (Chile) or Little Penguin Shiraz (Australia) with brie on toasted French bread;
- Moscato d'Asti (Italy) with Gourmandise cheese with cherries and walnuts or with sugar cookies or a dessert such as cake or fruit tart.

If this is a pre-dinner party, one bottle for each "course" should suffice. Total cost: about $50 for the wines and $40 for the cheeses. If your wine shop doesn't carry some of these wines, ask for a substitute in the same price range.

A simple maneuver can turn this gathering into a casual dinner—add roast beef finger sandwiches after the brie course and step up to an even bigger, better (and more expensive) Cabernet such as SIMI Alexander Valley at $25 a bottle or Tudal Clift Vineyard Napa Valley at $45 a bottle.

In lieu of a wine and cheese tasting, host a casual wine and food dinner. Of course you can use the same wines, but to fancy it up to the $200 level, try this:

- J or Iron Horse sparkling wine with pate and/or smoked salmon canapés
- Duckhorn Sauvignon Blanc with goat cheese crostinis or canapés
- Patz & Hall Pinot Noir with turkey-and-Swiss finger sandwiches
- Robert Mondavi Napa Cabernet or Casa Lapostolle Merlot Cuvée Alexandre (Chile) with roast beef-and-cheddar finger sandwiches with light horseradish spread. At this point, if you're serving the above-mentioned Merlot, bring up the "little problem" with Miles in *Sideways* stating vehemently that if anyone ordered Merlot, he was leaving. The fact is, his "sacred" 1961 Chateau Cheval Blanc (which he surreptitiously enjoyed by himself) is about 2/3 Cabernet Franc and 1/3—you guessed it—Merlot!
- Blandy's 10-year-old Boal or Malmsey Madeira, or Taylor 20-year-old Tawny Porto with crème brulee or crème caramel.

WHAT IS TERROIR?

Terroir, a French word, has been described as the combination of all the natural elements prevailing in a vineyard. Components of terroir include type and quality of soil, elevation, slope, direction the vineyard faces, amount of annual sunshine, winter freeze (or not), variance in daytime and nighttime temperature, annual rainfall, drainage, presence of fog, etc. Sometimes the contributions of a vineyard manager and winemaker are added to the mix, including practices regarding thinning, space between vines, natural vs. cultured yeasts, little oak vs. lots of oak, and generally being a minimalist in the winery vs. attempting to sculpt the juice into some particular outcome other than expressing the terroir. In other words, it's safe to say that no two vineyards are exactly alike.

A true devotee of terroir generally believes that the goal should be to do everything possible to bring out the unique aspects of a vineyard. In fact, there are certain wines of the world that some say cannot be duplicated nor even matched in quality by the same grape. I agree with the duplication part, but it's easy to belie the notion that the quality can't be matched.

All one has to do is pour through wine magazines and find out who wins, for example, international Rhone-style tastings—hint, it's sometimes not a Rhone wine—or a Bordeaux-style tasting—hint, sometimes it's not a Bordeaux.

BANKING ON THE TERROIR

An interesting component I've added to the subject is that one's banker may actually be a part of a vineyard's terroir. If improvements must be made, such as drainage, pest control or hand sorting, and the lender won't approve a loan, then the bank has played a direct role in affecting the terroir.

There is no question that sustainable farming, organic farming, certified organic farming and the mystical biodynamic farming will add to rather than subtract from a vineyard's terroir. After all, just about any foreign substance, including pesticides and inorganic fertilizers, is going to detract from the naturalness that would otherwise prevail.

On the other hand, installing owl houses and hawk stands for controlling moles and voles is not introducing a foreign substance—it's enhancing a native substance. Likewise, recycling crushed grape peels, seeds, leaves and stems back into the vineyard would not be considered adding a foreign substance.

There are those who live and die by terroir, and those who understand the ramifications of the word but don't think it's that important. Obviously, those with century-old vineyards in the Old World are more inclined to stressing the importance of terroir than a New World vintner who has just planted 10 varietals in a new vineyard location.

In blind tastings, it sometimes is not too difficult to guess a grape or even whether it's Old World or New World. But it's a horse of a different color to guess the soil type from which the grape derived.

I get a kick out of a story about a $100 California wine named Fourteen. One expert is said to have taken a sip and exclaimed the virtues of the terroir of the obviously fabulous, perfectly situated vineyard from which it came. Interesting. Fourteen is a Cabernet blend from 14 different vineyards representing 14 different appellations in the Napa Valley!

In closing, a connoisseur supposedly once guessed the mortgage on a particular vineyard after taking a sip of the current release. The owner must have been in financial trouble and over-cropped the vines, and by the amount the connoisseur perceived the over-cropping, he guessed the amount the vintner borrowed against the vineyard to continue in business!

Chapter 12
DECIPHERING THE
WINES OF GERMANY

Imagine yourself wine shopping and picking up a bottle with a label that reads, "Scharzhofberger Riesling Trockenbeerenauslese Erzeugerabfullung Egon Muller xw Scharzhof Qualitatswein Mit Pradikat Mosel-Saar-Ruwer." You may be inclined to put it back and continue down the aisle toward the California section. But you might pause if you know that Germany has been on an historic run of excellent vintages since 2001! Skipping right over that label, let's investigate some facts about German wines that might encourage and inspire you to stop and make a selection for your next wine purchase:

- There are 13 wine regions in Germany, most of which are located in the western portion of the country. The premier wine regions are the Mosel, situated along the Moselle River (Mosel in German), and Rheingau, Rheinehessen and Pfalz. The latter three are along the Rhine River (Rhein in German).
- The Mosel wines are fresh and crisp with an amazing fruit/acid balance. They are found in green bottles.
- The Rhein wines have more color, body and depth. They are distributed in brown bottles.
- *er* stands for *from*; therefore, a wine called Scharzhofberger comes from the town of Scharzhofberg. Same with Bernkasteler (Bernkastel), Piesporter (Piesport) and Niersteiner (Nierstein).

- The best German wines are designated Qualitatswein mit Pradikat (QmP), which means quality wine with a special attribute. The attribute is listed on the label as follows (in ascending order of sweetness):
  1. Kabinett—Normal harvest;
  2. Spatlese—Late harvest;
  3. Auslese—Individually selected bunches of overripe grapes;
  4. Beerenauslese—Individually selected, extremely overripe grapes, sometimes affected by the beneficial mold botrytis cinerea;
  5. Trockenbeerenauslese—Individually selected, botritized (not botricized) grapes;
  6. Eiswein—Individually selected, frozen grapes of at least Beerenauslese quality (since 1983).

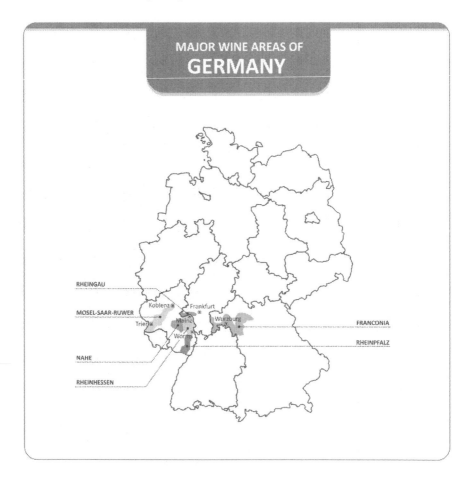

The residual sugar levels of these wines can run from around 2 percent for a Kabinett to 20 percent or more for a Trockenbeerenauslese or Eiswein. Because so many German wines are perceived as too sweet for most foods, some new wines were introduced as drier alternatives. Although wonderful, they have failed to catch on with the public and instead caused more confusion. "Trocken" means dry and "halb-trocken" means half-dry. Unfortunately there was Kabinett trocken and halbtrocken, Spatlese trocken and halbtrocken and Auslese trocken and halbtrocken. Very few even tried to sort that out.

In 2000, to identify and elucidate what a reasonably dry, German white wine might be for the consumer, the term Classic was established. The Classic logo appears next to the grape variety on the label, and fortunately no sesquipedalian vineyard name follows. A classic wine contains no more than 15 grams per liter of sugar and has substantial alcohol and substance. More important, it is food-friendly.

Along with the classic designation are the new Selection wines. These are wines of even less sugar and of much higher quality (Auslese at harvest), with a superior fruit/acid balance.

To even further muddy the waters, the description Grosses Gewächs is used in most regions to designate a top dry wine. And a Goldkapsel or Gold Capsule denotes a substantially sweeter or more delicious version of a normal Prädikatswein.

Following are some top producers to seek out: Dr. H. Thanisch; J.J. Prum; Dr. Loosen; Egon Müller; Dr. Pauly-Bergweiler; Müller-Catoir, Hermann Dönnhoff and Schäfer-Frölich (the latter two being producers in the Nahe region).

Finally, I must mention Germany's neighbor Austria. A longtime producer of top-quality Rieslings, Austria, like Spain with its Albariño, shocked the world some years ago with another great white wine, Gruner Veltliner. It has been touted as the world's best wine with vegetables! My favorite producers of both varietals are F.X. Pichler, Prager, Nigl, Franz Hirtzberger and Brundlmayer.

OTHER SPARKLING WINES

Spain is the largest producer of sparkling wines, and Freixenet (fresh uh net) is the largest producer in the world. Priced very reasonably at $12, Freixenet's Cordon Negro has always been a favorite. Freixenet owns Segura Viudas, and the Segura Viudas Brut Heredad Reserva, at around $20 a bottle, is among the best made in Spain. This particular cava has a heavy, pewter-like base and a seal on the label. Most importantly, it's excellent.

The big difference between Spanish Cava and Champagne are the grapes: Xarello, Macabeo and Parellada, instead of Pinot Meunier, Pinot Noir and Chardonnay. Almost all of Spain's cavas come from the Penedés region and are made by the Champagne method.

Italy and Germany, on the other hand, produce sparkling wines that are mostly made by the less-expensive Charmat method—the secondary fermentation takes place in large, sealed tanks, not in the bottle. In Italy, the best-known sparkler is Asti Spumonte, which is actually a nice, pleasant dessert wine. Even better to me are the Moscatos, which are very slightly sparkling dessert wines. Prosecco, a dry wine, is also well-known, and a good one like Bisol can be an excellent bargain.

Germany's sparkling wine is usually dry and is called sekt. It has a slightly different taste because of the German grapes. There is also some sparkling wine made in Alsace (Cremant) and in the Loire Valley (sparkling Vouvray).

In the United States, the traditional sparkling wines were those of Gallo (primarily André) and those from New York, derived from other than vinifera grapes. These sparkling wines were made by the Charmat method, and considered the workhorse sparklers for years. Korbel was one of the first to use the method champenoise, which didn't necessarily involve the Champagne grapes—that innovation is credited to my late friend Jack Davies and his wife, Jamie, of Schramsberg in the Napa Valley.

Most California wineries have attempted to produce wines that rival Champagne using Chardonnay and Pinot Noir almost exclusively; however, that changed when Domaine Chandon (from Moet & Chandon in Champagne) started up in the Napa Valley in 1973, adding Pinot Meunier.

Two of the very best California sparklers are made by Iron Horse and J Wine Company. Iron Horse boasts one of the most beautiful vineyards in California. The winery has just undergone a multi-million dollar replanting program. Its Pinot Noirs and Chardonnays are not just for producing sparklers—the still wines are also top notch. The Wedding Cuvée and Russian River Cuvée are among the best known of all California sparkling wines. The J Wine Company is owned by Tom Jordan's daughter, Judy. Every wine is excellent. Visiting the "Bubble Room" is a well-spent wine-tasting experience with the winemaker and/or chef, tasting through sparkling wine, Pinot Gris, Chardonnay and Pinot Noir (call ahead to make reservations). My other favorite sparklers are those made at Mumm Napa, Roederer Estate and Gloria Ferrer.

HOW TO LEARN MORE ABOUT WINE

Along with reading up on the subject, the best approach to learning about wines is the empirical method: Purchase bottles of wine made from the same grape, but from different countries. My first of six examples is California Sauvignon Blanc vs. Sancerre or Pouilly-Fume from the Loire Valley. You could also throw in a New Zealand Sauvignon Blanc.

Purchase two bottles of each wine, taste the first group and write down anything you smell or taste. You may find that the California wine has the most fruit and is the most luscious by itself; the French wine exhibits less fruit but more acidity and is possibly more food-friendly; and the New Zealand wine has more pronounced flavors of either grapefruit, wild grass, hay or even gooseberries.

A week later, taste all of them again, but this time blind. Possibly for the first time, you will be able to tell which is which, and more importantly, you'll know why. And yes, you can cheat and bring your notes from the first tasting!

Switching gears, you can sample different grape varieties. Try a Pinot Noir vs. a comparably priced Zinfandel and Cabernet Sauvignon. Go through the same two-week exercise, taking notes the first time and subsequently guessing blind.

You may find that the Pinot Noir is lighter and has a bouquet of cherries, mushrooms, earth, leather and truffles. The Zinfandel may be all berries and spice and the Cabernet might exude black currants, cassis, mint, chocolate and a pronounced vanilla in the finish. Or not. Whatever you come up with, write it down.

The next week, when facing these three wines blind, with notes in hand—you may have written that the Cabernet smelled like fresh creosote stains on a sweaty saddle blanket—you will at least have your personal annotations. When you try these wines, you will also learn a thing or two.

Following is a sample eight-week program—the first week taking notes while tasting, and the second week tasting blind.

WEEKS
  1 and 2—Pinot Noir vs. Zinfandel vs. Cabernet Sauvignon
  3 and 4—Riesling vs. Sauvignon Blanc vs. Chardonnay

5 and 6—Sangiovese (Italy) vs. Tempranillo (Spain) vs. Grenache (Australia or France)

7 and 8—Shiraz (Australia) vs. Merlot vs. Malbec (Argentina)

And if you really want to get esoteric, try Albarino (Spain) vs. Gruner Veltliner (Austria) vs. Garganega (Italy)! Meanwhile, have fun. It's not exactly work!

If you're also searching for a comprehensive education on wine, or a quick refresher course, I recommend Kevin Zraly's *Windows on the World Complete Wine Course*—over 3 million copies sold!

THAT'S WHAT MAKES HORSE RACES

I once read a wine article in which the writer quoted a wine retailer as saying that instead of reading wine guides or reviews, you should just trust your own palate. That's an interesting idea, except it could take 10 wine purchases before "your own palate" finds a great value.

There's no question that different writers appeal to different consumers. I've had recommendations from wine shop salespersons and wine writers that were perfect, and just the opposite. When you do find someone in the know with whom you agree most of the time, better stick with him/her!

The writer of the above-mentioned article outlined the exact temperature and humidity percentage that is ideal for storing wine. I have no problem with quoting a range of temperatures or humidity levels, but the ideal conditions also depend on what's in your cellar. In fact, there is no perfect temperature or humidity percentage, nor is there an optimal temperature to drink a red or white wine.

Another writer recently decried the fact that since 2000, Chianti producers have been allowed to add up to 20 percent Cabernet Sauvignon or other authorized grapes. He proclaimed that Chianti doesn't taste like Chianti anymore, "austerity" being the key attribute he enjoys in the wine. Traditional Chianti lovers may find some truth in this assertion, but austerity is one of the key traits most Americans wish to avoid in a wine.

The 2000 law probably results in more Chiantis being enjoyed by Americans. Good for us, and there are plenty of traditionalists in Chianti who are not blending in 20 percent, or even 1 percent, Cabernet Sauvignon.

In France, there is the argument against California-style wines—opulence over elegance—to achieve higher scores from the major wine critics, thus driving up sales in the U.S. It's certainly happening, but there are plenty of winemakers who do not participate in this endeavor, and their wines can be enjoyed by the traditionalists.

It's funny that Robert Parker gave the 1990 Chateau Montrose—an opulent, rich, tender- tannin, lower-acid Bordeaux—a score of 100, whereas some European writers have gone out of their way to denigrate the wine. It's ironic that some of the greatest vintages in Bordeaux, such as 1982, 1990 and 2000, came from warmer weather and more sunshine—sounding like California?—producing richer, more opulent offerings as opposed to the more tannic, austere vintages.

There is a company named Enologix that specializes in helping a winery increase its ratings. Those who think wine is only about bringing out the terroir of each specific vineyard, microclimate, etc., hurl nothing but pejoratives at the idea of hiring Enologix to obtain a better score from Robert Parker—even if it does make the wine "better." In truth, it would be sad if all the wineries in the world started making rich, opulent, 15 percent alcohol, low-acid, soft-tannin wines.

But I'm not the least bit concerned. There are tides—ebbs and flows—in life and in winemaking. I remember the 1974 Cabernet Sauvignon Reserve from Robert Mondavi. It was a blockbuster, made with little fining or filtration, and didn't start showing its best until around 1980. In the early 1980s, Mondavi told me he was "sculpting" his wines—making them lighter and more elegant because that's what people wanted. By 1984, he had come full circle; his 1984 and 1985 vintages were analogous to the 1974 style.

One time I was at Mayacamas with owner Bob Travers, and although I'm a big fan of his red wines, I mentioned that I didn't really care for the white wine we were drinking and explained why. He cared not in the slightest. He has and always will make his wines one way—the way he thinks they should be made. The fact that his Cabernets sometimes don't "turn the corner," as he puts it, for 15 years is irrelevant. There are plenty of oenophiles out there who cellar wines for years. I mean, what's a cellar for anyway?

Finally, there are winemakers who produce their wines to bring forth the terroir, others who produce wines for great Parker scores or to appeal to the public, and still others who make wine the way they want. I don't think we're in serious danger of all wines tasting the same anytime soon!

Chapter 13
SOUTH AFRICAN WINES

It's amazing to look at a world map and find the South African wine regions at almost the same latitudes as those of Mendoza Argentina to the west and Australia to the east. South Africa's wine regions are actually similar to Oregon's Willamette Valley and France's Burgundy in the northern hemisphere.

The original rootstocks for wine were brought to South Africa by Willem Van Stel, governor of the Cape. The Dutch East Indies Company sent him there to be governor because this was a refilling station for ships sailing from Europe to the Far East. He requested rootstocks mainly so he could make vinegar to pickle the meats for the long ship journeys, but he also wanted to make some wine.

The first rootstocks were planted at Groot Constantia. Some original wine buildings still stand from the 1700s. Subsequent to this, many French Huguenots, who were being persecuted in France, fled to England. Not knowing what to do with this sizeable group, England offered them land in South Africa. The people greatly expanded and modernized the fledgling wine industry from their knowledge of wine and wine-growing techniques in France. An interesting fact: after his exile, Napoleon could no longer get wine from France, and the wines from Groot Constantia became his mainstays.

After working to form export markets for years, South Africa lost most of it around 1928 due to the world depression. From that time until the late 1960s, the non-white population was prohibited from drinking alcoholic beverages. Ralph Leibman opened the first self-serve retail liquor store for non-whites in 1967 in the town of Pretoria.

For some 60 years, ending in 1992, a cooperative called KWV (still in existence) regulated wine by controlling allowed varietals, growing methods and production. A certain percentage of each winery's grapes had to be sold to the KWV each year. Since this co-op could not begin to make and sell wine from all these grapes, it made brandy from the ubiquitous Chenin Blanc and Ugni Blanc grapes. Even though the forced sales to it are now over, KWV maintains a huge brandy operation.

When Nelson Mandela was released from prison in 1984, there was a change of government, which decreed that the KWV had to sell its assets. Since the grape farmers owned the co-ops, they issued shares of stock in KWV on the Johannesburg Stock Exchange at one rand per share. As an interesting aside, sheebens were the illicit bars in the townships where non-whites socialized and drank wine, beer, etc. One of the government decrees was that the sheebens had to buy shares in the KWV. Since most of them did not have the money, the grape farmers loaned them the funds to buy shares. According to some, in a couple years when the value of the shares reached about one and a half rand, the sheebens mostly sold, paid back their loans (actually, they were probably collateralized) and made a nice short-term profit.

Going back to around 1955, Sydney Back was the first individual to open an estate winery with first-class dry wines. Prior to this, the main wines of South Africa were sweet muscatel, hanepoort (sweet Muscat of Alexandria) and another sweet wine called jeripigo. While Americans were drinking rum and coke in the U.S. in the 1950s, most everyone in South Africa who consumed alcoholic beverages drank brandy and coke or sweet white wines. As an aside, both then and now, the primary snacks to serve with wine in South Africa are biltong (dried beef) and dried sausage.

During Apartheid (government-enforced racial segregation), the KWV does get credit for opening up the modern export markets for brandy and sweet wines in England, Norway, Sweden, Finland and Canada. As the modern, upscale wineries started production, they were able to piggy-back to some extent on this opening. After Apartheid, the estate wines made tremendous strides as the world's markets opened to them. With new sales and inflows of cash, the wineries acquired new technology and expanded their production.

The South African wine industry also is able to take advantage of its Nietvoorbij Research Station, which provides almost everything to the wineries from professional advice to rootstocks to production methods. This station governs, along with the winery and vineyard owners, quality control for exports. Now all exported South African wines have a seal of authenticity—a neck sticker stating "Certified—Wine Spirit Board."

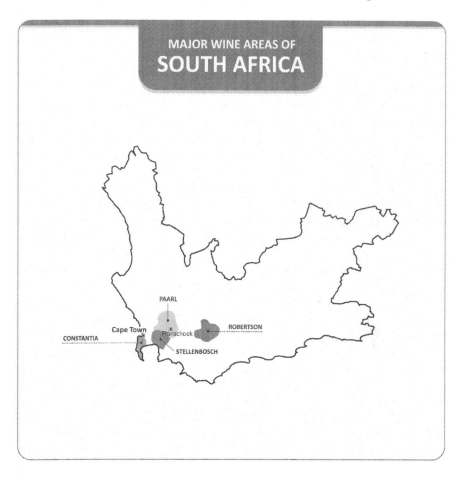

MAJOR WINE AREAS OF
SOUTH AFRICA

PAARL

Cape Town

CONSTANTIA

Franschoek

ROBERTSON

STELLENBOSCH

Following are the primary wine regions. Each region is listed with one winery with two excellent wines (the first wine is under $20; the second, over $20):

Paarl—Fairview Merlot and Cabernet Sauvignon
Constantia—Groot Constantia Pinotage and Gouverneurs Reserve Shiraz

Frannschoek—Rubert & Rothschild Classique Cabernet/Merlot and Baron Edmond Cabernet/Merlot

Robertson—DeWetshof Bon Vallon Chardonnay and Bateleur Chardonnay

Stellenbosch—Saxenburg Sauvignon Blanc and Shiraz Select.

OTHER EXCELLENT SOUTH AFRICAN WINES

Mulderbosche Chardonnay
Hamilton Russell Pinot Noir
Graham Back Sauvignon Blanc
Fairview Goats du Roam
Warwick Cabernet Sauvignon

USING COMMONSENSE IN WINE SENTIMENTS

I read once with great interest an article that explored the topic of whether wine and cheese really go together. Several famous winemakers and/or chateau owners (in France no less) were "for" and others "against." Some who were against avowed adamantly that wine and cheese never should be served as a pairing. So who was wrong? Everyone!

The reason I can state this with such certainty is simple: There is no universal answer to the question. Let's face it: Some like the match-up and some don't. The subject is similar to other wine deliberations:

- Is 52 degrees the perfect cellar temperature?
- Is 65 degrees the perfect temperature to serve red wine?
- Is 50 degrees the perfect temperature to serve a great white Burgundy?
- Does Pinot Noir go with lamb?
- Is sweet white Zinfandel only for people who haven't really learned what great wine is all about?
- If you're not into the "elegant, classic" wines of Bordeaux and Burgundy, but prefer the high-alcohol, big, bold, fruit-forward wines of California and Australia, are you lacking in class and taste, and in immediate need of a course in European culture?
- If you like any sweet wines other than dessert wines, such as German Kabinetts and Spatlesen, off-dry American Rieslings, some Texas Chenin Blancs, etc., are you a wine novice?
- If one of your favorite wine/food matches is Beaujolais-Villages with ham and cheese sandwiches, are you a wine slob?
- If you mention that the reason you know the second "i" in Lafite-Rothschild is a long i (instead of being pronounced a long e, as would be commonly thought in French), is because Baron Eric de Rothschild pronounced it that way himself at a luncheon with you once, are you a wine snob?
- If you like Chateau Margaux with hamburgers as Malcolm Forbes did, are you a wealthy wine weirdo?
- If you don't read voluminous wine periodicals every month, but instead just want to know what wines to buy every so often so

as not to spend money on bad wines, is there something wrong with you?

• If you don't open the wine to let it breathe, are you a numbskull?

Now I assume you get the message. Many of these points are personal, aren't they? Nobody can tell me that my favorite wine/food combinations don't work for me. I have a friend who has tried everything and settled on Sauvignon Blanc. Even with steak. He likes it that way. So who am I to tell him he's wrong (even though to most that would be a lousy combination)?

I cringe when I read some didactic statement about some wine that "must" breathe for 17 minutes before being served, or about who is or isn't a wine snob, etc.

Unlike in most of Europe, where wine and food are merely a part of the ebb and flow of life, a mystique has taken hold in America that breeds feelings of inadequacy in making wine selections, and great care is taken by some to avoid serving a wine or a wine/food pairing that might not be to someone else's liking. Relax and enjoy wine and food however you like it. There are several incredible wine/food combinations I've picked up while dining at friends' homes that I never would have thought of nor read about. So experiment and have fun!

A WEEKEND IN THE LIFE OF A MAJOR WINE FESTIVAL

Banff, Alberta, situated south of Edmonton and northeast of Vancouver, is possibly the most beautiful site in North America. My personal two favorite views in the world are:

1—from the Fairmont Banff Springs Hotel looking down upon the Bow River, with leviathan snow-capped mountains looming near and far;

2—of the lake, mountains and glacier in the mountains from the Fairmont Chateau Lake Louise, about an hour north by car from Banff.

It is impossible to describe the scenes one beholds at these heavenly spots. It is truly worth the trip just to be surrounded by this majesty of nature. And for an oenophile, add an Annual Fairmont Banff Springs Hotel Festival of Wine and Food, and now we're talking about Heaven!

Just fly into Calgary, rent a car and, in less than two hours, you're in a gorgeous castle-like edifice ensconced in the midst of scarcely believable beauty.

My wife and I have attended this festival around the end of October more than once, and the program one year included the following:

- A 1961 Bordeaux tasting with James Sichel of Chateau Palmer
- A tasting of eight Taylor-Fladgate Ports, including the 30-year-old Tawny, 1998 Quinta de Vargellas and 1977 Vintage, with partner and vice president Huyshe Bower
- A tasting of 10 wines from Joseph Drouhin, including a Grand Cru Chablis, a Clos des Mouches Blanc and a Hospices de Beaune Cuvée Maurice Drouhin with the director of Maison Drouhin, Gerald Uhlen
- A tasting of eight Fontannafredda wines, including four Barolos, with winemaker Danilo Drocco
- A cooking demonstration and wine pairing with Banffshire Club Chef Daniel Buss and club manager and wine director David Walker
- A tasting of eight wines from Cakebread Cellars with Bruce and Karen Cakebread, including the Pinot Noir Anderson Valley and the Cabernet Sauvignon Howell Mountain

- A "Wines of Austria" tasting with Gruner Veltliners and Rieslings from Huber, FX-Pichler, Prager and Brundlmayer with winemakers and owners
- Two awesome luncheons with seven wines at each
- A gourmet gala dinner with 11 wines—remember, nobody had to drive home—and courses such as the following: "Pan seared Aux Champs d'Elise Foie Gras, Warm Lobster, Local Organic Cinderella Pumpkin, Chestnuts, Hotchkiss Farm Greens and Chestnut Sauce" and "Roasted Kobe Classic Wagyu Beef Tenderloin, Truffled Braised Veal Sweetbreads, Poplar Bluff Potato, Local Vegetables, Wild Mushrooms and Perigord Truffle Sauce."

All of the vintners "hung with the group" from Friday afternoon until Sunday after lunch, answering any questions. Each of these celebrities was affable, courteous and pleased to dispense his or her considerable wine wisdom!

The event takes place each fall. The Fairmont Banff Springs was voted as North America's leading resort, *Travel and Leisure* has designated the Willow Springs Spa at the resort a "World's Best Award," and the resort is a 5 Diamond AAA and a 4 Star Mobil Award winner.

Chapter 14
ISRAELI WINES ENAMOR
THE SENSES

In mid-February 2010, I was fortunate to join a small group of global importers and wine writers on a trip to Israel. The journey was chock-full of delicious meals and wine tastings, including The Third International Wine Exhibition in Tel Aviv. Another highlight was touring some of the foremost wineries of the two preeminent wine regions, Galilee (including Golan Heights) and the Judean Hills. These regions have the most complementary growing seasons for the best Israeli reds—Cabernet Sauvignon, Carignan, Merlot and Shiraz.

Twenty-five years ago, Israel had around 20 wineries—roughly the same number of wineries that existed in Texas. Today the Lone Star State has around 200 and Israel boasts even more—but what qualifies as a winery? Some are not tiny, but teeny-weeny. Today, the five largest wineries of Israel produce 85 percent of the grape tonnage. In descending order they are: Carmel, Barkan (including Segal's), Golan Heights (including Yarden and Galil Mountain), Teperburg and Binyamina. All of the large wineries are kosher (note: it is illegal to sell non-kosher wine in Israeli supermarkets). The boutiques and micro-wineries, however, are not kosher. Producing kosher wines is costly, thus the boutique wines can't be found in supermarkets.

ISRAEL

Nazareth

Tel Aviv

Jerusalem

Gaza

1. Galilee
2. Shomron
3. Samson
4. Judean Hills
5. Negev

BARKAN WINERY

Situated almost 2,000 feet up in the Judean Hills, Barkan produces 9 million bottles a year. It exports around 30 percent of all Israeli wines exported and also owns Segal's.

Barkan Chardonnay Reserve 2008—2/3 barrel fermented, 1/3 tank fermented. Only partial malolactic (to preserve some of the bright natural acidity) and aged nine months in French oak. $18

Barkan Shiraz Superieur 2006—Very low-yielding vineyard. Luscious! Top-rated wine I tasted in Israel. $55

Barkan Cabernet Sauvignon Superieur 2006—Also excellent. The "flagship" wine for Barkan. $60

Segal's Argeman Rehasim Dovev Vineyard 2006—The only Israeli grape (Argeman) is a cross between Carignan and a Portuguese varietal, Sousao. It was created as a high-yielding, relatively inexpensive varietal; however, when treated with care and harvested under optimal conditions as was done here, the end product is fascinating. One of my great surprises of the trip. $30

ELLA VALLEY WINERY

Located between Barkan Winery and Jerusalem (sort of), this winery is inside a wealthy kibbutz. The owners tried going the organic farming route, but it just didn't produce the results for all the extra effort. The winemaker here worked for Jaques Prieur in Meursault, Burgundy. Little wonder that my favorite wine is the Chardonnay 2008, part of which, like at Barkan, went through malolactic. Aged mostly in French oak, the wine successfully tasted like a very good white Burgundy. $24

On another day, we ventured to the Galilee Region, saw the Sea of Galilee (massive) and crossed the Jordan River (only a trickle at that crossing). The wineries we visited were:

ADIR GOAT FARM AND WINERY (A TWOFER)

This winery was the perfect setup for a wine and cheese tasting.

ADIR Cabernet Sauvignon Kerem Ben Zimra 2007—The higher-than-normal residual sugar, for a Cabernet, was masked by the excellent acidity. $26

ADIR Plato 2007—I thought this wine was named for the philosopher, so I asked if there was also an Aristotle! Actually, it's named after the plateau upon which the vineyard is ensconced. The vineyard is roughly 2,800 feet above sea level. The wine won a double gold medal at the Mediterranean International Wine and Spirit Challenge in 2008. Lovely, expressive fruit flavors, 14.2 percent alcohol, harmonious. Memorable finish. $50

DALTON WINERY

Stopped in for a visit on the way from ADIR to Golan Heights. Producing 900,000 bottles annually, this winery either owns or manages all of its vineyards.

Dalton Unoaked Chardonnay 2008—A very good value at $12.

Dalton Merlot Reserve 2006—Aged in French oak. $30

Dalton Matatia 2006—200 percent new oak (aged in new oak barrels for a year, then removed and aged in a new group of new oak barrels for another year). Super blend of best blocks in the vineyard. Low yields, superb fruit, excellent balance. 2006 was an excellent vintage for this wine. $100

GOLAN HEIGHTS WINERY

This winery has the type of growing season (because of the altitude) that can be found somewhere between Napa and Oregon! All soil is volcanic with classic Mediterranean climate (hot summers with very little rain from April through October—wonderful for ripening grapes).

Golan Heights produces 5 million bottles a year and exports to 30 countries. Zelma Long, former winemaker at Robert Mondavi Winery in Napa and consultant to Golan Heights, said the wines of Golan Heights combine New World power with Old World elegance. Yarden and Galil Mountain wines are also produced here.

Yarden Blanc de Blancs non-vintage—100 percent Chardonnay. Champagne method. Elegant and crisp with excellent acidity and toasted brioche flavors. Comparable to some non-vintage brut Champagnes. $29

Yarden Gewurztraminer 2009—A semidry Gewurz that exhibits fresh kiwi and litchi flavors. Complements fish and even spicy seafood dishes. $15

Galil Mountain Viognier 2008—Bright fruit flavors. Peaches and apricots. No malolactic (why screw up the natural malic acid when it's this good?) Fresh and full. $15

Galil Mountain Rosé 2009—Mostly Sangiovese and Barbera. Another crowd-pleaser. Strawberries, apples and red currants. All-purpose wine for summer days on the beach or by the pool. $15

Golan Heights Cabernet Sauvignon 2008—Aged in American oak. Blackberry and black currant flavors. Good structure with ample tannins. Try with beef tender with Bordelaise sauce! $27

Yarden Merlot 2005—Dark purple in color. Unfiltered with lots of character. Sage and plums! $20

Yarden Syrah Yonatan Vineyard 2007—Pepper and spice. Perfect wine for prime rib. Lengthy, notable finish. $50

Yarden Heights Wine Gewurztraminer (Galilee) 2007 (half bottle)—Picked at 42 percent sugar and bottled at 21 percent residual sugar. Amazing dessert wine made from frozen clusters of grapes. In the style of classic ice wine. Serve by itself as a dessert or with something akin to crème brulee, fruit tart, sugar cookies, etc. $29

OTHER EXEMPLARY WINERIES

I was particularly enamored with two wineries that I did not visit; however, I met the owners/winemakers. The first is Saslove Winery in Kibbutz Eyal in Tzuriel, which is owned by Barry Salove, who grew up in Canada and later taught winemaking courses in San Francisco. While there, he spent lots of time in the Napa and Sonoma wine country. My favorites here are the lovely Adom Cabernet Sauvignon 2008, $28, and a big, rich red with hints of chocolate and currants, Aviv Cabernet Sauvignon 2008, $50

The second is Tulip Winery. CEO Roy Itzhaki recalls his traveling days as a youth, accompanying his parents as they visited wineries around the world. While in college studying economics and business management, Itzhaki wondered why his family couldn't operate a winery. He wrote up a business plan, and the rest is history. The winemaker here since 2003 has been the talented Tamir Arzy. My favorites here are: White Tulip 2008 (Gewurztraminer and Sauvignon Blanc) $19.99; Mostly Cabernet Franc $27.99; Syrah Reserve 2007 (with a whopping 15 percent alcohol) $39.99; and Black Tulip $47.99.

One winery I found that offers some excellent values is Recanati. I particularly like the Jasmine White 2009 $7; the Rosé 2009 $10; and the Merlot 2008 $13. Another winery provided me with two of the three biggest surprises of the trip—Vitkin Winery. The prices were moderate, and the Carignan 2007 and Petite Sirah 2007 were each outstanding.

EVALUATING WINES

Evaluating and judging wines is a worldwide phenomenon that has proven to be both beneficial and injurious to the wine industry.

In the 1970s, the primary scoring method in the U.S. was the 20-point scale. Some did and still do use "puffs," four stars, five stars, etc. My favorite method was a friend's two-word system, yuck or yum.

Robert Parker started the 100-point scale, which I and others have praised primarily because most people in this country understand what a 90 or 95 means, particularly when the groupings are defined, i.e., 90-95 is outstanding; 96-100 is extraordinary. A numerical system is a big plus for consumers who don't have time to read through voluminous monthly or bimonthly publications that rate wines. Another argument for a numerical rating system is that it forces the taster to take a pretty stark position for the world to see.

On the other hand, a numerical rating is an objective score, which presents a problem. Although tasting a wine to determine if it has too much sulfur, too much tannin or not enough fruit is a matter of objectivity—yes or no—tasting a wine to deem it as a great value is subjective. While current scores are helpful for the buyer who wishes to purchase and drink now, scores for newly released wines to be cellared are more suspect. For example: several days ago, I looked up a writer's scores for a wine in my cellar. This writer had scored the wine three times over a four-year period. The first score, 90-92; the second, 91-94+; and the third, 96. Now the difference between a 96 and a 90 for this particular wine is about $150 a bottle! However, it takes guts to place a score on a wine, so I can't knock it.

When I was writing *Moody's Weekly Wine Review*—a weekly compilation of 10 great values in all price ranges—a score was not necessary. All the wines were great values, and if a wine needed several years to smooth out or 10 years in the cellar before it was drinkable, I said so! Also, a score could change for any blind taster hourly or daily, depending on the time of day, the company and atmosphere, and the food, if any, tasted with the wine.

My usual method of evaluating wine involves selecting three or four wines of a certain type that I think, from years of experience and reading, should be good values. Mrs. Moody marks the bottles and glasses with dots to track which wine is in which glass. I then taste the wines blind, attempting not only to guess which is which, but primarily to find a truly great value from the group.

Sometimes all are good, but none make the cut. And it almost never happens—I'd save a lot of money if it did—that all three or four are great values. Many times the least expensive or at least a lesser-expensive wine is not only the best value but the best wine!

After I taste the wines blind with a neutral cracker between tastes, the wines either go to the dinner table or are consumed with a cheese that complements that varietal. Occasionally, a wine that didn't quite make the grade with a cracker will "improve" so much with the right food, it will catapult itself into being named a great value. In such a case, I will mention these facts. The wine most likely to fit into this category is Sauvignon Blanc, which can have too many wild grapefruit or hay smells or be too acidic by itself, but with goat cheese or a veggie salad, can soar into the "zone" and create a synergism.

WINE DESTINATIONS

Napa County and Sonoma County are obviously distinguished as the prime wine destinations in this country. There is so much to do, so much to see, and oh so many outstanding wines to taste. I've been to each locale on at least 30 occasions, yet I've barely scratched the surface.

Another wine excursion I recommend is a summer visit to the Finger Lakes District in upstate New York, about an hour drive from either Rochester or Syracuse. In fact, you're close enough to run over and see Niagara Falls! Next in this country would be Santa Barbara County.

If visiting Portland, make time for a day visit to the nearby Willamette Valley, especially if you are a fan of Pinot Gris and Pinot Noir. But in Washington State, besides visiting Chateau Ste. Michelle and a handful of others in Seattle, head off the beaten path and spend several days in Walla Walla!

Since all 50 states now have wineries, make use of the Internet before visiting any of the 50. For example, near San Antonio or Austin, a one- or two-day wine trip to the Hill Country wineries is fabulous. In fact, the Texas Hill Country American Viticultural Area is one of the largest and most frequently visited appellations in the United States. Michigan, Virginia, Idaho and others produce seriously good wines, primarily because high-quality grapes can be shipped to winemakers from long distances. Witness the Pacific Rim Riesling – it is made with grapes from Washington State and Germany!

When researching wine destinations online, just go to your favorite search engine, type in the name of your state followed by the word "wineries" or "wines" and see what happens. Also, at your state.org, you may find all you need to know under the Department of Agriculture. For Texas, every state winery is listed alphabetically, by county and by city, at www.agr.state.tx.us under "Marketing."

Regarding wine festivals, if it's been awhile since your last attendance, you're in for a shock. If you were a computer geek and had attended a seminar featuring Bill Gates and the late Steve Jobs, not only as the main speakers but also as your dinner companions, would you not have come away with some incredible new insight into the world of technology? The same is now true of wine festivals. For example, at The Grand Wine and Food Affair in

Sugar Land/Houston one year, participants could attend a Master's Class on Bordeaux wines held by the leading authority in the world on Bordeaux, Michael Broadbent from London. Not only that, he was available for hours on end to socialize and answer questions from any participant. The fortunate patrons at his seminar have a perspective on Bordeaux wines that few in this country can claim.

Top winery owners and winemakers from around the world can be found at wine festivals in such places as Napa, Sonoma, San Luis Obispo, Nashville, Jackson Hole, Aspen, Austin, Banff, Naples (Florida) and, of course, New York. For the "foodies," it's quite possible that Wolfgang Puck, Tyler Florence, Daisy Martinez or another renowned chef will appear. At the grand event at many wine festivals, 40 or 50 wineries will be showcased along with 20 or more of the premier chefs from the region or other countries!

Wine events provide the perfect opportunity to learn about wine at an elevated level that's impossible to achieve otherwise. The Grand Wine and Food Affair in 2006, for example, featured a Riedel wine glass seminar with Georg Riedel himself. There were also two incredible tastings hosted by Mary Ewing-Mulligan, the first and, at the time, one of only two American women Masters of Wine, and her husband, Ed McCarthy, C.W.E. (Certified Wine Educator). One tasting spotlighted Chianti Classico (the couple wrote *Italian Wine for Dummies*). The other highlighted Champagne – Ed is probably the leading authority on Champagne in the United States!

Where else can people who are passionate about a subject have complete access to the most famous celebrities in the world in that field over a several-day period?

WINE IN THE BIBLE

The first project that Noah undertook after he hopped off the ark was planting a vineyard. I imagine at that time, a vineyard somewhere on Mount Ararat was equivalent to a vineyard today in the Napa Valley!

In the King James Version, I Timothy 3:8, the apostle Paul says, regarding Deacons, they "should not be given to much wine." (Notice he doesn't say "no wine.") In I Timothy 5:23, Paul tells Timothy to "use a little wine for thy stomach's sake and thine often infirmaries." (early medical prescription using wine). Matthew 11:19 seems to make it clear that even Jesus drank wine; therefore, why do a number of churches prohibit their congregants from drinking wine? Probably because of the conflict that is presented when Paul says in Romans 14:21, "It is good neither to eat flesh, nor drink wine, nor anything whereby thy brother stumbleth, or is offended, or is made weak." But in the prior verse, Paul teaches that it is evil to eat "with offense." Surely he doesn't mean we should never eat a hamburger or a piece of fried chicken because it might make our brother stumble. I believe these passages point out that Paul is talking about avoiding gluttony and drunkenness, not shunning wine altogether.

What is the greatest wine ever produced? For me, it's the 1870 Chateau Lafite-Rothschild. For others, it's the 1947 Chateau Cheval Blanc. And how about 1921 Chateau d'Yquem? Not a chance. For his first miracle, at the wedding at Cana, Jesus turned water into wine (second chapter of John). I don't know of any winemaker in the world who would want to compete with Jesus for producing the best wine ever made!

PHOTO GALLERY 2

Joy Sterling gets her after-lunch hug from me in 2004 in the Eden-like gardens owned by her parents, Audrey and Barry Sterling, most congenial hosts and founders of the spectacular Iron Horse Vineyards. Joy and her brother Lawrence now run the winery.

My friends since 1977 and 1979, respectively, Michael Broadbent (left), former chairman of the wine department at Christie's in London, and Kevin Zraly (right), author of Windows on the World Complete Wine Course—over 3 million copies sold—with me in 2006 at The Grand Wine and Food Affair Sugar Land/Houston.

After a fabulous luncheon in 2006 at the Taylor Fladgate offices in Villa Nova de Gaia, Marijo and I pose with Alastair Robertson, current owner and president of the 300-year-old family firm. The city of Oporto appears in the background.

With the always-gorgeous Marijo after a convivial, enchanting dinner in the amazing wine cave at Clos Pegase in the Napa Valley in 2007, with owner Jan Shrem and a group of friends.

In between visits to Israel's wineries, I visited the Western Wall (also referred to as the Wailing Wall) in Jerusalem in 2010. I closed my eyes and touched the wall to pray, and immediately saw the stunning image of Jesus Christ. My life's most memorable experience.

183

Nicolas Catena (left), the "Robert Mondavi of Argentina" and the author at the 130-year-old Catena Family Estancia in Mendoza in October 2010.

In 2010 I watched as the indefatigable, unrivaled wine glassmaker Georg Riedel had some fun with his newest decanter named Eve, prior to our luncheon at Reef Restaurant in Houston.

On the patio in 2011 at Artisans of Barossa with possibly the greatest winemaker in Australia, John Duval (right). His Plexis (Rhone-style) and Entity (Shiraz) are two of the greatest "under-$40" wines in the world. We sampled the 2008s, which are substantial, luscious and unrivaled in that price range.

OTHER DESSERT WINES

Chapter 15

~🍇~

Few dessert wines ever attain the zenith reached by the best wines of Sauternes (Semillon and Sauvignon Blanc) and Germany (Riesling). Two exceptions, however, spring to mind: Napa's Dolce, produced by the partners at Far Niente, is pretty much a dead ringer for the top wines from Sauternes; and Dr. Konstantin Frank Bunch Select Late Harvest Finger Lakes (N.Y.) Riesling is as good as the best of Germany. In fact, a specially made 9-liter bottle of the 2008 recently sold for $35,000 at The Houston Livestock Show and Rodeo International Wine Competition Auction.

Hungary's Tokaji or Tokay (no kin to Tokay d'Alsace or Australia's Tokay) was famous for hundreds of years, but the quality was vitiated by communist rule. After 1990 in post-communist Hungary, several important wine persons, including Hugh Johnson, author of *The World Atlas of Wine*, became investors. Within several years, the quality of Tokaji wines had soared to an all-time high.

Tokaji Szamorodni is normally dry or off-dry and not that appealing to some. Tokaji Aszú is another story. Shrivelled Aszú berries affected by botrytis are picked separately, and the amount (measured in puttoños—approximately 50-pound basketfuls) of these added to a barrel of regular-harvest wine determines the level of sweetness. Wines labeled 3 puttoños are more like an auslese from Germany—a little too sweet to go with food (maybe cheese and nuts by the pool)—and not sweet enough to be a dessert wine. 4 puttoños is very close, especially with a not-too-sweet dessert, but 5 and 6 puttoños definitely make the grade at around 10 percent residual sugar or more. An even sweeter, albeit much more costly, Tokaji is Essencia, made from the free-run juice of Aszú berries and stored in cask for at least 10 years. It is very low in alcohol and has been regarded in the past as a panacea; however, as amazing as it is, Essencia tastes more like thick, sweet, honeyed juice than wine. A 500-ml bottle of Essencia retails for more than $200.

Many wine aficionados know that the primary grape in Tokaji is the Furmint. But as an advanced oenophile, you now know that up to half of the wine can be Hárslevelü.

Following are other delectable dessert wines to seek out:

Alsatian Sélection de Grains Nobles—Although some Alsation wines are labeled "Vendange Tardive" (late harvest), these wines are not nearly sweet enough to be dessert wines—just picked riper, resulting in richer and sometimes only slightly sweeter wines. But those labeled Sélection de Grains Nobles are among the great, and very expensive, dessert wines of the world. The S.G.N. Rieslings are fabulous and the S.G.N. Pinot Gris can be unusually rich, sweet and hedonistic.

Vouvray Moelleux and Liquoreux—Dessert versions of Loire Valley's Vouvray, made from Chenin Blanc. Age extremely well.

Quarts de Chaume and Bonnezeaux—Both from the Anjou district of the Cotes de Layon in the Loire Valley. Limited quantity but excellent dessert wines made from the Chenin Blanc grape.

Jurançon—From Southwest France, this sweet white is a good value dessert wine made from the Petit Manseng grape. Jurançon Sec is the dry version.

Monbazillac—Also from Southwest France (within the Bergerac District), made with the same grapes as Sauternes, but lesser in quality and price.

Moscato d'Asti (slightly sparkling)—This is an extremely well-received dessert wine. It is sweet, sprightly, relatively inexpensive and only around 5.5 percent alcohol. My favorite producer of Moscato d'Asti is Saracco.

Moscato is currently on a blitz in the U.S. The best article I've seen on Moscato is by wine icons Jay McInerney and Lettie Teague, published in the Jan. 14, 2012, issue of the *Wall Street Journal.*

FOOD AND WINE SYNERGY

Food and wine pairings are all the rage. After all, we're always looking for a synergism in which both the wine and food taste better together than either one possibly could by itself.

Some of the old favorites are oysters and Vouvray from the Loire Valley in France; goat cheese and Sauvignon Blanc, including Pouilly-Fume and Sancerre from the Loire Valley; rack of lamb with Bordeaux; fowl with Pinot Noir; and paté or caviar with Champagne.

The saying that "white wine goes with fish and red wine goes with meat" is generally correct, in my opinion. But there are many exceptions. For example, grilled salmon is excellent with Pinot Noir, particularly from California or Oregon. A local trout cooked in red wine with a great red Burgundy was a smashing success at the Hotel de la Poste in Beaune, France. And halibut and swordfish can go well with a Bordeaux.

Some people serve Chardonnay as a house wine with paté, caviar or smoked salmon. Unfortunately, Chardonnay really doesn't complement these hors d'oeuvres as does Champagne. If serving a white wine instead of, or along with, Champagne, Sauvignon Blanc is a superior selection.

I once matched some wines and foods for a school auction item. My only fee for such "difficult" work was that I be there to enjoy the fruits of my labor. The pairing that created the most excitement was a chicken and sausage paella with a Bodegas Arzuaga, one of the excellent Tempranillo-based reds from the Ribero del Duero in Spain.

Another fabulous match is the generally forgotten consumé along with Madeira. From driest to sweetest, Madeira is labeled (with several exceptions) Sercial, Verdelho, Bual or Malmsey. Even though Sercial works well, the perfect match is Verdelho, particularly with pheasant consumé. And for a dessert wine, try a Bual or Malmsey with crème brulee, bread pudding, etc.

Every once in a while, I discover a new combination. One year after the Sonoma winegrowers' big tasting event in Texas, most of the vintners ended up at our house. I pulled out a couple of great vintage Ports. The only thing I could find to pair with the Port was Vanilla Wafers and peanut butter. OK, laugh, but it was wonderful!

Experiment. Try Bargetto's Ollolieberry wine with cheesecake. Pour some Pedro Ximinez Sherry on vanilla ice cream. Have fun!

VALUE WINES VS. ELITE WINES

At a well-known wine festival years ago, I moderated a panel of wine experts that included the late, famous wine writers Alexis Bespaloff and Robert Lawrence Balzer. The topic of discussion was value versus elite— three pundits on each side of the debate.

The seminar heated up when one speaker not only arrogated to the value side a definite superiority, but also decried those who purchased elite wines as label buyers and collectors. With that, Martin Sinkoff— at the time a wine wholesaler in Dallas—rose to compare favorably a great dinner and beautifully matched elite wines to an evening at the symphony or opera, enjoying the occasion with all the senses versus just seeing and hearing. He expounded on this theme for about five minutes with dramatic and sincere passion—an unscripted one-man performance. This not only drew a spirited round of applause, but vitiated the "value" proponent's assertion.

Many years later—in 2005 to be exact—I moderated a panel at The Grand Wine and Food Affair in Sugar Land/Houston on the same subject. This time the panel included Michael Broadbent, Chairman Emeritus of Christie's wine department; Kevin Zraly, author of *Windows on the World Complete Wine Course*; and Karen McNeil, author of *Wine Bible*. Less rowdy, but just as informative!

There are few worldly delights more enjoyable to me than matching, say, a 1982 Cheval Blanc with a perfectly prepared rack of lamb (which I actually did at Mark's Restaurant in Houston one evening). As one of the lucky few who regularly drank the fabled vintages starting in the mid-1970s, I can verify that the elite group has a major point.

Among the greatest I've been fortunate enough to enjoy:
- Chateau Lafite-Rothschild 1870 (Magnum). This one was stored at Glamis Castle for almost a century, and was said to be undrinkable for the first 50 years!
- Chateau Pétrus 1947. Even better than the more heralded Chateau Cheval-Blanc 1947.
- Chateau Pétrus, Palmer, Latour, Mouton, Haut-Brion and Margaux 1961 at Dr. Lou Skinner's first 1961 tasting in Coral Gables in 1981 (50 1961s).

- Chateau Mouton-Rothschild, Latour and Pétrus 1945 (all served in magnums), Romanee Conti 1945 (served in one of only three jeroboams produced) and Taylor Fladgate Port 1945 at Dr. Frank Komorowski's birthday dinner in Vermillion, Ohio, in 1995.
- The perfect 1899 and 1900 Chateau Margaux served at a private dinner in 1983 with the owner Corinne Mentzolopoulos and her famed consultant Emile Peynaud.
- Romanée-Conti 1942 on my (and its) 40th birthday.
- Chateau Lafite-Rothchild 1959 and 1949, tasted as often as possible in the 1980s and 1990s.
- Grange Hermitage 1955, tasted in Sydney at the Third Triennial International Wine and Food Society Convention in 1980.
- About half of the unbelievable 1959s served by Steven Kaplan from his own cellar over two days with unforgettable meals at the Four Seasons Hotel and the Intercontinental Hotel in Chicago in 1994.
- B.V. Cabernet Sauvignon Private Reserve 1951, tasted on three occasions—once with Andre Tchelistcheff, who made the wine.
- Heitz Cabernet Sauvignon Martha's Vineyard 1968, tasted from the late 1970s through the early 1990s.
- Gruaud-Larose 1819—"Astonishing preservation," exclaimed Clive Cotes, M.W. Tasted with the owners at Marvin Overton's massive Gruaud-Larose tasting in Fort Worth in 1990.

Chapter 16
PORT

By Bartholomew Broadbent

Bartholomew Broadbent is one of America's top wine educators and trend builders. In June 1997, *Decanter* magazine named Bartholomew one of the "fifty most influential in the wine world…the faces to watch in the new millennium." This was reaffirmed by *Wine&Spirits* magazine (2008), which polled leaders throughout the industry and named him one of 10 in the world to be "driving the most revolutionary changes in wine." Bartholomew has expanded from his pivotal role in the growth of Port and Madeira to "exert a profound influence on the US wine market," says Decanter. Profiled by *Wine Spectator* in 1986, *Market Watch* "The Pioneer of Port" May 2008 and Forbes.com (2009), Bartholomew, son of legendary Michael Broadbent, is now one of America's leading wine importers, Broadbent Selections, Inc. (www.broadbent.com), representing such famous brands as Chateau Musar. His speaking circuit includes major cruise lines, wine festivals, including being the Reserve Tasting Director at the Food&Wine's Classic in Aspen. Bartholomew is classic rock KFOG radio's "Wine Guy" in San Francisco. He is the permanent expert for www.intowine.com webtv. Bartholomew makes Port, Madeira and Vinho Verde in Portugal under the Broadbent name, as well as Malbec in Argentina and Gruner Veltliner in Austria. As the 50 percent partner in Dragon's Hollow, a pioneering winery in China, he helped launch the first nationally available Chinese wine in the U.S. market. Bartholomew enjoys an active web presence on Twitter and Facebook (www.facebook.com/broadbentselections) and welcomes new friends.

The Douro is a stunningly beautiful wine region in northern Portugal along the Douro River. The area is best known for its Port and boasts a history of winemaking that dates to pre-Roman times. Port, or Oporto, is the great fortified wine of Portugal. Although outside of the country it has not always been a front-runner on the international wine scene, Port is unabashedly a historical gem in the world of wine.

PORT: A BLEND OF PORTUGUESE AND BRITISH HISTORY

Port wine is named after the coastal town of Porto, where the Douro River ends its journey and spills into the Atlantic. Port traces its roots back to the 17th century, during the wars between England and France. In 1679, the British were prohibited from buying Bordeaux when the English Parliament imposed an embargo on French wine. So the British went in search of wines from elsewhere in the world. Their quest led them to Portugal's Douro Valley, which produced the greatest wines outside of Bordeaux. The British fortified the wine with brandy to protect it during the long sea journey to England. Though they infused more spirit into the wine, the English could not exactly lay claim to this idea. An abbot at a monastery in Lamego, Portugal, had been making a wine named Pinhão using a similar method: by adding brandy to the cask during fermentation.

Kopke is the oldest Port house, established in Portugal in 1638; however, it wasn't until around 1730 that fortification went into general practice. It eventually became law, against the wishes of many great wine merchants, most notably the Baron de Forrester. The Baron was an influential character who created maps of the Douro and decried the practice of fortification. But he is probably best known for having perished in the Douro River in 1861, weighed down by a money belt as his boat capsized.

The definition of Port was not actually agreed upon until 1905, initiated by the British, and it became law in the Anglo-Portuguese Commercial Treaty Act in 1914.

PORT PRODUCTION

Port today is made with the addition of a brandy that has no color, smell or taste. The brandy is simply a fortifying agent made from distilled table wine of approximately 77 percent alcohol. This brandy, which can be distilled anywhere within the European Community, is added to the fermenting must when the alcohol has reached approximately 7 percent, within 24 to 48 hours of harvesting. During these first two days, there is a rush to extract as much color as possible from the skin of the grapes, traditionally by foot treading, by pump-over every 15 minutes in "autovinificators," or by mechanical devices designed to simulate foot pressing. The grapes are generally picked and fermented together, especially as the old vineyards are randomly planted with combinations of over 100 indigenous grape varieties.

When vineyards are replanted today, there is a focus on half a dozen grape varieties, the most important being Touriga Nacional. Other heralded varieties are Tinta Roriz, Tinta Francesca, Tinta Barroca, Tinta Amarela and Tinta Cão.

White Port exudes greater variety in sweetness levels. For instance, Lagrima is super sweet, but most white Port is medium sweet to off dry. The most common use of white Port is as an aperitif, mixed with tonic with a twist of lime, though it can be served on the rocks or mixed into cocktails. White Port can age very well but is mostly consumed young. It is usually bottled at three years of age but can be bottled at 10 years.

Fermentation increases the alcohol content from around 7 percent to 19 percent or 20 percent, thus killing the yeast so that fermentation stops and the unconverted sugar remains as residual sugar in the wine. This is why Port is always sweet, although some houses may produce a slightly dryer style by adding brandy when the fermentation is further advanced, say at 7.5 percent alcohol.

Port is aged for at least two years in stainless-steel or oak barrels. The majority of Port is bottled at three years of age, either as Ruby Port or Tawny Port. These two are inexpensive and relatively simple wines. They are made from vineyards that don't produce wines with great aging capability, generally closer to Porto than Spain.

The finest Ports are defined by when they are bottled. Vintage Port, bottled at two to three years of age from deep-colored wines, is designed to age at least 50 years in the bottle. It is only made in the best years from the best vineyards, accounting for about 2 percent of all Port produced. Vintage Port can be consumed young with chocolate desserts or it can be aged. The oldest-known Vintage Port still available is the Ferreira 1815, which is still in great condition, but the Port generally peaks at 15 to 50 years of age.

Vintage Port is bottled in opaque black glass bottles to prevent light from penetrating the wine. It is not filtered or fined, so in time it will show sediment and require decanting. Prior to bottling, Vintage Port can be aged in a stainless steel cask or oak barrel, depending on the house style.

Vintage Ports are usually blends of multiple vineyards. The Port shippers "declare" that they are going to release a Vintage Port, which generates great interest. However, in years when a Port is not declared, shippers often produce small quantities of Vintage Port for their own consumption, for families who want to give a traditional gift of Port to a newborn child, or simply because they only have a small amount of Vintage-quality wine. Often, these Vintage Ports from non-declared years are produced from single vineyards, such as Graham's Malvedos or Taylor's Quinta da Vargelas.

Port that is kept in the barrel for four to six years prior to bottling is designated a Late Bottled Vintage (LBV). There are two types of LBVs. The first is the largest-selling category of Port in England. It is, therefore, made in vast quantities by most of the English brands to fill the needs of the English supermarkets. This type of LBV is a step up from basic ruby Port. It is filtered, fined and bottled in regular bottles—designed for immediate consumption.

The other type of LBV is equivalent to a step down from Vintage Port. These Ports tend to be produced by the Portuguese houses that do not produce vast quantities for the UK market. However, two English houses, Warre's and Smith Woodhouse, also take pride in producing these wines. These

Ports are bottled for aging unfiltered in the opaque black bottles. In fact, these wines can age extremely well and are almost indistinguishable from true Vintage Port, but a fraction of the price.

RESERVE PORT

Once referred to as Vintage Character Port, Reserve Port wines vary greatly in quality. These Reserve wines have proprietary names and are produced in either large or small quantities. A Reserve Port is a blend of several vintages and bottled on average between three and six years. The best-known examples include Graham's Six Grapes, Warre's Warrior, Broadbent Auction Reserve, Cockburn's Special Reserve, Taylor's First Estate, Ferreira's Dona Antonia, Fonseca's Bin 27 and Sandeman Founder's Reserve. These wines are designed to be consumed soon after bottling. They are often the biggest priority for any given Port house as a commercial brand-building wine. Crusted Port is a similar wine in terms of production, except it is bottled unfiltered, perhaps akin to the unfiltered LBV in the realm of Reserve Ports.

TAWNY AND VINTAGE PORTS

Port that mellows in a wooden barrel for seven years or more can be bottled as a barrel-aged Tawny. Not to be confused with inexpensive Tawny, it is bottled with an indication of age. Some old Tawny Ports are bottled with the name Colheita (Portuguese for vintage). The most notable producer of Colheita Port is Niepoort.

Most wood-aged Tawnies are bottled at either 10 or 20 years of age, and some are bottled at up to 40 years of age. The 20-year-old Tawny is considered the finest with the ideal balance of fruit and age. The leading 20-year Tawny producer is Portuguese-owned Ferreira. The winemaker's Duke de Braganca 20-year Tawny is a blend of Ports that have been aged for 15 to over 40 years.

In both the UK and U.S., Vintage Port tends to be considered the finest of the Ports. There is no question that a suitably aged Vintage is one of the finest wines in the world. In the UK, it is served mature with Stilton cheese or nuts, or on its own after dinner. In the U.S. it is served younger, usually as a dessert wine or after dinner.

In Portugal, Tawny Port is considered the finest Port and for good reason. Vintage Port was the creation of the British, and most of the Vintage Port was bottled by wine merchants in the UK until the practice was banned in the 1970s.

However, the Portuguese truly respect Tawny Port because it is so difficult to make, taking generations to develop and requiring considerable investment in aging the wines. Tawny Port can be served chilled as an aperitif, but is more frequently served as a dessert wine, with nuts, on its own after dinner or as a nightcap.

STORING PORT

A very old Vintage Port, perhaps 50 years old or more, should be consumed within a day or two of opening. However, a young Vintage Port can be kept open much longer. A Vintage Port in its first decade of life might benefit from being open for a month or so.

Tawny Ports, having been exposed to oxygen for 10 or 20 years, do not benefit from being bottled. In fact, they slowly die over the ensuing years. A tawny can stay fine for many months after opening. Ports do not turn to vinegar like a table wine does. Frankly, I've served Ports that have been open for a year or more...but in our house, a Port that's opened is consumed in about 10 minutes!

After a successful run in the 1980s and 1990s, Port sales are suffering today. This may be due to the fact that table wines frequently have alcohol levels of 14 percent to 16 percent, as opposed

Douro Table Wines

The pioneering non-fortified Douro wine Barca Velha was first produced in 1952. But the region's popularity for table wines took off in the 1990s, when winemaker Quinta do Crasto won the International Wine Competition in London. Quinta do Crasto began receiving previously unimaginable scores from *Wine Spectator* for its Douro wines, even being named the number three wine in the publication's Top 100 Wines of the World. Crasto proved that the Douro can produce some of the finest wines in the world.

to 12 percent to 12.5 percent two decades ago. Who wants to drink a glass of wine at 20 percent after polishing off half a bottle of table wine at 15.5 percent? The tide has changed, at the time of writing, and alcohol levels in table wine are beginning to come down again. Certainly Port's time will come again.

PORTS OF THE TAYLOR FLADGATE PARTNERSHIP

Taylor Fladgate and Yeatman, as it is sometimes called, was founded in 1692. It is a family concern that has never been bought, sold or taken over, although I'm sure there are large corporate buyers who would drool over the prospect. Michael Broadbent, Master of Wine and former chairman of the wine department for Christies in London, describes Taylor as the Chateau Latour of Port. Not only does the Taylor Fladgate Partnership own Taylor and Fonseca, it also has Croft and Delaforce in its stable. And as late as 1968, there was just one owner (part of the family, naturally).

Since 1968, Alistair Robertson has been chairman and partner (responsible for sweeping, positive changes) and Huyshe Bower, vice president and partner. The other partner from the same vintage as the above two, Bruce Guimaraens, is deceased, but his son, David, is now a partner and the winemaker. Curiously, only one offspring of the Robertsons (Natasha) and one of the Bowers (Robert) work there; so in all probability, in 30 years there still will be one Robertson, one Guimaraens and one Bower running the partnership.

Year after year, one of my favorite three Ports is Taylor's (or in the U.S., Taylor Fladgate) vintage Port. In the 1980s, at a vintage Port tasting, about the 10th Port served was a Graham's 1945. On the scale of 1 to 20, I gave it a 19. Another Port was served blind as a mystery wine. It was so outstanding that it almost transcended a score, so I gave it a 20. Everyone present seemed impressed when I announced that it was the '45 Taylor and correctly so.

It really was easy to guess. The color mirrored the Graham, indicating that the mystery wine was somewhere around the same age. Since it was even better, it had to be another '45—nothing else was possible. The only '45 better than Graham's would be Taylor or possibly Fonseca. Since I had tasted the '45 Fonseca several years prior and had given it a 19, this one had to be the Taylor!

In June 2006, Marijo and I made the three-hour jaunt by train—for the first time—from Lisbon to Oporto for a tasting and lunch. Later we meandered, by train again, up the Douro River eastward for another three hours to the Vargellas Station. We were fortunate enough to have been extended an invitation to visit the Quinta de Vargellas, the coruscating jewel of the Taylor Fladgate Partnership holdings.

At the preliminary tasting in Oporto, the wines that stood out were two from Delaforce: His Eminence's Choice 10 Year Old Tawny and the vintage 2003; three from Fonseca: Siroco (a white aperitif Port), 40 Year Old Tawny and the Quinta do Panascal 2001; and three from Taylor: Late Bottled Vintage 2000, 20 Year Old Tawny and the vintage 2003.

The ride up the Douro reveals some of the world's most gorgeous vineyards, terraced hundreds of feet high into the hills around the river. There is also a fabulous homestead perched in the middle of a huge Quinta (estate with vineyards in this case) about every five miles far up the river. The panoramic views, especially from the tops of the mountains in the area around Vargellas, are incomparable. At one mountain top, my eyes beheld more than 5,000 acres of terraced vines in the 360-degree sweep.

Speaking of vines, the grapes that go into "real" Port are grown exclusively in the Douro Valley, one of the oldest appellations in the world. The most concise and accurate descriptions of the primary grape varieties I've seen are listed in a brochure from Delaforce:

"Touriga Francesca—Intensely aromatic, low yield, small berries, tight clusters.

Tinta Barroca—Profound colour, precocious and rich in sugar, good productivity, opulent, round and supple.

Tinta Roriz—Very fine and aromatic, giving complexity, elegance and a firm structure.

Touriga Nacional—Wonderful concentration and scale, small berries, tight clusters.

Tinta Cao—A very old vine varietal with good acidity and colour, generous in alcohol—a trustworthy variety."

One type of Port that generally is unfamiliar to the American public is the single Quinta Port. Since Vargellas is the jewel of Taylor as well as the Douro, I'll use it as an example. In the "declared" years, that is, the three or so vintages every decade that have such concentration and longevity that a vintage Port is made, the wines from the Quinta de Vargellas, "firm and exotically scented," are blended with the wines of the Quinta de Terra Feita, "round, opulent and fruity," to form the vintage blend.

In several of the other six or seven vintages in a decade, when the grapes at Vargellas are amazingly great (possibly three or four of those years) but for some reason a vintage is not declared, a limited amount of Quinta de Vargellas with a vintage date will be released. Sometimes this wine can be as good as a declared Taylor vintage. For the best example, Clive Coats, M.W., scored the 1995 Quinta de Vargellas a 20!

While at Vargellas with Alistair and his wife, Gillyane, in response to being queried, I guessed a vintage Port served to be a 1975 Taylor. Alistair responded, "Oh, it's from a magnum." So I said, "Then it's the 1970."

On another occasion, after a lovely al fresco dinner, another vintage Port was served. Again queried about the vintage after being told that it was a Fonseca from a magnum, I guessed 1970 once again. Two guesses combined with a great degree of luck!

There is no question in my mind that Port from the Duoro is the greatest fortified dessert wine made in the world.

WINES TO CELLAR

There are wines to drink now, wines that can be consumed now or cellared for further development, and wines to avoid now but cellar for a future revelation.

At Stephen Kaplan's incredible 1959 wine and food event in Chicago in 1994—59 of the best '59s—most of the wines were still fabulous. And at Dr. Frank Komorowski's "Dinner of the Century" in Vermillion, Ohio, in 1995 (he was 50 and the wines were 50), with all 1945s in magnums or larger bottles, the wines were perfect. In fact my favorite food/wine course of all-time was served. Komorowski had flown Wolfgang Puck to Ohio to assist the French Chef at Le Francaise, and the dish was a mushroom risotto with white truffle shavings with one of the three jeroboams produced of 1945 Romanée-Conti. Tasting these wines was the ultimate evidence for the culinary, historical and gustatory riches to be gained from cellaring wines.

Before the 1982 vintage in Bordeaux and the advent of "tender tannins," a top Bordeaux from a great vintage—especially a "hard" vintage like 1952—could take decades to smooth out. This was certainly true for pre-phylloxera Bordeaux wines and some of the later "vintages of the century," 1945 and 1961. But every vintage is different.

I attended Dr. Lou Skinner's first 1961 tasting in Coral Gables, Fla., in 1981. He had acquired 50 cases of the best Bordeaux wines. They were astounding. I gave perfect scores to: Pétrus, Palmer, Latour and Margaux. However, in reading about some of his follow-up tastings later in the 1980s, I discovered that a few of the wines were beginning to show their age.

For my first contribution to show the benefits of cellaring, I took the cue from Dr. Skinner and collected and donated 55 bottles of the finest 1974 California Cabernets—one of the best vintages ever—to raise money for public radio in Honolulu. In a spirit of good will and dedication, I forced myself to join the group of purchasers at the Halikulani and taste the wines. This was in early 1988, and at least the top-tier wines were at their peak. In descending order, the top seven, which were spectacular, were: Joseph Phelps Insignia, Robert

Mondavi Reserve, Diamond Creek Volcanic Hill, Ridge Monte Bello, Heitz Martha's Vineyard, Mt. Eden and Mayacamas.

Wines in half-bottles, while very practical—half-bottle of white with appetizer, red with entrée (enough for a couple)—will never develop as well in such a container. From my experience and that of many others, the optimal container for long-term aging is the magnum.

There are many bottles that are only for the cellar. Generally, the big Bordeaux wines from great vintages are best suited for cellar bottles, while the best fortified wine candidates are the vintage Ports. Both of these can develop complexity, drinkability, charm, depth and marvelous nuances over the years that just can't be found in any young wines. Although some wines can age for many decades, most of these top wines peak in 15 to 30 years.

Other wines perfect for cellaring are the big reds from Burgundy, Rhone, Tuscany, Piedmont, Australia and Spain, as well as the best Cabs from great years in California. The best whites for cellaring are the big white Burgundies from great years and dessert whites.

Chapter 17
MADEIRA, THE FORGOTTEN ISLAND WINE

by Bartholomew Broadbent

The volcanic island of Madeira, situated approximately 435 miles off the coast of Morocco in the Atlantic Ocean, was discovered in 1419 by the Portuguese. The island was covered with dense forest, hence the name Madeira, meaning "wood" in Portuguese. As trees and vegetation were set ablaze to make room for farming and settlements, the island smoldered for several years, creating a fertile soil in which vines were planted.

Madeira is also the name of the wine produced on the island.

The island is located directly in the trade winds between Europe and America, providing a welcome stopping point for ships sailing to North America and the West Indies. Barrels of Madeira were once used as ballast in the bottom of the boats.

One day, a boat returned to the island after having forgotten to unload its cargo of Madeira. Tasting the wine, the shipmates found it had, in fact, developed. The consensus was that the wine had improved after being heated in the holds of the ship while crossing the ocean twice.

The result of this discovery was a law that prohibited Madeira wine from being sold until it had been shipped around the world twice. Madeiras were, in those days, named not after the producer or the grape, but after the vessel in which they sailed.

While this wine may be unknown to many Americans, Madeira may be considered the most historic wine in U.S. history. America was by far the largest market for Madeira, until Prohibition destroyed the customer base. The wine is referenced in numerous books on American history. George Washington was known to drink a pint of Madeira every day with dinner. The Constitution and Declaration of Independence were both toasted with Madeira. Betsy Ross kept a glass of Madeira on her side table while she sewed the flag. Thomas Jefferson and virtually all the Founding Fathers drank Madeira regularly.

Although Madeira is no longer shipped around the world twice before its release, production of the wine simulates the journey to North America. Madeira is heated to 113 to 122 degrees for a minimum of three months, followed by a settling period of at least 90 days. This heating process, called "estufagem," is accomplished by heating the wine in stainless-steel casks in two ways: by warm-water coils that heat the wine from within, or with warm-water blankets that are wrapped around the cask's exterior. Madeira also is heated using the "canteiro" method, which occasionally is used as an alternative to the estufa. This heating takes place over a two-year period on the upper floors or in the attics of buildings. The casks heat up naturally during the summer.

THE MAKING OF MADEIRA

Madeira is a fortified wine. The addition of brandy to arrest the fermentation is performed immediately prior to heating and is timed to result in the desired sweetness of the wine. Madeira can be very dry or very sweet—and anything in between. The sweetness level is controlled in two ways. The drier wines are made from grapes grown at higher altitudes, whereas the sweetest wines come from riper grapes grown almost at sea level. In addition, the earlier the Madeira is fortified, the more residual sugar is left in the wine. The brandy used to fortify the fermenting must is produced from distilled table wine. It has no color, smell or taste.

Whether made from red wine or white wine, Madeira always turns brown after heating. There are three main red grapes used to produce Madeira: Tinta Negra, Triunfo and Complexa. The white grapes include Sercial, Verdelho, Bual [Boal], Malmsey [Malvazia], Terrantez, Moscatel and Bastardo.

In addition to being grape varieties, Sercial, Verdelho, Bual and Malmsey also indicate sweetness levels. Sercial is always dry, Verdelho is medium dry, Bual is medium sweet and Malmsey is sweet.

Madeira is aged in old oak barrels that are well seasoned by previous owners. At Justino's, for instance, the barrels come from the Scotch producers. Those same barrels were acquired by the Scotts from Port producers who no longer used them for Port!

TYPES OF MADEIRA

Madeira is bottled at various ages. It can be sold at:
- Three years of age (seleccionado, commonly called Fine Rich);
- Five years of age (Reserva, a blend of vintages that must be at least five years of age but below 10);
- 10 years of age (Reserve Especial, must be at least 10 years of age but, though possibly containing older wine, should not taste like a wine older than 15 years of age);
- 15 years old (Reserva Extra);
- 20 years of age;
- 30 years of age;
- Over 40 years of age.

The word Vintage is not used on bottles of Madeira because Port shippers have trademarked the word in Portugal, reserved exclusively for their Vintage Ports. However, a Madeira is referred to as a vintage when it is made from grapes of a single year (or 85 percent of the wine, according to EU law) and has spent at least 20 years aging in oak casks.

Colheita is a relatively new category. It is a wine indicating a single vintage but can be bottled after aging for five years. Colheita is typically bottled at seven years of age. This category was introduced to allow Madeira to be more competitive with Port. A Vintage Port holds an unfair advantage because it can be sold at two years of age, whereas a vintage Madeira must be 20 years old.

Rainwater is a lighter Madeira that is usually bottled at three years of age and officially should not age for more than five years. However, Rainwater has occasionally been bottled after 10 years. The origins of the term Rainwater remain unknown, but the two most popular theories are: 1) A gentleman in Charleston, South Carolina, once tasted a Madeira and declared that it was "as fine as rainwater"; and 2) Some casks of Madeira were left outside during a tropical storm without their bungs, and the wine took on a lighter style when diluted with rainwater.

Solera Madeira was first created after the island of Madeira was devastated by phylloxera. Before production resumed, when the cure of grafting vines onto American rootstock was discovered, Madeira producers stretched out good vintages by adding older wine. The rule was and still is that 10 percent of the wine from a vintage could be sold in a year and replaced with a younger wine of equal quality. This could be done a maximum of 10 times, resulting in a high-quality blend.

LONG LIVE MADEIRA

Madeira is known as the longest lived wine in the world. It is virtually indestructible. A bottle can be opened, tasted and then kept for years for a special occasion.

Madeira is also versatile. It has two unique properties, the first being its high natural acidity. Madeira can be paired with almost any dish or dessert, even if the dessert has citrus ingredients. Madeira even stands up to balsamic vinegar! Second, although the richer Madeiras are sweet, they do have a dry finish. This means they can be paired with sweet desserts without clashing. Dessert is sometimes known to kill dessert wine, making it taste horribly dry. Not so with Madeira.

Few Madeira houses remained after the disastrous Prohibition, but large stocks of ancient wines did survive in the cellars on the island. There are eight remaining Madeira companies, including The Madeira Wine Company. The company acquired 18 firms with a total of 33 brand names! Today's brands to look for include Barbeito, Blandy's, Borges,

Broadbent, Cossart Gordon, Henriques & Henriques, Justino Henriques, Leacock's and Miles.

Following the repeal of Prohibition, shipping methods had changed during World War II and the island lost its place as an automatic stopover. The wine became the forgotten island wine. In 1989 the Symington Port family purchased the Madeira Wine Company and, as their employee in America at that time, I was tasked with re-creating the market and educating Americans.

Prior to 1989, the only restaurant in America known to be serving Madeira was Masa's in San Francisco, offering a glass of old vintage Madeira or Chateau d'Yquem with foie gras. We launched Madeira with a remarkably well-attended trade tasting at the Four Seasons Clift Hotel in San Francisco, which resulted in almost every great restaurant in the Bay Area adding Madeira to its wine list. For instance, TraVigne in Napa Valley poured no less than seven Madeiras by the glass! I spent the next several years of my life traveling the United States educating Americans about Madeira, and the rest, as they say, is history!

WINE—BAD NEWS AND GOOD NEWS

Wine is not for everyone. For those who enjoy an alcoholic beverage, I recommend it be consumed with a complementary food, whether it's beer with Mexican or Chinese food, a mixed drink with hors d'oeuvres, iced vodka with caviar or a cava with tapas. This creates a synergism in which both the food and the drink taste better than either could by itself. And physiologically, one functions better if the alcoholic beverage is taken with food.

For those who choose to consume alcoholic beverages, there are pitfalls. The major one, of course, is the possibility of becoming an alcoholic. Other downfalls that come to mind are:

1. As one ages, the deleterious effects of drinking too much become more noticeable
2. Alcoholic beverages are obviously not complementary to driving or many other tasks
3. Too much wine can negatively affect sleep patterns
4. Alcohol consumption can be an expensive habit
5. Alcohol may add unwanted calories
6. Alcoholic beverages give some people a bad headache

One of the primary benefits to consuming wine in moderation is often referred to as the "French Paradox"—an observation that although the French indulge in foods rich in saturated fats, their incidence of heart disease is much lower than in America. Many, including the writer, believe this is because of the moderate wine consumption, particularly red wine, in a large percentage of the French population.

Some studies show that just one or two alcoholic beverages per day of any type can be beneficial. However, more and more studies suggest that red wine is the very best. This is probably due to the antioxidants, some of which, like resveratrol, appear to be present in high enough quantities in red wine only to be beneficial!

Some other benefits:

1. It is a civilized and enjoyable way to spend time—particularly on a summer vacation—sitting on a terrace oceanside, having Champagne or white wine with hors d'oeuvres.

2. It can provide great pleasure using all the senses, unlike the opera, theater or symphony: sight, smell, touch, taste and even sound in clinking wineglasses.

3. For oenophiles, it is never boring because each vintage is distinctive, and every wine differs at least slightly from all other wines. In addition, the multifarious soils, climates and microclimates produce innumerable nuances to experience in wine.

4. Each vineyard manager and winemaker—often the same person— does something to inject an individuality, personality and philosophy into each wine.

5. Wine, stamps, coins and antiques may rise in value if purchased well and held for some period. However—think about this—wine is one of the only collectibles that if chosen well and stored properly, actually becomes "better" as it gains value.

TRAVELING WINEMAKERS

It happens now more than ever. Winemakers and winery owners from the world over are visiting major markets, hosting tastings and/or meals with their local representatives, the wine media and the public. Within a short period, each of the following came to Houston, saw, tasted and conquered—"veni, vidi, gustati, vici?": Michael Martini of Louis M. Martini; John Clews of Clos du Val; Michael De Loach of Hook and Ladder; Kent Rosenblum of Rosenblum (all from California); Howard Rossbach of Firesteed (Oregon); Maria Martinez-Sierra of Bodega Montecillo (Spain); Robert Eymael of Monchof (Germany); and two Frenchmen, Laurent Drouhin of Joseph Drouhin and Bertrand Denoune of Lucien Albrecht, from Burgundy and Alsace, respectively. I've tasted wine with each one, and let me tell you, this is very hard work!

Following is a sampling of traveling winemakers I've encountered, and from whom I've acquired not only some wine wisdom, but occasionally an esoteric fact.

Michael Martini informed me that his dad was a graduate of U.C. Berkeley's 1941 class. At a reunion in the late 1960s or early 1970s, he, Charles Crawford of Gallo, Myron Nightengail (then of Cresta Blanca), Zeb Halprin of Christian Brothers and another classmate who represented wineries in the vast San Joaquin Valley computed the number of cases of wine that they or their companies produced: 85 percent of all the wines made in California!

Howard Rossbach in Oregon started in the 1990s with a virtual winery—no vineyards and no winery. He just knew what kind of grapes to contract for and had them made at another winery for years. Today, Firesteed is the third-largest producer by volume in Oregon and, yes, Rossbach now has his own winery.

John Clews, a native of Rhodesia, was an accountant in London in the 1970s, but his passion for wine led him to U.C. Davis where he was awarded the prestigious M.A. Amerine Research Scholarship. He worked at three California wineries prior to joining Clos du Val in 1999. Since then, the wines there have improved vastly, my favorite being the Pinot Noir.

Michael DeLoach grew up at the DeLoach Winery but after college entered the film industry. He primarily filmed commercials. One day he thought, "Someday maybe I'll be able to retire and start a winery." Then it hit him, "We already have a winery!" So, he eased back into the family business just at the point when his father really needed his help. After DeLoach sold its brand and some of its wineries to BOISSET America, the DeLoaches started their new winery, Hook and Ladder (in honor of founder Cecil DeLoach's firefighting career), enjoying instant success.

Kent Rosenblum is a trained veterinarian. Although he produces many different wines, his title is "The King of Zin." In three consecutive vintages alone, 25 of his wines scored 90 or above in *Wine Spectator*. After moving from Minnesota to California in 1970, Kent began making wine at home. From his adoption of cold fermentation practices in 1973 to his trips to the winegrowing regions of France, Italy and Germany in 1974, he constantly expanded his skills. In 1978, along with a small group of friends, he started Rosenblum Cellars. His success, among other things, has been in contracting with top growers from various California appellations. I'd call it a well-diversified portfolio of vineyards!

As an aside, I recently dined with Joel Peterson, owner of Ravenswood Winery and the "Godfather" of Zinfandel. Apparently he and Kent Rosenblum are buddies—The King and The Godfather!

Maria Martinez-Sierra is an amazing woman. In a country of male-dominated winemakers, she has been at the helm of Bodega Montecillo for 30 years! Her title is "The Queen of Rioja." Although Martinez-Sierra produces three levels of wine: crianza, reserva and gran reserva (the latter only in great years), she produces none of the above if the vintage is not good enough. In 1999, for example, she didn't even produce a crianza.

My dinner with Bertrand Denoune of Lucien Albrecht in Alsace was special. When he arrived, just for fun I wore my blue ribbon with a small wooden wine cask—the second degree of the Confrerie St.-Etienne d'Alsace. He grinned and said he never thought he would see a member of the Confrerie in Houston, since there are only two chapters in the U.S.

Chapter 18
SHERRY AND OTHER
FORTIFIED WINES

Sherry seems to have lost much of its luster in this country. That was my sentiment until March 2006, when I attended an Osborne Sherry tasting and dinner at Rioja Restaurant in Houston to a packed house.

Sherry is a wine that is produced in Spain's southern Andalusia, the most famous town being Jerez de la Frontera. Palomino grapes once made up around 70 percent of plantings in Sherry, but now comprise closer to 90 percent, with the balance in Moscatel and Pedro Ximinez (PX).

The last article I read about Sherry was so complicated that I remembered virtually nothing of importance when I was finished. The description of soils such as albarizza and barro, containing up to 80 percent chalk with sand and clay on the one hand, and about 30 percent chalk mixed with iron oxide on the other, is mostly useful knowledge for taking a Master Sommelier or Master of Wine exam.

So let's tackle the fundamentals. The basic types of Sherries are: fino and amontillado, manzanillos from Sanlucar; olorosos and dessert.

The first step in making Sherry is to decide whether it will become a fino or an oloroso. It was once assumed that the road a barrel of juice would take could not be predicted, but this is no longer the case. There are different avenues of approach that will determine the course.

First, wines from certain areas and the use of free-run juice are now known to produce the best finos. Procedures for handling the juice in the winery also determine the outcome. For example, after fermentation, the wine is bland and contains around 12 percent alcohol. Wines destined to be finos are fortified with a spirit similar to brandy to no more than 15.5 percent alcohol. With finos, natural yeast forms a thin coat on the surface of the wine called flor. If higher alcohol is attained, the development of flor will be inhibited and presto—no more fino.

A fino is a very light-colored wine that is generally bone dry and delicate, with a tart, rather oxidized taste that in some instances must be "acquired." It should be chilled and is best when very young, but will keep in the fridge for several days after opening. Salty almonds and olives, plain or marinated in garlic, are the perfect pairing; however, a fino can be an appetite-enhancing aperitif by itself.

Finos that lose the covering of flor become amontillados. This can occur naturally or through killing off the flor by fortifying to over 16 percent alcohol. Compared to a fino, an amontillado is deeper in color with a more profound aroma and complex taste. It is a perfect match with shrimp sautéed in olive oil, salt, spicy pepper and garlic. While finos have an average age of three or four years, the best amontillados age for several years more.

A fino called manzanilla comes from the district of Sanlucar. It is the lightest in body and the palest in color of all the finos. Its saltier taste makes it a better match with seafood than a regular fino. A manzanilla can also become an amontillado.

Olorosos are Sherries that do not (or are not allowed to) develop flor and are fortified to between 18 percent and 24 percent alcohol. They have a darker color and more bouquet and body than finos. Olorosos can be dry, medium-sweet and sweet. If you spot a Sherry called palo cortado, this is a special type of oloroso that typically is very dry and complex. Olorosos usually present flavors of nutty almond, walnut and even smoke, along with discernible oak flavors from barrel aging. This wine can be enjoyed by itself, with nuts and olives, or even with an entrée, especially a dish cooked in olive oil, pepper, onions and garlic.

Sweet Sherries are usually labeled abocado (medium-sweet), amoroso, pale cream or cream. These olorosos are sweetened and can be served as dessert, with dessert, alone or with cigars after the meal. One of the best sweet Sherries is made from the PX grape.

In addition to Osborne, Lustau, Gonzales Byass and Pedro Domecq are the Sherries I most often enjoy.

Now we will delve into other praise-worthy fortified dessert wines that span the globe.

AUSTRALIAN LIQUEUR MUSCAT

When I returned from Australia in 1980, I had a small dinner party for Michael Broadbent, then chairman of Christie's Wine Department. At the end of the meal, I thought I would really throw him off by serving "blind" a Morris "Show" Muscat I had brought back with me. He took one sniff, looked up at me and said, "Northeastern Victoria Muscat."

The Muscat was, in fact, Muscat Blanc à Petits Grains, found in northeast Victoria, Australia. It is fortified like Port and normally scores over 90 for a half-bottle that costs around $16. The ultimate accompanying dessert is pecan pie. The wine actually exudes a pecan pie nose! I recommend adding a tablespoon of hot, melted butter over a warm pie slice before serving. My favorite Australian Muscats are Brown Brothers, Morris, and Chambers.

MÁLAGA

The town of Málaga is east of Cadiz, Jerez, in southern Spain. The principal grapes are Pedro Ximénez and Muscat of Alexandria. Málaga never fully recovered from the phylloxera epidemic. The small industry that is left produces a fortified wine in the Port method, unlike in the old days when the grapes were first laid out to dry. There are different types of Málaga, from dry to sweet, but other than for their local market, there is not much interest today.

MARSALA

Although better known than Málaga, this product of western Sicily in Italy has also become moribund. From large quantities exported in the late 18th and 19th centuries, production, especially of the best versions (Superiore and Vergine), has slowed to a trickle. If you're searching for a dessert wine like Port, avoid the "seco" and go for the "sweet" (more than 10 percent residual sugar). Some semiseccos are sweet enough to be classified as a dessert wine, but you'll have to guess which ones (they're allowed to be 4 percent to 10 percent).

ROUISSILLON

Located in southeast France, Rouissillon boasts four fortified dessert wines:

Muscat de Rivesalts—Largest Muscat area in France, using both Muscat of Alexandria and Muscat Blanc à Petit Grains.

Rivesalts—Wide variety of reds and whites with Grenache Noir, Grenache Blanc, Grenache Gris, Maccabeu, etc. The best are from Domaine Gauby and Domaine Cazes.

Maury—Both red and white, similar to Rivesalts, except 75 percent Grenach Noir necessary for the red. Mas Amiel is the best producer.

Banyuls—My favorite of the four. Some swear this is the best wine with chocolate. Banyuls is only red and is at least 50 percent Grenache Noir for the regular and 75 percent for the Banyuls Grand Cru. Top producers are Mas Blanc and Chapoutier.

COMMANDARIA

Cyprus boasts of having the possibly oldest, continuously produced wine in the world, Commandaria (or Commandaria St. John), with roots dating back to wines made from sun-dried grapes (which fits this wine) and mentioned by the Greek poet Hesiod. It is made from Mavro (red) and Xymisteri (white) grapes. After a week or so of drying in the sun, the grapes are crushed, fermented and fortified to around 20 percent alcohol.

MORE WINE AND FOOD PAIRING WISDOM

What can be more frustrating and uneconomical to a wine and food enthusiast—besides a "corked" wine that smells like moldy cardboard—than sitting down at a restaurant and choosing a wine that doesn't complement the food?

The wine/food match—or mismatch—that provoked this article is one mentioned by a famous pairing expert as one of his favorites: a 15- to 20-year-old Premier Cru Burgundy with prime rib. Don't get me wrong—nobody can argue that this isn't a great match for him. For example, I love peanut butter on Nilla Wafers with vintage Port, and nobody can tell me I don't!

However—and this is what makes wine the versatile, complex, intriguing subject that it is—to me, a 15- to 20-year-old Premier Cru Burgundy with prime rib is almost akin to a Beaujolais or Dolcetto with beef tenderloin. Now a Cote Rotie or Hermitage with prime rib is the perfect match in my book. Who's right? He's right for him and I'm right for me. Trial and error—hopefully before you order that $50 bottle—is the only way you'll know for sure.

Another controversial dish is lamb, which many enjoy with Pinot Noir. The perfect match for me, especially rack of lamb, is Cabernet Sauvignon or Syrah. But that's my conclusion. When I was at SIMI once having lunch with SIMI's chef, Mary Evely, she stated emphatically that Pinot Noir is overwhelmed by lamb.

In the past, I've written about some of my favorite food/wine pairings such as goat cheese with Sauvignon Blanc, plain Danish havarti with Chardonnay, grilled salmon with new world Pinot Noir, Italian food with olive oil and tomato sauce with Chianti Classico, and crème brulee with tawny Port.

Following are some other pairings to try:

WHITE WINE
Pork—Dry Riesling. Pork with fruit sauce—semisweet Riesling

Ham and corn casserole—Gewurztraminer with 1 percent to 2 percent residual sugar

Vegetable plate—Gruner Veltliner (Austria) or Semillon (Australia)

Chicken Curry—slightly sweet Riesling

Shrimp in white cream sauce—Chablis or Albariño

Light fish in butter/lemon sauce—Pinot Gris

RED WINE

Pizza with Italian sausage and extra tomato sauce--Zinfandel

Pasta with veggies (mushrooms included)—Pinot Noir

Halibut or rare tuna—Cabernet Sauvignon

Chicken in pesto sauce—Merlot

Barbecued beef—Southern Rhone

Braised beef—Barbera d'Asti or d'Alba

DESSERT WINE

Southern pecan pie—Australian Muscat, such as Chambers or R.L. Buller.

For my favorite wine and food pairing app, visit *www.nataliemaclean .com/mobileapp.*

THE TWILIGHT OF A WINE'S LIFE

There is nothing worse than purchasing a wine and letting it languish in the cellar until it's no good.

A high-quality California Cabernet from an excellent vintage will improve in a proper wine cellar for up to 12 years or more from the vintage date. The better Cabernets from the outstanding vintage of 2001 are mostly at peak; however, some of the 1997s from an equally excellent vintage are not showing so well. With a number of exceptions, significant aging after the 12th to 14th years can be cause for concern.

To optimally enjoy the aging of a nice California Cabernet, purchase a case from a top vintage like 2008 and then try a bottle each year starting about 2012. Sometimes I start out with the intention of doing just this, only to find a few months later that all 12 bottles have disappeared—discipline being my problem. Early over-consumption will not be an issue with the top Bordeaux because of the wine's occasional surfeit of tannin in its youth, not to mention the higher acidity. Sometimes this wine is no fun to drink for up to seven or eight years.

Back to the California Cabs. Let's say the 2008 Napa Cab is already drinking well on the first tasting in 2012. You then notice the wine improving every year as the tannins resolve and the wine develops lovely complexities and nuances. Then, in 2016 or 2018, the wine either tastes almost exactly like the one from a year earlier—which would indicate that it may have peaked—or the wine has improved yet again to the point that it's about perfect. In either case, this is a wine to begin trying every month or so, and if it appears you are right, have a party and drink some of it up.

This plan certainly will prevent a negative experience such as the following. Around 1978, I acquired two bottles of Sebastiani Cabernet Sauvignon Proprietor's Reserve from the outstanding 1968 vintage. I tried one and it was perfect, especially for a very inexpensive wine. I opened the other one about one year later and it was completely sapped! I've never known a wine to go to pot that quickly. Had I bought the wine in 1972 and tried a bottle every year, I would have known by 1974 or so that there was no need for further aging.

I've never encountered a great Bordeaux from a top year that has crashed like this. The plateau for an exceptional Bordeaux from an excellent vintage might be reached in 20 years and remain there, more or less intact, for another 10 or 15 if stored properly. It may then slowly sink into oblivion over a period of another 10 years or so.

Having said that, the single greatest dinner I ever attended highlighted the awesome 1945s from large bottles at 50 years of age. To view the unbelievable list of wines, see Dinner of the Century—the last article of the book. And although I've enjoyed Bordeaux wines that were 25, 50, 75 and even over 100 years old, over the last 10 years or so, I have been disappointed in many of the "old timers." Intact wines from the 1920s, 1940s 1950s and 1960s—there wasn't much worth drinking in the 1930s except for the occasional '34 and '37—are becoming harder to find. Provenance is key here, that is, knowing how the wines have been stored.

A person who has been storing a 1961 Chateau Latour—a $2,000+ wine if stored properly—for 20 or 30 years at room temperature at home will be very disappointed upon opening said bottle. Many a friend has been given a great bottle (particularly my doctor friends) that has languished in a home awaiting a proper time for opening. One problem is that "room temperature" isn't usually constant. Our home, for example, fluctuates between 68 degrees and 73 degrees, and when we're out of town, it may reach 75 or higher. A few years of that may not be a problem, but 10 years, or even five years, at these temperatures will have a deleterious effect on the wine.

A study I once read showed that wine ages exactly twice as fast at a constant 70 degrees as it does at a constant 52 degrees. This may be true for several years, but after that, the wine at 52 degrees, if a great red from a great year, will hardly age at all for a number of years, while the one at 70 degrees will begin to deteriorate at a much more rapid pace.

So drink your wines too early rather than too late. Even better, plan ahead, test occasionally and catch as many as possible at their best!

ASIA'S WINE SCENE. IT'S THE WILD WEST IN THE EAST

Chapter 19

by Debra Meiburg,

Master of Wine, chairman of Meiburg Wine Media Ltd.

www.debramasterofwine.com

A longtime resident of Hong Kong, Debra Meiburg is a celebrated wine journalist, TV personality, wine educator and speaker. A widely respected wine judge, she recently founded and is director of the largest pan-Asian wine competition, the Hong Kong International Wine & Spirit Competition.

Debra is Chairman of Meiburg Wine Media Ltd, a multimedia wine edutainment platform that encompasses weekly print media commitments, an online video interview series *Meet-the-Winemaker*, branded media outlets, *Grape Cues* wine tips in-journey for China's metro-taxis, and a suite of chic DebraMasterofWine branded wine educational products. Debra is also producer and presenter for *Taste the Wine*, an entertaining and lively wine television show on Cathay Pacific Airways. Debra also launched the first ever *Guide to the Hong Kong Wine Trade*, a resource for trade professionals.

Not a week goes by without Asia grabbing attention for its record-breaking wine auction prices. It's the home of fine wine, deep pockets and big cellars.

Asian markets are exciting, if not a touch overheated. It has been said that if the population of China walked past you single file, the line would never end because of reproduction. The line of international winemakers hoping to enter this market seems equally as long.

There are hundreds of new Hong Kong importers as a result of the recent elimination of wine duty. Hong Kong leadership is determined to position Hong Kong as the wine hub of Asia. It is the only major wine-trading metropolis in the world to have taken such a bold step. The region's wine activity—which has always been robust—has been propelled into hyper speed. I have records of some 350 importers actively trading this year.

Wine producers who are keenly interested in exporting to Asia might consider sharing a booth at the Hong Kong International Wine Fair in November. In its fourth year— and already Asia's largest wine exhibition—the event attracts imports from around the globe.

Throughout Asia, red wine is seen regarded as healthy, lucky, auspicious and appropriately expensive.

More than any other culture—excluding, perhaps, the French—the Chinese avow they "live to eat." A common Chinese greeting is *ni chi le mei you*—have you eaten yet? Due to China's vast size and ancient reverence for food, opinions differ as to how many distinctive regional cuisines exist. The most simplistic subdivision suggests salty cuisine in the north, sweet in the south, sour in the east and spicy in the west.

Hong Kong's wine market is uniquely dominated by restaurant activity (there are some 8,000 dining venues). Accordingly, Hong Kong restaurants drive the majority of wine sales. Most Hong Kong Chinese do not entertain or drink wine in the home. In all of Asia, wine is a celebration beverage, to be given as a gift or consumed with clients, family and friends on occasions where it is important for the host to show one's respect to others. Wine is typically consumed in groups of 10 or more (Chinese dining style). Many women will not drink wine, as blushing cheeks are considered unsightly; however, a new mini-trend is for female consumers is to drink one glass of wine before bedtime to improve one's skin and health. I would add that it's probably good for the marriage as well!

While the growth rate of Chinese wine consumption is astounding, most of these successes have been in China's "first tier" or metro-cities: Shanghai, Beijing and Guangzhou. Shanghai's astounding economic development makes it the wealthiest city in the mainland and a core market for the wine trade. Due to a longtime affiliation with European culture, Shanghai was quick to accept wine as an important part of the dining experience. The Shanghainese pay more attention to wine value and quality than consumers in other provinces of China.

Meanwhile, as one of my friends put it, "Beijing people are living at the foot of the emperor's palace." Far less influenced by foreign culture, they drink more white liquor or beer. Wine taste in Beijing is strictly Francophile, and unless professionals intimately introduce Australian or South African wines, few Beijing people venture outside a Bordeaux list. The interesting markets to explore are the so-called "second tier" cities, such as the relatively unknown Chongqing, which has a piddling population of 31.4 million.

In Asia's wine retail market, 70 percent to 80 percent of sales are driven by the gift-giving tradition. Most wine purchases take place prior to the Mid-Autumn Festival in September or October and the Lunar New Year holidays in January or February. Retail shelves are dominated by pre-packaged wine boxes in bright red, gold, or pink—all considered auspicious colors in Chinese culture. Also unique to China is the practice of buying boxed wines as gifts for the elderly. The gesture is made to extend a wish of good health.

Asia is not a winemaker's utopia, but as Asian consumers explore new tasting experiences, the region could become the most important market to any wine-producing country's future in wine exports.

NARRATIVES OF MOMENTOUS WINE
TASTINGS/DINNERS

I have been very fortunate to find myself involved in some of the most significant wine tastings/dinners ever held. One was the 1994 tasting of 59 of the top 1959 wines from the cellar of Chicago collector and philanthropist Stephen Kaplan. The tasting took place over two days with consummate dinners at the Four Seasons and Intercontinental Hotels, prepared by Charlie Trotter and other heralded chefs. Other tastings included such superstars as Lafite-Rothschild wines, and still others consisted of verticals and horizontals of the unrivaled Burgundies from the greatest vintages of the Domaine de la Romanée-Conti.

Putting the WOW factor aside, I have taken a practical aspect to presenting these wines, hoping that a number of you will emulate, in some ways, the preservation and appreciation of great wines. For example, the next time a vintage of, say, California Cabernets is universally recognized as being great, round up 10 of the best ones and hold them until they are 10 years old. Then, in 2022, you can auction off a tasting of the best 2012 (assuming that's a great year) California Cabernets with the proviso that you would attend and maybe even discuss the wines. It doesn't have to be a behemoth tasting, such as the 1974 tasting in Honolulu described later in this chapter.

Another approach is to purchase three bottles of a nice current vintage Champagne, three bottles of a great current vintage of a major white Burgundy, and three bottles of a great current vintage of red Burgundy or Bordeaux and three half bottles of Chateau d'Yquem. Wait five or 10 years, and coupled with a caterer who wants some publicity, auction off a dinner for 10 (for best results, at the beautiful home of a well-known member of the charity you're supporting...of course, you have to be in attendance). You will be serving wines that may have appreciated three or four times the original purchase price.

Regardless if it's a charitable event, you will simply find it fun to host a tasting in 10 or 20 years of valuable wines that might be impossible to find, possibly out of your price range and probably vastly improved with age!

FIFTY 1961 CLARETS

1961 is one of the vintages of the 20th century for Bordeaux, along with 1900, 1929, 1945, 1947 (Pomerol and Saint-Emilion only) 1959 and 1982. On the 21st and 22nd of February in 1981, 20 wine connoisseurs gathered for a tasting of the 20th year of maturation from 50 bottles of 1961 clarets.

The host, the late Dr. Lou Skinner of Coral Gables, Fla., possessed one of the most complete collections of 1961 clarets in the world. I had discussed such a tasting with Lou on no less than 10 occasions, beginning in 1975 in Coral Gables, continuing in 1977 in Bordeaux and Paris, and ultimately in Australia and New Zealand at the Triennial Convention of the International Wine and Food Society in 1980.

Lou wisely arranged this most fascinating degustation to take place on a date that coincided with Michael Broadbent's vacation schedule. Michael, then chairman of Christie's Wine Department in London, conducted the tasting.

At 11 a.m. at the David Williams Hotel, the first 17 wines were served. Michael announced that we would start with the looser knit wines of Saint-Emilion, work toward the firmer Pomerols and complete this first sitting with the earthy Graves with "tobacco on the nose and hot pebble taste."

The following descriptions are taken from the notes of yours truly and those of several others. In addition, Michael's comments will be referenced throughout. At the time of the tasting, a scale of 20 was used for scoring.

SAINT-EMILION

Pavie: Medium-brick red with light-brown rim. Slightly musty and alcoholic on the nose with only medium fruit. Taste is almost stemmy. Possibly past its prime. 14

Belair: A bit deeper. Almost red-black color with orange hue. Distinguished, but a little dryish. Still very tannic. One taster thought it had "lots of fruit in the middle and a really good future." 16

Clos Fortet: Deep red-black, no browning at the rim. Classic, mature claret nose, vitiated somewhat by high acidity. Definite hint of bell peppers. At this point, bottle variation becomes apparent. Two bottles of each wine are served. The late wine writer Alexis Bespaloff suggests each be poured in alternate glasses so that if one is bad, the neighbor could share the good one. Michael thinks this wine is the worst of the day. 12

La Gaffelière: Same deep color as the Clos Fortet, but brighter and more depth of hue. Very slight browning on the rim. Fruity flavors with excellent balance and good tannin for an excellent future. Michael refers to this as "high-toned style" because of the hint of volatile acidity, which downgrades the wine. 17.5

Magdelaine: Bottle variation apparent again. The first is lighter in color and the tannin is inharmonious with the rest of the wine. The second is darker in color, full flavored and quite well balanced. Good fruit but somewhat faded richness. Michael sees some little beads on the rim (possibly the first bottle) and suggests the wine is breaking up. 15.5

Figeac: Deep red and really closed up when first poured. Restrained, fruity bouquet develops in 10 minutes or so of swirling. Very young with lots of tannin. New York importer Julius Wile says his wine can't be improved on, but the second bottle is considerably lighter. 17.5

Cheval-Blanc: "Ripeness and plumpness" is the description of one taster. Really spicy with a roasted quality. Beautifully knit, very elegant. Not as big as expected. Michael says all the components are there, but it certainly won't develop like the '47. 18

POMEROL

Clos l'Eglise: Excellent, deep, almost black color with brown-orange edge. Rich nose with sweet, velvety taste. John Avery from England and several others think it is charming also, and John says that we tend to take the first wine in a series not seriously enough. Michael describes it as "Cabernet-Franc style on the nose but fleeting." 15.5

L'Evangile: Possible bottle variation. Similar outstanding color with deep, firm, plummy nose. Michael says this is the first wine in which we notice different texture, silkiness and sweetness on entry, which great Pomerols have. 17.25

Vieux-Chateau-Certan: Lighter in color than the above two, but very distinguished nose, although somewhat closed. Excellent fruit in a somewhat lighter style. Balanced with excellent tannin for future consumption. Michael had little say about it. 16.5

Gazin: Brick, red-brown with browning edge. This wine evoked the most disagreement on a wine so far, with Michael and Dr. Marvin Overton from Fort Worth, Texas, the leading advocates. Michael expresses that the wine has a "real punch and may be great in 15 years." Leaner style with refined, fruity nose. Again, some bottle variation. Best of the two bottles. **16.**

Trotanoy: Deep red-black color with somewhat closed, firm, fruity nose with truffles and pepper. Still young – rich and velvety. In January 1979, I tasted this at La Caravelle in New York and scored it 18 with the prediction that it would be at its best around 1983. If that is true, it should have a long plateau after that. Gaining on its prime. Wile finds a "great sweetness in taste." **18.5**

Pétrus: First really deep, almost black color. Huge, overwhelming, freshly roasted prime sirloin strip nose. About as good as a wine can ever be in the big style. Perfect harmony of all components. Man o' War! Michael describes it as opulent and says it may be as fine as the '47. Julius Wile adds that it will get much better. Around $300 a bottle at that time. **20**

GRAVES

Domaine de Chevalier: Very fine, medium body, classy "wax" flavor. Bouquet slightly closed with a hint of pepperiness. Michael says we change gears now to the "hot pebbles" taste of Graves. Julius Wile finds a "hayfield" bouquet that suggests young vines. **16.75**

Pape Clément: Medium, brown-brick red on color with a hint of tobacco on the nose. Almost searching for a fault with these Graves – all four of which show very well – the wine seems a little over-fruity, over-plummy, or possibly lacking the balancing acidity of the others. Michael, elegant and consistent himself, briefly describes Pape Clément as elegant and consistent. **16.5**

La Mission-Haut-Brion: Deepest hue of color of the Graves with ruby edge. No hint of 20 year age. Fresh, clean, sand-gravelly nose, even though still somewhat closed. **18**

Haut-Brion: Apparent bottle variation here. I had pepper and spiciness on the nose, but it just has not come together like the La Mission. At first, thoughts prevail that it doesn't show as well by virtue of following the La Mission. Still excellent. **17.75.** The second bottle is a great wine at its peak, but should hold. Beautiful and complete. Although biased by the first bottle, I scored the second higher. Michael comments that as opposed to the immensely impressive, concentrated, rough-textured La Mission, the Haut-Brion is elegant, and one of the most consistent of all wines since 1945. He adds it has perfect weight in the mouth and is "pretty close to the Pétrus." **18.5**

In the review period, which follows each sitting, Michael recites that it is almost impossible to pronounce upon wines such as these on first impression, regarding the complexity, length and development. One sign of a great wine, he adds, is how it develops in the glass after 10, 20, 30 minutes.

Looking back at the noses, Michael advances that the Figeac did very well and the Cheval-Blanc achieved a marvelous fragrance; Julius Wile singles out the Belair for its positive development in the glass.

Wine writer Terry Robards doesn't believe the majority of the Saint-Emilions are ready to drink. Michael adds that he expected them to be plumper and less dried out.

British retailer John Avery declares the Magdelaine to be "lovely... possibly people tend to condemn a '61 that is totally ready now."

The second sitting begins at 4 p.m., giving us one hour and 20 minutes to taste 17 wines and 40 minutes to engage in further examination, review and discussion.

The wines are poured two and three minutes apart with slightly longer pauses between areas. Michael is the general of this fabulous maneuver through Bordeaux. Everyone follows his lead, except for Alexis Bespaloff, who apparently is tasting the wines blind.

Michael decided earlier that if the wines were tasted blind, participants would spend an inordinate amount of time guessing the wines' provenance rather than analyzing and appreciating. Michael explains that we start with the Saint-Juliens—most fairly close to each other geographically with consistent style and weight—"the fulcrum against which one compares all the rest of the Médoc." We complete the day with Margaux.

SAINT-JULIEN

Lagrange: Deep brick-red color with browning edge. Fairly well-balanced wine with tannin seemingly predominant. Didn't seem to develop in the glass, except in the negative. Michael thought more of the wine and predicted it should develop well. 14

Brainaire-Ducru: This wine and Beychevelle are the lightest in color of the first five (served together in one tranche). Very little browning at the rim. Very good, fruity nose and sweet entry. Well balanced, quite enjoyable. Michael refers to Brainaire as less known and probably the most high toned of the Saint Juliens. **15.5**

Langoa-Barton: Excellent, deep black-red color, but a bit off in the nose at first. Depth and character are evident. Excellent development in the glass. Very promising future. Michael says this is the "first wine of the sitting with classic sweetness and gentleness on the nose…well made, pure." Possible bottle variation. **16.5**

Saint-Pierre Bontemps: Medium-dark color with good floral bouquet. Balanced components. Medium weight and texture. Michael suggests this wine is unfairly underrated and is "crisp, fruit bush character on the nose…peppery…a little bite." **16**

Beychevelle: More to offer than medium-light color and slightly singed or even seaweed nose indicates. Expecting more. **15.5**

Gruaud-Larose: Bright, medium-dark color with only a tiny bouquet of flowers at first, but coming on a bit. Well balanced with good concentration and harmony of flavors. Lacks finesse and complexity. **16**

Léoville-Poyferre: Similar in color to the Gruaud with discernible browning at the rim. Very good sweetness and weight; excellent overall impression. **17**

Léoville-Barton: Slightly deeper red than the two above with embryonic stage of orange in the rim. Outstandingly fruity nose. Vinous and very fine. Best of these first eight. Elegant flavor, almost perfect balance. Michael says, "harmonious, four square." **18**

Léoville-Las-Cases: Very deep red-black color with almost no browning. More closed than the Barton. Cedary, big bodied, rich and tannic. **18.25**

Ducru-Beaucaillou: Similar in color to Las-Cases but deeper hue and a trace more of browning. Sweeter on entry. Most immediately seductive of the Saint-Juliens. Possibly less future than Barton and Las-Cases, but charming now. Michael describes as "gentlemanly firm body. Meatier and chunkier than the rest." **18.5**

MARGAUX

Cantemerle: Deep brick-red color with orange rim. Michael puts it in a "class of its own…delicacy, charm, lack of aggressiveness…great gradation of color…gingery." **16.5**

Rausan-Ségla: About the same color as Cantemerle with more red in the rim. Slight technical problem in the nose defies description; otherwise very good all the way through. Probable bottle variation. Michael says it's a bit manufactured or stewed. **16.5**

Giscours: Lighter than the Rausan with orange-brown edge. Fragrant with slightly burnt flavor. Michael finds nice acidity but a touch of rawness–possibly from new vines. **15.5**

Malescot-Saint-Exupéry: Same excellent, bright color as the Cantemerle. Sweetness on entry. Well-made, harmonious wine. Michael finds it flavorful but austere without much finesse. **16.5**

Brane-Cantenac (magnum): Light color with orange on the rim. Dishwater nose at first, but develops agreeably enough. Somewhat oxidized–surprising for a magnum–several find it "tired." Terry Robards describes Brane-Cantenac usually as either very good or very mediocre. Weak for a second growth. **13.5**

Palmer: Deep dark-black color with tinge of brown at the rim. Nose immediately reminiscent of the '61 Pétrus. Like the Pétrus, perfect all the way through. Superb sweetness from perfect ripe berries. Huge, rich, exciting wine. Michael agrees it is almost in the Pétrus class and states it will be a "delicious and velvety mouthful for years." **20**

Margaux: Not as overpowering as Palmer, but unbelievably seductive at first sight, sniff and taste. Deep red-black color with very refined nose of restrained elegance. As good in middle taste with less powerful, but arguably more pleasing aftertaste. Michael describes it as firm, gentle, delicate, finesse. **20**

In the review period, Michael says there is some danger that the '61 Saint-Juliens may dry out and not make it, i.e., Lagrange. But he feels the '61s will overtake the '45s.

David Milligan of Joseph Seagram & Sons, New York, finds the Margaux wines much more advanced at this stage than the Saint-Juliens.

I found it impossible to fault the Palmer and Margaux. Tom Whelehan of Dublin, an enthusiastic lover of wine and lover of life, later told me that he really preferred the Margaux to the Palmer. Of the perfect 1961 Chateau Margaux, Whelehan said, "When I want to be overwhelmed, I drink a Romanée-Conti or other great Burgundy. With great Bordeaux, I want to be beguiled and intrigued."

Saturday evening found all who had retained their bearings at the Bath Club in Miami Beach at a black-tie dinner hosted by Lou and his fellow members of the local International Wine and Food Society chapter. All the wines except the first and last were provided by an extremely generous member, Jim Redford.

The wines with brief comments:

Perrier-Joet Flower Bottle '75: Excellent, much better than the '73.

Corton-Charlemagne, J. Drouhin '73: Excellent, although I would have interchanged this and the fourth wine.

Bual, Solera 1878, I.E.C.: This Bual, from the International Exhibition Cooperative Wine Society, was excellent. More like something between a Bual and a Verdelho.

Clos de Mouches, J. Drouhin '78: This wine placed No. 2 in a "Chardonnay Shootout" of more than 100 Chardonnays from around the world. Very good now. Needs around three years of age.

Echezeaux, J. Drouhin '72: Very good.

Charmes-Chambertin, J. Drouhin '72: Good. Lighter style, more like a '73. These two served with lamb; the next two with cheese.

Cote Rotie, J. Vidal-Fleurey '61: Very good, beautiful at late middle age.

Hermitage, J. Vidal-Fleurey 1962: Excellent–rich, chewy, opulent. If these are indicative of age on great Rhones, one should relish the idea of tasting the great '78s in 1998.

Chateau Climens 1970: Very good.

Up at 8:30 a.m. for a jog to clear the acid, tannin, alcohol and residual sugar from the brain and body, I prepared for the finale with an infrequently staged breakfast of bacon and eggs.

Michael begins immediately at 11 a.m. describing the hardness of the fruit in the Saint-Estèphe wines. This is peculiar since all are very close to Lafite, with the possible exception of Phelan-Segur, whose whereabouts, Michael, only to show that he too is human, has forgotten.

SAINT-ESTÈPHE

Phelan-Segur: The only Cru Bourgeois of the tasting–in retrospect, Gloria would have been a good substitute for the Lagrange–this wine shows ample, medium brick-red color with an orange-brown rim. Michael's comments suggest praise for a Bourgeois. "Reasonable depth of color, nice open style, but near the sea, slightly cheesy, medicinal character. Will develop." 14.5

Lafon-Rochet: About the same color as the Phelan with hints of tobacco and leather in a very good, but slightly closed bouquet. Good depth. Almost an extra point for development in the glass. 16

Calon-Ségur: Deepest color and biggest of the first three. Possibly one of those that will never come around. Lack of fruit, somewhat disappointing. Michael cites Calon as a Chateau that has been fading in recent years. 14.75

Cos d' Estournel: Good, medium-dark brick-red color. Restrained but elegant nose with layers of flavor discovered only with some work. By far the best of these in middle body, aftertaste and future. Michael describes as having "depth of fruit on the nose, ripeness at entry–has charm. You can throw a stone from Cos to Lafite." 17

Montrose: In retrospect, should have preceded the other wines, or at least the Cos. Darkest color of these five, but unbalanced with almost no fruit showing in the nose, but hints of underlying flavor are apparent. Way too much tannin and lack of fruit presage little future. 14.5

PAUILLAC

Lynch-Bages: Cedary in the nose with some mintiness that really develops in the glass. Beautiful balance, breed, future. Michael reminds us that for the first time, the Cabernet flavor is more marked. 17.5

Batailly: Noticeably browner than the Lynch-Bages with an orange edge. Probably at its peak. Obvious bottle variation. Michael says, "style here open and plummy – consistent but a watery meniscus. Not great, but very good." 16

Haut-Batailly: Most depth of the first three, although a shade lighter in color. Charm and refinement on the nose. Elegant, almost in the outstanding category, but something holds it back. Michael finds it "absolutely exciting...intensity of color and fragrant...most attractive... distinct ripeness and sweetness coming into mouth...silky texture compared to Batailly." Probably at peak, but should hold. 16.75

Mouton-Baron-Phillipe (magnum): First wine with a big California Cabernet nose – not like Ridge, but B.V. Private Reserve. Fine, deep color. I describe it as medium style. Michael explains that this wine can be very ordinary in some years and relays a tale about a watery '73 tasted recently. Probably at peak. **17**

Grand-Puy-Lacoste: Similar in color to the above wine. Nose is off at first but develops well in the glass. Fruity, well-balanced wine with slight overabundance of tannin at the end. Probably has a good future. **15.5**

Pontet-Canet: Medium-dark red-black color with start of orange at the rim. Good, but closed nose. Full flavored in the mouth, but no outstanding qualities. Firm, fleshy. **16**

Pichon-Longueville-Baron: Dark brick-red with brown-orange edge. Rich, charming wine. Cedar and spice. Everything nice! Not so, says Michael, "the wine is pricked" (meaning volatile acidity to a fault). Nobody in the room has noticed. Dr. Nils Sternby of Malmo, Sweden, agrees with Michael and says, "I didn't see it at first, but now that you mention it, I believe you're right." John Avery agrees. To me, a flaw that is widely unnoticed is not enough to worry about currently. Michael's almost casual dismissal of the wine as "pricked" does give rise to some worry about its future. **18**

Pichon-Lalande: Slightly lighter in color than the above wine, but less signs of age on the rim. Closed up at first, it develops into a fabulous, seductive, intriguing claret with an excellent future. **18.5**

Mouton-Rothschild: Deep black-red color with only a slight hint of age. Big, rich, closed-in Cabernet nose. Excellent acidity and tannin. Michael describes as "pronounced gingery Cabernet nose...great depth of fruit and crispness." **19.25**

Latour: Outstanding, almost black color. Darkest of all. Huge, rich, complex and in complete harmony. Very young and of the finest quality imaginable. Chocolate, spice, tobacco, eucalyptus and mint on the nose, reminiscent of Heitz Martha's Vineyard 1968, but even more opulent. Michael adds, "great length." **20**

Lafite-Rothschild: At first look, closed up and probably going through a stage, or, just unfair when following Mouton and Latour. My first impression is 17. After 30 minutes in the glass, the wine undergoes a transformation similar to what occurred with a '59 Lafite from a magnum in March 1975–a beautiful flowering in the glass. After one hour in the glass, even better! Michael says, "This is all that Lafite should be

– very delicate. Lots of finesse. Old Latours are more reliable, but great old Lafites sometimes have more nuances. Color less intense, nose gentle, and slightly more cheesy and cedary than Mouton and Latour…Ivy leaf character and an iron character from the soil." **18.5**

To wrap up the event, each attendee introduced himself or herself. Dr. Sternby correctly asserted that almost all the wines were served in the proper order.

Terry Robards of *New York Times* fame proclaimed that this was a very unusual, important event in the history of wine. He thought the '61s lived up to their expectations with most not ready to drink, and added, "We were probably overly critical of many by comparison to the top ones."

I mentioned that probably nobody else in the world could have staged such a smooth and workable tasting of 50 1961 clarets as the extraordinary, talented and experienced Michael Broadbent. Everyone applauded Michael and we formally ended, naturally, with a toast to Lou Skinner. I toasted Lou with the Lafite. After an hour in the glass, the wine was still improving.

REVIEWS OF THE REVERED 1974 CALIFORNIA CABERNETS

The 1974 vintage was originally praised as a great year for California Cabernet Sauvignon. But subsequently, there was widespread doubt to the acclaim. Were some of the wines merely going through awkward stages?

Twelve wine aficionados gathered in 1988 at Honolulu's Halekulani Hotel to taste 53 California Cabernets from the '74 vintage in conjunction with the KHPR Public Radio Wine Classic Auction and Tasting, conducted the following day. Wine Classic director Archie McClaren and co-chairmen Dennis Foley and Walter Emery, all of San Francisco, were at the tasting. I contributed the wines to KHPR several months beforehand to give the bottles ample time to rest, and the results were explosive!

The attendees repeatedly commented that the wines tasted much younger and better than expected. The verdict now, judging by this tasting, is that the best of the vintage are stupendous wines. Seventeen of the 53 wines were truly exciting.

My two favorites were the Robert Mondavi Reserve and the Joseph Phelps Insignia. The Ridge Monte Bello and Diamond Creek Volcanic Hill tied for second, and the Heitz Martha's Vineyard was third. But this is splitting hairs. I feel more comfortable with a five-way tie for first place. A poll of the tasters placed the Insignia first; Ridge, second; Mondavi Reserve, third; and Diamond Creek and Heitz Martha's Vineyard tied for fourth.

My tasting notes follow, with ample borrowing from the notes of McClaren, Foley, Emery, and Honolulu attorney and former professional football player Robert P. Richards. The ratings are mine.

26 TOP SCORING WINES REVIEWED

98. Joseph Phelps Winery 1974 Insignia, Napa Valley. What a treat! "Awesome complexity," noted one taster. All components of a great wine are present, from deep, rich color through an elegant and seductive middle taste to a long, rich, sweet finish.

98. Robert Mondavi 1974 Cabernet Sauvignon, Reserve, Napa Valley. The media attention surrounding this wine upon its release was unprecedented. Bob Mondavi once said that this wine would be nearing perfection in 1990. It appears he was right! Mint and eucalyptus in even more harmony than the Heitz, combined with profoundly rich texture and flavors. Nearly perfect.

97. Diamond Creek Winery 1974 Cabernet Sauvignon, Volcanic Hill, Napa Valley. Almost perfection in the bouquet. The weight and texture in the mouth were equally impressive. Gorgeous, full flavors abounded throughout the tasting experience. Great future; best possibly between now and 1995 with a five- to 10-year plateau.

97. Ridge Vineyards 1974 Cabernet Sauvignon, Monte Bello. Almost perfect, medium red-black color. Lovely Cabernet fruit in the bouquet. Deep, powerful wine with layers of flavors and rich texture, like a fully developed Chateau Latour from 1964 or even 1961. Lingering, luscious finish.

97. Heitz Cellars 1974 Cabernet Sauvignon, Martha's Vineyard, Napa Valley. Deep garnet-red color. Rich, possibly too-concentrated mint and some eucalyptus evident in a unique, enticing bouquet. Loads of fruit with depth and complexity and a long finish. A beautiful wine lacking only a synergism and components and the super-power or sublime elegance to push it all the way to the top.

95. Mt. Eden Vineyards 1974 Cabernet Sauvignon, Saratoga. Inky, purple-black color of a four- or five-year-old Cab. Concentrated varietal character. Long finish. Could get better and last for years and years.

95. Mayacamas 1974 Cabernet Sauvignon, Napa Mountain. I have always been a strong supporter of the '74. Purple-black color, similar to the Mt. Eden. A reservoir of flavors are straining to get out. In taste and finish, this wine has come together better than the Mt. Eden and displays a unique array of concentrated fruit flavors. Should continue to age well and could get even better. My best guess is to drink it between now and 1995, but it could hold for five to 10 years after that. The uniqueness of the flavors added points for some judges and subtracted points for others.

93. Stag's Leap Wine Cellars 1974 Cabernet Sauvignon, Stag's Leap Vineyard, Cask 23, Napa Valley. Medium-dark garnet red. Hints of mint and eucalyptus. Similar to the Ridge Monte Bellow but with less clout. Very classy, well-made wine that has reached its peak but has not started downhill. Drink between now and 1990 for best enjoyment.

92. Beaulieu Vineyard 1974 Cabernet Sauvignon, Private Reserve, Napa Valley. Some brown starting to develop in the color. This wine was not made by Andre Tchelistcheff, who made the '70. The '74 is nonetheless rich and chocolatey in taste and has some mint and other harmonious qualities in both bouquet and taste. Whereas the '70 is at peak and hopefully will plateau for five years or more, the '74 is already beginning to show wrinkles it didn't have three or four years ago. Drink within the next couple years.

92. Simi 1974 Cabernet Sauvignon, Reserve Vintage, Sonoma. Medium-dark garnet color. Excellent bouquet. It has a hint of more depth and possibly a better future than its sister wine listed below.

91. Simi 1974 Cabernet Sauvignon, Special Reserve, Sonoma. Nearly identical to the Reserve Vintage. Both wines were made under the consulting genius of Andre Tchelistcheff while he was at Simi.

90. Chateau St. Jean 1974 Cabernet Sauvignon, Sonoma. Almost identical in appearance to the Montelena below. Excellent open bouquet. Medium bodied, with noticeable length in the finish. No reason to cellar any longer; drink by 1990.

90. Clos du Val 1974 Cabernet Sauvignon, Napa Valley. Deep garnet color with medium body and wonderful taste. The fruit is very good now but probably will not last too much longer.

90. Tedeschi 1974 Cabernet Sauvignon, Napa Valley. Produced by a man who now makes pineapple wines, sparkling wines and Beaujolais-type wines on Maui (and some are very good), this was the No. 1 surprise of the tasting. Nobody was quite ready for this unknown, medium-dark red-garnet beauty with sweet, ripe fruit and multidimensional flavors. Only about 200 cases were made. The last time I tasted this wine in 1986 it seemed to be at the end of its peak, but this bottle had at least a three- to five-year plateau ahead. Sleeper of the vintage?

90. Sterling Vineyards 1974 Cabernet Sauvignon, Reserve, Napa Valley. Very deep garnet color. Subtle heat in the taste slightly mars an otherwise great wine. Complex and fruity. No rush to drink.

89. Clos du Bois 1974 Cabernet Sauvignon, Second Release, Dry Creek, Sonoma. The most elegant and best of the three Clos du Bois Cabs from this vintage that were tasted. Good length in the finish. Should hold well for another three or four years.

89. Freemark Abbey 1974 Cabernet Sauvignon, Napa Valley. Surprisingly better than its famous relative from the Bosché Vineyard, this wine had lots of life and soft, elegant flavors. Good short-term future.

88. Sterling Vineyards 1974 Cabernet Sauvignon, Napa Valley. Less depth of color than the Sterling Reserve. Very closed nose. Mature Cabernet fruit is just right for current drinking. Will not improve but should hold well for another four to five years. An impressive if not exciting wine.

88. Burgess Cellars 1974 Cabernet Sauvignon, Vintage Selection, Napa Valley. Similar to the Sterling in color and overall quality, with better bouquet and equal or slightly better taste, but slightly fading in the finish by contrast. Very good drinking now, but don't be surprised if it starts to decline soon.

87. Chateau Montelena 1974 Cabernet Sauvignon, Sonoma. Beautiful garnet color. Restrained but fruity bouquet. Medium body; possibly a bit too tannic. Probably will not improve but very good now and should hold well for several years.

86. Robert Mondavi 1974 Cabernet Sauvignon, Napa Valley. Originally a fabulous wine that was meant either to be drunk soon after release or cellared for five to 10 years. This wine scored consistently in the low- to mid-90s until three or four years ago, when it started fading. Still very good if well stored, and still eminently drinkable. Very consistent scores by the tasters.

86. Clos du Bois 1974 Cabernet Sauvignon, Proprietor's Reserve, Dry Creek, Sonoma. Excellent depth of color. Better balance and length of flavors than Clos du Bois' Unfined Cab reviewed below. A fairly big style, but the components didn't seem compatible with a long future. Very good now.

86. Chateau Chevalier 1974 Cabernet Sauvignon, Napa Valley. Deep, rich garnet color. All parts blend together well for an above-average, mature Cabernet with no noticeable faults other than some sharpness in the mouth. Very good balance. At its peak; drink now.

86. Sonoma Vineyards 1974 Cabernet Sauvignon, Alexander's Crown Vineyard, Sonoma. This was the first Alexander's Crown Cabernet, made from three- or four-year-old vines. It was heralded early on by at least one well-known writer. Medium-dark garnet now, with slight browning. Moderately fruity bouquet with some tannin, both beginning to fade slightly. Drink within the next year.

85. Inglenook 1974 Cabernet Sauvignon, Cask D-2, Napa Valley. Better color than Inglenook's Cask A-11 was a harbinger of better fruit and a degree of richness the other wine lacked. Could last another three years or so at the same quality level.

85. Chappellet 1974 Cabernet Sauvignon, Napa Valley. Good dark color. Some tasters noted vegetal smells. Ample fruit and tannin for a very good wine for current consumption, without much future.

THE RENAISSANCE OF CHATEAU MARGAUX

On the evening of November 11, 1983, a wine tasting and dinner of historical significance took place in Houston, Texas. Houstonians Bill Sharman and Lenoir Josey, each an accomplished authority on food and wine, hosted a "fairytale" evening in conjunction with the owners of Chateau Margaux and their famous wine consultant, professor Emile Peynaud. The Mentzelopoulos family purchased Chateau Margaux in 1976 and produced their first vintage in 1977. Daughter Corinne Mentzelopoulos-Petit ran the show then and still does!

This degustation and dinner is not only important as a record of the wines tasted, but also because of the comments by Peynaud, who at the time was unrivaled as a wine consultant (a possible exception is Andre Tchelistcheff in California).

The tasting event included 38 wines of Chateau Margaux, scored using the 20-point scale. The guests were greeted by the following menu:

Chateau Margaux Wine Tasting and Dinner

Charley's 517 Restaurant

The Wines

Reception Pavillon Blanc 1980

Flight A

Chateau Margaux

1980	1967
1979	1966
1978	1964
1975	1962
1970	1961

Flight B

Chateau Margaux

1959	1950
1957	1949
1955	1947
1953	1945
1952	1934

Flight C

Chateau Margaux

1929	1920
1928	1911

1926   1906

1924   1900

1921

Flight D

Chateau Margaux

1899   1892

1893   1887

1875

Le Programme

Reception 7:00 – 7:30 pm

Chateau Margaux Flight A

Chateau Margaux Flight B

Discussion

Le Diner

Zuenelles au Saumon Fumé au sauce a l'aneth

(Pavillon Blanc 1979)

Supremes de Faisau et Ris de Veau

Au jus avec Lherbs

(Chateau Margaux 1981)

Baron d'Agneau avec un Bouquetiere des legumes

(Chateau Margaux 1977)

Chateau Margaux Flight C

Chateau Margaux Flight D

Discussion

Les Desserts

Carte aux Noixettes Mont Blanc

Charlotte aux Fruites: Poires, Framboise, Fraises

Truffles au Chocolat

Demi-tasse

We began with a Pavillon Blanc 1980. It was clean, refreshing, fruity and harmonious in its balance and components. I was much more impressed with it than I was with the 1978 at its release several years ago.

The first "flight" of five reds included the 1980, '79, '78, '75 and '70.

1980: Already has an excellent floral bouquet, and is considerably further along in its development than I would have imagined. (The 1980 Palmer is also quite good and surprisingly mature.) Chateau Margaux may be the best '80, although I have heard that Latour is excellent and possibly even better. 17

1979: Someone muttered, "class in the glass," and I would not challenge that. It is certainly the best '79 I've had, and Robert Parker of *The Wine Advocate* agrees. Another fast-maturing wine, this one shows considerably more depth and beauty than the '80. 18

1978: Much more closed up than the '79. A wine that caused some dissension – several not caring too much for it in contrast to the more immediate seductiveness of the '79. As it developed in the glass, however, and as it was enjoyed with a bite of cheese and cracker, I concluded that it was superior overall, even though not the better of the two to drink for the next three to five years. In fact, the '78 probably needs another 10 years for proper development. 19

1975: I was at Chateau Margaux in 1977 and tasted this one from the barrel. This was pre-Mentzelopoulos, and even though from an excellent vintage, the wine was just not properly made or cared for by the previous owners. (In fact, Chateau Margaux from 1967 to 1976 produced wines that were not up to first growth standards and were, and still are, terribly overpriced for the quality). This one is way off compared to '75 Lafite, Latour, Ducru-Beaucaillou and several others. The wine seems even worse by contrast to the '79 and '78. Probably at its peak. 15.5

1970: Significantly better than the '75. Nearing full maturity and will possibly improve. 16.25

Professor Peynaud spoke briefly after each flight of wines. From the first Mentzelopoulos vintage in 1977, Peynaud has directed the character of Chateau Margaux from his vantage point as wine consultant. The Mentzelopoulos family has charted the destiny of Chateau Margaux with an infusion of capital and the vision to employ professor Peynaud.

As Andre Tchelistcheff had made many wines and wineries famous, such as B.V. Private Reserve Cabernet Sauvignon, Jordan and others, and is regarded as the "dean" of California winemakers, professor Peynaud enjoys the same reputation in Europe.

Peynaud opened by stating that wine was a perfect machine or tool to take us back in time—here—to many vintages of memories. The best possible use of the sun, he said, is to transfer it into wine. "We're really drinking 36 summers and vendanges. None of these has enough evolution to hit a maximum. Although I've had each of these separately, we meet them anew every time we taste them."

He is most impressed with the '78, saying that he achieved his goal producing this wine and hopes that he can do this again and again. He scores it 20. He also likes the '79, but finds it less generous and round. He is astonished by the '80, saying that the bouquet will get better. "This was not a light vintage for Chateau Margaux," he said, "and should be enjoyed most in five to 10 years."

He mentions that the color of the '75 has undergone quite an evolution and is quite light for a '75, with considerably less tannin than before. He observes that the '70 looks the same or even younger than the '75.

"The wines are speaking to us and you should listen to them, not to me," he summed up jovially.

Next came the '67, '66, '64, '62 and '61.

1967: Lightish, not perfectly ripe fruit flavors. Very little aftertaste. Drink quickly. **14**

1966: A really unusual year. Typically a great year, such as '61 and '45, produces huge wines, full-bodied, closed up and with layers and layers of tannin. Many think '66 is a great year, but '66 certainly is not like '61 or '45. Some of the '66s, such as Lafite and Pétrus, are arguably not even outstanding. The '66 Chateau Margaux is outstanding. It boasts of a rich, sweet bouquet, and is a very substantial wine with more class and charm than clout. It is probably the best, or tied with the best '66s (La Mission-Haut-Brion and Palmer are excellent also). Just about perfect. Drinkable now, but no rush. **19**

1964: Surprisingly good, especially following the '66. A little more "chewey" but not as harmonious. Also ready to drink, but without the same staying power as the '66. **16.5**

1962: Beautiful bouquet. Very similar in style to the '66, although not quite the same quality. Probably at peak. Very substantial and one of the best '62s, the Latour being the only one to come to mind that is better. **17.5**

1961: Power, charm, majesty, elegance. This wine is so fabulous, it makes one wonder how the others got such high scores. Actually, there is a great chasm between a wine that scores a 17.5 and one that scores a 20. The '61 is, along with Pétrus, Palmer and Mouton, a 20, although definitely of a different style. Whereas the Pétrus and Palmer are almost overpowering, and the Mouton is enthralling in its strength, the Margaux, even though powerful and rich, is uniquely beguiling and seductive. 20

Professor Peynaud commented that this is the time these wines should be enjoyed. "About 10 years of development is needed for Margaux wines – here, we're climbing steps and reaching the peak of quality at the '61.

"We have changed the vinification techniques at Chateau Margaux. First, we select the grapes in steps:

1. In the vineyard;
2. After picked on the truck;
3. In the vat room on a big table.

"This allows us to get out grapes that are too ripe, too dry, rotten or whatever. Each plot is picked separately and put into a separate vat, for example, young Merlot from one plot goes into one vat, old Merlot from another plot goes into another vat. This is the basis of the job of a great growth. Also, control of temperature during fermentation is very important.

"The aim is to get the best extract from the seeds and skins possible, but not too much! If kept in vats too long, the wine will become bitter and vegetal. But it must be kept long enough to get body. Then, regulation of total acidity is very important. The higher the tannin, the lower the total acidity should be. Then, the art of tasting and blending from the vats cannot be overemphasized."

Peynaud thinks the '61 is certainly the most beautiful of the group, coming from the best possible climate and only half the normal crop for a very rich and concentrated wine with lots of body.

More important than the percentage of Cabernet, Merlot, Cabernet Franc and Petit-Verdot, he explains, is taking the best vats without regard to the grape variety. For example, in 1982, the Merlot was superior, so a higher percentage of Merlot was used. In 1983, the Cabernet was the choice grape, so more Cabernet will be present. The vines are approximately 70 percent Cabernet, 20 percent Merlot, 4 percent Cabernet Franc and 1 percent Petit-Verdot.

The next wines served were the '59, '57, '55, '53 and '52.

1959: Sweet, well-developed bouquet. Remarkably similar in style to the '62 in middle and aftertaste. Good balance and ready to drink. 17.25

1957: Considerably better than any '57 I've tasted. From a year that has produced some harsh and acidic wines, this one delivers some substance and pleasure. 15

1955: Definitely superior to the '57, but nowhere near some of the great '55s such as '55 Mouton, Latour or Cheval-Blanc (when stored well). 15.5

1953: Charming, floral bouquet and well balanced in the mouth. Only real negative is a perceptible weakness in the aftertaste. Drink now. 17.5

1952: Very similar in quality to the '53, but different style because of the vintage. A little less bouquet, but a little more depth and more length in the aftertaste. No rush to drink this one. 17.5

Professor Peynaud reminded us that these vintages are becoming extremely difficult to find. He doesn't like the '55 because it is too light. He thinks the '53 is very fleshy, fresh and well developed and that the '52 has lots of alcohol and is a big, warm wine.

Peynaud mentioned that 1959 was very hot, making vinification difficult due to lack of the ability to control temperatures during fermentation. '59 was thus the last of the old wines and '61, in a way, was the first of the new; the problems associated with '59 precipitated the purchase of modern equipment that was used for many of the '61s. He said the '57 has no finesse or elegance and is a bit coarse, but is a successful '57 and a "pretty" '57.

The last flight before dinner" 1950, '49, '47, '45 and '34.

1950: The bouquet "jumped" out of the glass and met me before I got there! Lightish color with lovely, unique bouquet. Sprightly, dancing wine. Not full bodied or polwerful, but well balanced with attractive flavors. Extra point for uniqueness. This is touted as the best '50. 18

1949: Up to this point, I had spit most of the wines to retain as much sober objectivity as possible. I was going to spit this one as well, but couldn't. The voluptuous roundness and pure pleasure of rolling this wine around in the mouth quite frankly forbade anything other than swallowing and counting the seconds of the lingering aftertaste. Mouton's '49 is the best I've tasted, and Latour and Lafite are both exceptional – could the Margaux be far behind? 19

1947: The '47 vintage is overrated in the Médoc. Here is a perfect example. Some mention '47 in the same breath as '49, when they really should limit their superlatives for '47 mainly to Saint-Emilion and Pomerol. This '47, while lovely, can't stand in the shadow of the '49. 17.25

1945; Big, young wine. Here we encounter something akin to mint and eucalyptus for the first time in the tasting. At least as good and probably better in the long run than the '49. 19

1934: A decent wine, but below my expectations. I had a half-bottle at Windows on the World three years ago that seemed a cut above this one. Very good, but not going anywhere. As an aside, '34 and '37 were the only vintages of the '30s that might still be holding on. 17.25

Professor Peynaud declares the '45 to be of "extraordinary constitution." He finds it a little like the '61. He cites this '45 as a real example of what can be done at best (under the old method) with the attending problems of extreme heat, etc. He reminds us that the '45 was undrinkable when it was 20 years of age. It will last much longer, "til I'm 100," he chuckled.

"The flavor is better than the bouquet. It was very hard to make wines in all of these five vintages because of the heat and problems with malolactic fermentation. Most of these have a lactic smell of game. But remember, at the time, people really liked their wines this way, so there is a lot of historical value here, and that's why we can't be too hard on these wines. Now, we're more after the taste of the grape.

"The 1930s was the worst decade ever," he continued. "1930 to 1933 was a horrible period, with 1935 and 1936 not much better. The wines are mostly acid with poor color."

At this juncture, we stood up, walked outside into the first crisp-cold air of the season in Houston, and pondered our euphoria. Upon returning, we drank a '79 Pavillon Blanc which, I believe, is closer to the '78 in quality than the '80.

1981 and 1977: Our first wine upon resuming was the 1981. Not yet released, it is astounding. Inky and huge, it is already somewhat accessible and completely enjoyable – even with memories of the '49 and '45 dancing across a synapse somewhere between my olfactory and my brain. Difficult as it is to grade a wine at this early stage of development, it stood tall in the 18.5 range, possibly better. The '77, while by far the best

'77 I've had and considerably better than Latour, was just in the "very good" category, possibly 16.

The professor preempted my last bite of lamb with news that he had never tasted the '77 through '81 at one sitting, and it was interesting to try to find the same style or structure in each – a certain amount of tannin for flavor and power, low acidity for flesh and roundness (especially at first impression when the wine comes into the mouth).

"Most '77s have kept a grass taste, but here, we really have a pleasant smell of crushed leaves of Cabernet," said Peynaud. "The '81 was bottled three months ago. One of the most critical points in a wine's life is in the first year or two when it can get bottle disease. This one doesn't have it. It does have a very powerful smell and rich flavor. It is between the '78 and '79. Less classic than the '78, it is tougher than the '79. It will be a great race between the '81, '79 and '78; so, we should taste these three together every year from now on to see which wins out."

Now we come to the second-to-last flight: 1929, '28 (magnum), '26, '24, '21, '20, '11 and '06. The '11 and '06 do not merit discussion other than the '06 was terribly oxidized and the '11 was mediocre (although Peynaud liked it).

1929: Beautiful old-style claret nose. Still much to offer, but long past its prime. Yet a treat with some fruit and "meat." 16.5

1928 (magnum): Almost all the wines for his incredible tasting came from the cellars of Lenoir Josey and Bill Sharman. This was my lone contribution. Big, deep garnet in color and still young and tannic, this wine is an "oddly powerful" beauty. My first score was an 18.5 but it either failed to develop in the glass or it just didn't hold up when I came back to it after the gorgeous '21. I finally settled around 18.

1926: Some charm and interest, but fading very much like the '29. 16

1924: This was the first year the wine was bottled at the Chateau. It is slightly maderized but yields a chocolatey taste. This one has seen better days. 15

1921: Best of this group. Young, but not nearly as tannic as the '28. Beautiful color and balance. Seems to have some mintiness along with richness and concentration like the '45. 19

1920: Nose fairly subdued in contrast to the "fresh flowers" emanating from the '21. Very stylish and harmonious in middle and aftertaste.

Another outstanding wine with all the major components for a winner. 18.

Professor Peynaud said that we are "now seeing some wines losing color, losing tannin, losing body and getting thinner, some even skinny. Also, some are showing volatile acidity. '29 was a great vintage, but this one doesn't have quite as much color as we would like and possibly is not as clean as we'd like.

"The '28 has nice color and lots of tannin but does show a trace of volatile acidity. The '24 and '26 are both getting very thin, but are still supple. Tannins in them are becoming like mushrooms.

"Best are '21 and '20. Both have good definition and are soft, but have kept good tannin.

"We shouldn't be overly critical of some of these old wines, but respect them for what they are. Also, it is getting more difficult to taste these as our palates are becoming somewhat fatigued. It is hard to see nuances at this point."

And finally, the 1900, 1899, '93, '92, and '87 and '75.

1900: Beautiful color, deep, gorgeous bouquet, rounded and perfect in the mouth, perfectly mature and ready, smooth, long, elegant aftertaste. 20

1899: Further along in development than the 1900, but a ripe fruit and vanilla sweetness with an excellent taste and yet another lingering aftertaste of near perfection. 19.5

1893: Not really worth discussion other than the nose was off but the taste was passable.

1892: Curiously, the nose was acceptable but the taste was off; not so much oxidized as a bit of sourness. Again, not worth scoring.

1887: Not an old wine at all. Surprisingly hale and hearty. Hard to make any rational comments at 12:30 am after 37 wines, the last 20 or so not spitting, but this wine seemed more akin to the '47 and '34 than the 1893 or 1892. 17.5

1875: Unfortunately, this "dame" was no longer "grande." Barely enjoyable. Nothing more than a conversation piece.

Peynaud admired the 1900 as "very well kept, round, firm, full of finesse and lots of fragrance. The 1899 is more supple with less tannin. Just as good as the 1900 but in a different way.

"The 1893 is from an extraordinary vintage – the grapes were picked on August 15! It has nice color and good tannin. The 1892 is getting a bit mushroom-like. The 1887 is close to getting bitter, something that happens near the end of a wine's life. The 1875 is the image of a finished wine – like a house that's lost all its paint."

Corinne said that this was a great opportunity for all of them, because they had never tasted many of these wines. Her voice was somewhat hoarse, as she had been translating for Peynaud off and on for some 5 ½ hours, but her energy level and enthusiasm for her wines had not dwindled one bit.

I believe she is about the same vintage as the 1953 Chateau Margaux. As interesting and alive as the '53 Margaux is, it is no match for Corinne, who, in a reverse personification, more nearly resembles the '61.

Lenoir suggested we "meet back here in 2000 and do it again."

Bill Sharman thanked our honored guests and formally dismissed us.

I made my farewell rounds, walked up the stairs to the main restaurant to the smell of good food for the after-theater crowd at Charlie's, walked outside and invited the cold breeze deep into my lungs. I thanked God that I was allowed the blessing and the privilege of sharing this priceless, once-in-a-lifetime experience.

TASTING TWO CENTURIES OF CHATEAU GRUAUD-LAROSE

Following is my account of an incredible wine tasting I attended. The article appeared in *Wine & Spirits* in 1990 and is reprinted with the permission of the magazine.

In May 1990, Dr. Marvin Overton of Fort Worth, TX, orchestrated a Chateau Gruaud-Larose tasting of monumental proportions. The list of invitees included many from St. Julien, particularly from the Cordier family, owners of Gruaud-Larose in the Bordeaux region. Serena Sutcliffe and her husband, David Peppercorn, both Masters of Wine, were the official commentators.

The first event took place at Fort Worth's Le Chardonnay. Every vintage from 1989 to 1961 was included, with the exception of the useless '65 and '63, and the less-than-mediocre '72. The first incredible flight, which contained the '89, '88, '86 and '85, deserves special attention, since these wines can be purchased now.

The quality of the '89 and '86 makes it almost impossible to discern which is the best. The 1989 is purple-red with a flawless, youthful, somewhat closed nose with rich underlying fruit flavors. Tannins are plentiful, of the more tender variety, and harmony in the mouth is remarkable. It should develop beautifully. The finish is already exciting, and should lengthen to become increasingly luscious. The wine will be drinking well by 1997 and improve for 10 to 15 years after that time.

The '86 is dark garnet with some youthful purple still evident. Massive tannin and fruit, with what seems to be perfect balancing acidity, all evidence a wine that should burgeon around the year 2000 and remain at a high level of quality for another 20 years. Each of these two wines deserves a 95 or better on a 100-point scale.

The '88 has a slightly deeper color than the '89, with even more purple and a discernible hint of a bouquet already developing. A true blockbuster with richness and opulence; nevertheless, there is a trace of something lacking in the finish, and a hardness reminiscent of what has been written about many '28s and some '45s, leading me to believe the '88 will never show the quality of the '89 or '86.

The '85 was relatively controversial: the Europeans were more enthusiastic than many of the Americans. Although very open and stylish, and clearly a wine that will be drinkable before any of the others, it is just not up to the '89 and '86, and is about equal or possibly slightly inferior to the '88. I rate the '88 at 93 points, and the '85 at 92.

Other excellent to outstanding wines served, in ascending order of preference, were:

1964: Very sweet bouquet; excellent, fully mature; drink now.

1962: Lacking the power of the '66 or the opulence of the '61, but elegant and drinking well now.

1978: A controversial wine. Sutcliffe has a "weakness" for the '78s and found "tremendous aromatic complexity on the nose and surprising softness on the palate." Peppercorn preferred the '75.

1970: Almost identical in quality to the '66. Medium garnet color; very open bouquet and excellent fruit in the mouth. At its peak, but should hold well for at least five years at this level.

1966: Like '75, the '66 vintage has a reputation that surpasses its empirical quality in many instances. Lafite, Pétrus and many others are not worth one half of their exorbitant prices due to a lack of ripe fruit and an overabundance of austere tannin. To be fair, Peppercorn stated he really likes the '75 and '66 vintages. In any event, the '66 Gruaud-Larose is a racehorse; more open and approachable than most '66s. Peppercorn finds that is has "great flavor and classic power." I agree!

1982: "Tremendous ripe tannins with great fruit and charm, but bouquet not quite ready yet," concluded Peppercorn. A fabulous, rich wine, better than '88 and '85, possibly in the same class with '89 and '86. Already a pleasure to drink, but wait another four years and drink happily into the 21st century.

1961: A wine of immense and opulent proportions; an impression of sweetness from perfectly ripe grapes. Always one of the best '61s.

The next event of the tasting took place at the City Club, featuring eight flights of wines–31 in all–from 1959 back to 1819. Following are the wines that showed the best.

The top wine of the '50s was the '53, with the '59 just behind. Both were excellent. The '45 was the highlight of the next flight, extraordinarily enjoyable, a wine of complexity, weight, extract, and great flavor.

One of the great joys of the tasting was the flight of the '20s ('29, '28, '26, '24, '21 and '20). The '28, '26 and '24, one after the other, showed consistent high quality and youthful vigor. Each was in the excellent to outstanding range. The '28 and '26 in particular were youthful, tantalizing wines with beautiful fruit and spice. The '29, '21 and '20, while disappointing for famous years, were actually very good—'20 being the best—and probably suffered in contrast to the top three.

Now I will jump to one of the greatest of all vintages, the 1870. Not even a hint of oxidation, with good fruit still evident; fresh and clean on the palate, with elegance and a certain fullness of flavor. This wine would have been in the '20s flight and shown well! The 1865 was almost as good as the '70. Both were great years and both wines are holding up beautifully.

At least two superb ancient vintages are in the cellar at Chateau Gruaud-Larose: 1819 and 1815. The Cordier family happily offered to bring the 1815, but since that would have depleted the stock to only one bottle, Dr. Overton declined. Instead, the family brought the 1819, of which there is a larger, albeit limited, supply. The 1819 has been recorked and filled with more 1819 every 30 years or so, and remained otherwise unmoved at the Chateau for about 170 years!

The wine showed good color with a light rim and barely a hint of oxidation. It's possible the 1870 will appear and taste like this in 30 to 50 years. A most remarkable, very drinkable wine, it could easily pass for a wine 100 years younger.

Although there is no way to place a value on this wine, I'll guess it would bring around $50,000 a bottle at auction, as it is now a known wine of staggering qualitative and historical value.

David Peppercorn summed it up: "1819 was a fine year. I am amazed by the fresh vigor on the nose. No decay or senility. Wonderful harmony; rich. Astonishing preservation."

WINE DINNER OF THE CENTURY

Without a doubt, the greatest single dinner I have attended, and possibly one with the greatest appeal to many oenophiles, was hosted by Dr. Frank Komorowski on his 50th birthday in 1995 at Chez Francois in Vermillion, Ohio. Frank had long been securing large-format bottles from his birth year, 1945, for this dinner. And for added flair, he and the chef at Chez Francois worked with Wolfgang Puck on pairing the foods and wines, and, of course, Chef Puck was present to put the finishing touches on each course.

The two universally mentioned vintages of the century in Bordeaux are 1961 and 1945. The great vintages of the 1920s are now almost impossible to find.

But 1945, a very tannic year, had developed beautifully by 1995 in large-format bottles. The magnum is the optimal bottle for aging great Bordeaux.

One of the highlights of the dinner was the jeroboam of 1945 Romanée-Conti, one of only three produced. Dr. Komorowski retained one more in his cellar, and the whereabouts of the third jeroboam was unknown. The fabled wine was perfectly matched with a mushroom risotto with white truffle shavings. I would venture that the wine was valued at around $100,000. Following is the magnificent menu that was created for the evening:

Blinis with Beluga Caviar
Champagne Dom Ruinart 1945
Champagne Krug 1945
Moet & Chandon Champange 1945, jeroboam

Carpaccio with 50-year-old Balsamic Vinegar and Sautéed Porcinis
Clos des Lambrays 1945, magnum
La Tache 1945, magnum
Musigny Vieilles Vignes 1945, magnum

Risotto with While Truffles from Alba
Romanée-Conti 1945, jeroboam

Shanghai Lump Crab Salad with Ginger Vinaigrette
Champagne Krug 1985, Magnum

Salmon Filet in a Potato Crust with Pancetta and Napa Cabbage
Chateau Calon Segur 1945, magnum
Chateau L'Eglise Clinet 1945, magnum
Chateau Trotanoy 1945
Vieux Chateau Certan 1945, magnum

Grilled Wolf Ranch Quail with Sage Polenta and Caramelized Onions
Chateau Ausone 1945, magnum
Chateau Haut Brion 1945, magnum
Chateau Lafite Rothschild 1945, magnum
Chateau La Mission Haut Brion 1945, magnum
Chateau Margaux 1945, magnum

Roasted Saddle of Venison with Braised Chestnuts and Sun-dried Cherries
Chateau Cheval Blanc 1945, magnum
Chateau Lafleur 1945, magnum
Chateau Latour 1945, magnum
Chateau Mouton Rothschild 1945, magnum
Chateau Pétrus 1945, magnum

Caramelized Comice Pear and Toasted Walnut Upside-Down Cake
Chateau d'Yquem 1945

Stilton Cheese and Nuts
Croft 1945
Taylor 1945

APPENDIX A

THE CLASSIFICATION OF 1855

For the Médoc

FIRST GROWTHS

Vineyard	Commune
Chateau Lafite – Rothschild	Pauillac
Chateau Margaux	Margaux
Chateau Latour	Pauillac
Chateau Haut-Brion	Pessac

SECOND GROWTHS

Chateau Mouton – Rothschild	Pauillac
Chateau Rausan – Segla	Margaux
Chateau Rauzan – Gassies	Margaux
Chateau Léoville – Las – Cases	Saint-Julien
Chateau Léoville – Poyferre	Saint-Julien
Chateau Léoville – Barton	Saint-Julien
Chateau Durfort – Vivens	Margaux
Chateau Lascombes	Margaux
Chateau Gruaud – Larose	Saint-Julien
Chateau Brane – Cantenac	Cantenac-Margaux
Chateau Pichon – Longueville	Pauillac

Chateau Pichon – Longueville – Lalande	Pauillac
Chateau Ducru – Beaucaillou	Saint-Julien
Chateau Cos d'Estournel	Saint-Estèphe
Chateau Montrose	Saint-Estèphe

THIRD GROWTHS

Chateau Kirwan	Cantenac-Margaux
Chateau d'Issan	Cantenac-Margaux
Chateau Lagrange	Saint-Julien
Chateau Langoa-Barton	Saint-Julien
Chateau Giscours	Labarde-Margaux
Chateau Malescot-Saint-Exupéry	Margaux
Chateau Cantenac-Brown	Cantenac-Margaux
Chateau Palmer	Cantenac-Margaux
Chateau La Lagune	Ludon
Chateau Desmirail	Margaux
Chateau Calon-Ségur	Saint-Estèphe
Chateau Ferriere	Margaux
Chateau Marquis-d'Alesme-Becker	Margaux
Chateau Boyd-Cantenac	Cantenac-Margaux

FOURTH GROWTHS

Chateau Saint-Pierre	Saint-Julien
Chateau Branaire-Ducru	Saint-Julien
Chateau Talbot	Saint-Julien
Chateau Duhart-Milon	Pauillac
Chateau Pouget	Cantenac-Margaux
Chateau La Tour-Carnet	Saint-Laurent
Chateau Lafon-Rochet	Saint-Estèphe
Chateau Beychevelle	Saint-Julien
Chateau Prieure-Lichine	Cantenac-Margaux
Chateau Marquis-de-Terme	Margaux

FIFTH GROWTHS

Chateau Pontet-Canet	Pauillac
Chateau Batailley	Pauillac
Chateau Haut-Batailley	Pauillac
Chateau Grand-Puy-Lacoste	Pauillac

Chateau Grand-Puy-Ducasse	Pauillac
Chateau Lynch-Bages	Pauillac
Chateau Lynch-Moussas	Pauillac
Chateau Dauzac	Labarde
Chateau d'Armailhac	Pauillac
Chateau du Tertre	Arsac
Chateau Haut-Bages-Liberal	Pauillac
Chateau Pedesclaux	Pauillac
Chateau Belgrave	Saint-Laurent
Chateau Camensac	Saint-Laurent
Chateau Cos Labory	Saint-Estèphe
Chateau Clerc-Milon-Mondon	Pauillac
Chateau Croizet-Bages	Pauillac
Chateau Cantemerle	Macau

APPENDIX B

THE 1855 CLASSIFICATION OF SAUTERNES AND BARSAC

GRAND PREMIER CRU
Chateau d'Yquem

PREMIERS CRUS
Chateau La Tour Blanche
Clos Haut-Peyraguey
Chateau Lafaurie-Peyraguey
Chateau de Rayne-Vigneau
Chateau Suduiraut
Chateau Coutet
Chateau Climens
Chateau Guiraud
Chateau Rieussec
Chateau Rabaud-Promis
Chateau Sigalas-Rabaud

DEUXIÈMES CRUS
Chateau Myrat
Chateau Doisy-Daëne

Chateau Doisy-Dubroca
Chateau Doisy-Védrines
Chateau D'Arche
Chateau Filhot
Chateau Broustet
Chateau Nairac
Chateau Caillou
Chateau Suau
Chateau de Malle
Chateau Romer
Chateau Lamothe

APPENDIX C

GRANDS CRUS OF THE COTE D'OR (FROM NORTH TO SOUTH)

Village of Gevrey-Chambertin:

Chambertin

Chambertin Clos-de-Bez

Chapelle-Chambertin

Griotte-Chambertin

Latricières-Chambertin

Mazis-Chambertin

Ruchottes-Chambertin

Village of Morey-St.-Denis:

Bonnes Mares (one portion of the Bonnes-Mares vineyard)

Clos des Lambrays

Clos-St.-Denis

Clos de la Roche

Clos de Tart

Village of Chambolle-Musigny:

Le Musigny

Bonnes Mares (one portion)

Village of Vougeot:
Clos de Vougeot

Village of Vosne-Romanée:
La Romanée
Romanée-Conti
Romanée-St.-Vivant
Richebourg
La Tache
La Grande Rue

Village of Flagey-Échezeaux:
Grands-Échezeaux
Échezeaux

GRANDS CRUS OF THE COTE DE BEAUNE
Village of Aloxe-Corton:
Le Corton (red and white)
Corton-Charlemagne (white)

Village of Puligny-Montrachet:
Le Montrachet (one portion—white)
Chevalier-Montrachet (white)
Bâtard-Montrachet (one portion—white)
Bienvenues-Bâtard-Montrachet (white)

Village of Chassagne-Montrachet:
Le Montrachet (one portion—white)
Bâtard-Montrachet (one portion—white)
Criots-Bâtard-Montrachet (white)

ABOUT THE AUTHOR

After an unforgettable two-year stint working with U.S. Senator Lloyd Bentsen—the last year as his executive assistant in Washingon D.C.—Denman returned to Houston and was somehow drawn to two wine books, *The Signet Book of Wine*, by Alexis Bespaloff, and *The Wines of Bordeaux* by Sir Edmund Penning Rowsell. He recalls it was like being plugged into "the universal wine source."

Denman soon joined the International Wine and Food Society, and over the years has been an officer or member of The Confrerie St. Etienne d'Alsace, Chaine des Rotisseurs, Commanderie de Bordeaux, German Wine Society, Les Amis d'Escoffier and others. He founded the Houston and Austin chapters of the Brotherhood of the Knights of the Vine, and is currently a member of the Sacramento chapter.

In 1978, Denman started *Moody's Wine Review*. In the early 1980s, the *Washington Post* said, "*Moody's Wine Review* is certainly the best publication in this country for tracking the state of rare and exotic wines." During the same time period, *Food and Wine Magazine* said the three wine writers they enjoyed reading most were Robert Parker, Robert Finigan and Denman Moody.

In 1991, Denman was inducted into "Who's Who in Food and Wine in Texas—recognized as a major contributor to the field of food and wine in Texas" by *The Dallas Morning News* and the Texas Department of Agriculture.

From 1984 to 1990, Denman was the contributing editor on rare wines for *The International Wine Review* in New York. He has continued as a freelance wine writer and has been published in numerous magazines, including *Revue du Vin de France* in Paris, the *International Wine and Food Society Journal* in London, *The Wine Spectator*, and *Wine and Spirits*. He has written the monthly wine column for *Houston Lifestyles and Homes* since 2000.

Denman Moody can be contacted at denmanmoody@gmail.com

Made in the USA
Columbia, SC
31 October 2017